Ius Gentium: Comparative Perspectives on Law and Justice

Volume 145

Ius Gentium is a book series which discusses the central questions of law and justice from a comparative perspective. The books in this series collect the contrasting and overlapping perspectives of lawyers, judges, philosophers, and scholars of law from the world's many different jurisdictions for the purposes of comparison, harmonisation, and the progressive development of law and legal institutions. Each volume makes a new comparative study of an important area of law. This book series continues the work of the well-known journal of the same name and provides the basis for a better understanding of all areas of legal science.

The *Ius Gentium* series provides a valuable resource for lawyers, judges, legislators, scholars, and both graduate students and researchers in globalisation, comparative law, legal theory, and legal practice. The series has a special focus on the development of international legal standards and transnational legal cooperation.

Emma Suzanne van Aggelen
Editor

Retirement and Employment

Comparative Insights on Retirement Age, Retirement Regimes and Taxation

Springer

Editor
Emma Suzanne van Aggelen
Faculty of Law
UHasselt
Hasselt, Belgium

Faculty of Law and Criminology
KU Leuven
Leuven, Belgium

ISSN 1534-6781 ISSN 2214-9902 (electronic)
Ius Gentium: Comparative Perspectives on Law and Justice
ISBN 978-3-032-33560-9 ISBN 978-3-032-33561-6 (eBook)
https://doi.org/10.1007/978-3-032-33561-6

This Springer imprint is published by the registered company Springer Nature Switzerland AG
The registered company address is: Gewerbestrasse 11, 6330 Cham, Switzerland

Acknowledgements

A Sincere Word of Gratitude

This book and process would not have been possible without the help of many people. Our thanks and gratitude goes to the people of the ministry of social security and labour of the republic of Vilnius. During one week we drove them out of their offices and took their wonderful work places. We own them a lot of chocolates! It was their kind chancellor Ana Selcinskiene granting us permission to utilise their workplaces at the ministry. But above all we would like to thank Inga Buškutė for facilitating this collaboration. Her warmth, hospitality and friendship were key to the success of our project. She not only opened the doors of the ministry to our team but also provided us with a unique and welcoming environment. For this enterprise we also got financial support from Euroclear. Euroclear is a leading global provider of Financial Market Infrastructure services for domestic and cross border securities transactions and funds. The director of the Euroclear Pension Fund, Ellen De Laender, was so kind to open some doors for us and allow this voyage of legal scientific endeavour, whilst respecting our academic independence. Furthermore, it goes without saying that all views expressed in this book are solely the views of the authors and not those of Euroclear.

Contents

Introduction 1
Yves Stevens

Country Reports

Austria 7
Verena Zwinger

Belgium 17
Yves Stevens

Croatia 27
Ivana Vukorepa

Finland 41
Toomas Kotkas

Germany 51
Stamatia Devetzi

Switzerland 61
Jacques-André Schneider

The Netherlands 73
Emma Suzanne van Aggelen

The United Kingdom 85
James Kolaczkowski

Retirement and Employment

To Retire or to Work? That's the Question: Choice or Necessity!? 103
Yves Stevens, Emma Suzanne van Aggelen, Stamatia Devetzi,
James Kolaczkowski, Toomas Kotkas, Jacques-André Schneider,
Ivana Vukorepa, and Verena Zwinger

Pension Law and Labour Market: Key Features of the Narratives 153
Emma Suzanne van Aggelen

Conclusions and Insights from a National Perspective

Austria 159
Verena Zwinger

Belgium 163
Yves Stevens

Croatia 169
Ivana Vukorepa

Finland 173
Toomas Kotkas

Germany 177
Stamatia Devetzi

Switzerland 181
Jacques-André Schneider

The Netherlands 183
Emma Suzanne van Aggelen

The United Kingdom 187
James Kolaczkowski

Editor and Contributors

About the Editor

Prof. Dr. Emma Suzanne van Aggelen obtained her Ph.D. at the University of Leuven (Belgium). She is currently an assistant professor at the Faculty of Law of Hasselt University (Belgium) and holds a teaching affiliation at the University of Leuven (Institute for Social law). Her field of expertise lies in pension law and tax law. She is also board member of INPeR (i.e. the International Network of Pensions Research), and Netspar Fellow.

Contributors

Prof. Dr. Stamatia Devetzi studied law in Athens, Rome and Osnabrück, has a diploma in law from the Law Faculty of University of Athens (1994) and a Ph.D. from Osnabrück University (1998). After working as a legal expert with the German Pensions Insurance Institution (1998–2003), in 2003 she became professor of Social Security Law at Fulda University of Applied Sciences. From 2011–2016 she was delegated as professor for Public Law and European Social Security Law at Osnabrück University. She has been active in teaching and research in the fields of Social Security, European Law and Law Comparison for over 20 years. She is a director of the Fulda Masters programme (LL.M.) "Social Law and Social Economy" (Cooperation between University of Kassel and Fulda), director of CINTEUS (Center for Intercultural and European Studies) and a member of the advisory board of FNA in Germany (Research Institute of the German Pensions Insurance).

Dr. James Kolaczkowski is a Lecturer in the Law School at the University of Exeter in the United Kingdom. His research interest is in pension law and policy and he is a board member of INPeR, the International Network for Pension Research.

Prof. Dr. Toomas Kotkas is a professor on public law at the Faculty of Law of the University of Helsinki. His research interests lie in the field of social security law and fundamental social rights—from the perspective of both doctrinal and socio-legal research. He has also worked as a justice at the Supreme Administrative Court of Finland, and he is regularly consulted by the Constitutional Law Committee of the Finnish Parliament on bills concerning social security legislation.

Dr. Jacques-André Schneider was for decades a pension and social security lawyer, teaching part-time as Titular professor at the University of Lausanne. Till this day, he has an extensive experience in the governance and trusteeship of 2nd pillar pension institutions.

Prof. Dr. Yves Stevens is a full professor at the faculty of law and criminology of the KU Leuven in Belgium. He is also coordinator of the specialized "Pension Law Studies". His field of expertise lies in social and pension law with worldwide experience. He is the current chair of INPeR, the International Network of Pension Research and member of the Netspar's Scientific Council. His full publication list can be found here: https://www.law.kuleuven.be/isr/bibliografie-yves-stevens.

Prof. Dr. sc. Ivana Vukorepa is full professor of labour and social security law at the University of Zagreb. She has collaborated on several research projects, as well as in the European experts' networks such as: ESPN in the field of social policy (from 20014 to 2018), MoveS in the field of free movement of workers and social security coordination (since 2018) and ECE in the field of labour law, employment and labour market policies (since 2020). Her particular field of expertise lies in pension law. For more see: https://www.pravo.unizg.hr/en/ivana.vukorepa. Full publication list: https://www.croris.hr/crosbi/searchByContext/2/1457.

Dr. Verena Zwinger is at the Austrian Pension Insurance in the Business Division for Legal Affairs and Research, where she is the head of Research and Research Coordination. Her field of expertise lies in pension law, where she is regularly invited to speak at conferences and publishes in professional journals and books.

Introduction

Yves Stevens

1 General Topic

This book is a legal journey to understand the relation between retirement provision and work in eight European countries. It is a subject that has intrigued many for several years and is high on the political agenda throughout the world.

Eight countries underpin the content of this book: Austria, Belgium, Croatia, Finland, Germany, Switzerland, The Netherlands and the United Kingdom. The countries analyzed are—due to multiple reasons—still searching for a balance between (so-called) active participation in the labour market and leaving the labour market. Given existing challenges regarding sustainability (financial capacity to pay out), adequacy (decent income), labour market developments, and so on, the questions are multiple.

With this book, the authors try to clarify the legal relation between work and retirement from a comparative law perspective. In the book is reflected on the way the different countries shape the relationship between work and retirement, or, more specifically, the retirement age. How do work and retirement interact? Does retirement entail a full stop of work? Or not? Not only a descriptive approach is taken, it also wants to realize an evaluative and normative assessment. Therefore, not only is looked at the current regulations on work and pensions, but also looked for narratives that may affect the legal relationship between work and retirement.

Both statutory and occupational pensions are considered. The method employed is functional comparative law. Given the fact that socio-economic backgrounds play an important role in this matter and the eight countries involved are indeed set in very different socio-economic backgrounds, it is important to stress that this is a work written by legal academics.

Y. Stevens (✉)
Catholic University of Leuven, Faculty of Law and Criminology, Department of Social Security & Labour Law, Institute for Social Law, Leuven, Belgium
e-mail: yves.stevens@kuleuven.be

E. S. van Aggelen (ed.), *Retirement and Employment*, Ius Gentium: Comparative Perspectives on Law and Justice 145, https://doi.org/10.1007/978-3-032-33561-6_1

One of the discussions that is not raised in this book is the one on disability pensions. Although we see the clear links between disability schemes and pensions, we consider it important to indicate that these schemes fall outside of the scope of this work.

2 The Collaborative Writing Process

The writing of this book was done in a rather unconventional setting. During one week eight legal scholars went to Vilnius to discuss, write and review. Such collaborative process where multiple individuals work together to produce a single document or piece of content is rarely used by legal academics. In the process we divided work based on the strengths, expertise and/or interests of the individual members. We all contributed to the writing process, the sharing of the responsibility for the content and the quality of the texts. In this manner we learned from each other's perspectives and skills. This intense week of collaboration resulted in a strong foundation for the book.

But this week was only the start. The work continued afterwards. Refining, expanding, and improving the manuscript based on the many insights taken home. The final book finds its roots in that common week in Vilnius, and at the same time reflects the careful work and critical reviewing that has been done afterwards.

At the end of the day we believe that the book has led to the development of our own personal skills in combining writing styles, opinions and work habits, as well as to an improved quality of our work as we combined different viewpoints and expertise.

3 Structure of the Book

The approach used to address the topic of work and employment is based on three main components.

The first component (Part I) consists of a description of the pension system and, specifically, the factors relevant for the central topic of work and retirement. These descriptive analyses are set out in the so-called country reports. The country reports are based on the structure of the second component. However, each of the authors remained the individual freedom to highlight what is relevant for the analyzed country. Therefore, the country reports are similar, but not identical.

In the second component (Part II) the authors address various common themes. A total of eight common themes are discussed: pensionable age and labour market (1), "normal" retirement age or age of reference (2), deferred retirement (3), early retirement (4), partial retirement (5), retirement regimes for persons in arduous and hazardous jobs (6), retirement regimes based on means or income testing (7) and taxation (8). For each of these themes is looked for narratives that may affect the legal relationship between work and retirement. These narratives are highlighted within each of the themes discussed. For the analysis of the second components, parts of the country reports of the first component are used directly. For optimal readability, no use is made of internal references. The references can be found in each of the country reports.

The final and third component (Part III) are the individual insights and conclusions from the authors. Each author reflects on the insights and/or take home lessons from the common themes relevant for their own country.

The information in this book is updated up to June 1, 2025.[1]

[1] The functionality of the websites referred to in this book were checked upon 1 August 2026.

Country Reports

In each country report, the author looks from his/her own national perspective at the topic of retirement and employment. The country reports are kept intentionally short as they are not meant to be an exhaustive overview of all the national regulations related to the central theme of this book. The goal of these country reports is to offer the reader an overview of important characteristics of the national pension systems as these country reports form the basis for the second part of this book, being the part in which the authors reflect on the central theme of this book.

To ensure that each of the country reports deals with similar aspects of retirement and employment, the authors were asked to look at some main topics. The following main topics were agreed on: access to retirement (1), early retirement and deferral of retirement (also including partial retirement) (2), retirement regimes for persons considered to be in hazardous or arduous jobs and retirement regimes based on means or income tested benefits, (3) and taxation (4).

Even though four main topics were determined, the authors could add their own accents due to national particularities of their pension system. This freedom was considered necessary to properly understand the differences between the various pension systems. The structure of the country reports is, therefore, similar but not identical. This difference is for example present when it comes to the scope of occupational pensions. Not all countries have the same approach towards occupational pensions. For countries such as the Netherlands and the United Kingdom, occupational pensions are at the heart of the discussion in the relationship between work and retirement. In Finland, however, there is no such interference because the general pension structure is very different. Countries such as Germany, Austria, and Belgium are familiar with occupational pensions but the occupational pensions play a far less important role than in the UK or the Netherlands. All this is reflected in both the country reports and the common chapter.

Austria

Verena Zwinger

1 Introduction to the Pension System and its Narrative

The Austrian Pension System is a multi-pillar system that provides for both public and private pension provisions.[1] The first pension insurance act was adopted in 1906 with the aim of providing income replacement at old age and in the event of incapacity to work or survival.[2]

1.1 Statutory Pension System

Based on a pay-as-you-go system (Bismarckian approach), the statutory pension system is part of the Austrian social insurance, next to health and accident insurance. The General Pensions Act (*Allgemeines Pensionsgesetz or APG*),[3] in force since 2005, is universally applicable to the private sector, i.e. workers/employees[4] and

[1] For a more detailed overview on Austrian social insurance including statutory pension insurance with description of current benefits in English see Soziale Sicherheit (2023), Focus on Benefits, An Overview of Austrian Social Insurance 2023, 6–35.

[2] For a historical overview see Zwinger (2020) Devolution and Decentralisation in social security: the situation in Austria in Schoukens, P, Vonk, G (eds), Devolution and Decentralisation in Social Security, The Hague, pp. 57–71.

[3] As effective from 01.01.2005, introduced with the Pension Harmonization Act 2004 (BGBl 2004/142).

[4] General Social Security Act, Allgemeines Sozialversicherungsgesetz—ASVG, BGBl 1955/189.

V. Zwinger (✉)
Austrian Pension Insurance, Business Division for Legal Affairs and Research, Vienna, Austria
e-mail: verena.zwinger@pv.at

E. S. van Aggelen (ed.), *Retirement and Employment*, Ius Gentium: Comparative Perspectives on Law and Justice 145, https://doi.org/10.1007/978-3-032-33561-6_2

self-employed[5] (including farmers[6] and liberal professions[7]) as well as for contract employees and civil servants of the federal government.[8] In 2024, 4.4 million people have been insured in the statutory pension insurance.[9]

Statutory pension insurance operates on the insurance principle, with periods of insurance. These periods are crucial in determining pension entitlement and amount. Examples include compulsory insurance contribution periods (due to gainful activity), partial compulsory insurance (e.g., times of military service/social year or child care) and voluntary insurance (self-, continued-, and higher insurance).

The Austrian Federal Constitution stipulates that social security is governed by independent (self-governing) bodies,[10] being under no direct state control but subject to supervision by the respective ministries.[11] Statutory pension insurance is administered by three insurance institutions.[12]

Social security is funded primarily through contributions from insured individuals, based on their earned income.[13] There is a limit on the maximum amount of income on which contributions are required,[14] which amounts to 6.450 EUR (monthly) in 2025 for non-self-employed. For self-employed, it is 7.525 EUR (monthly) in 2025; however, if projected on a yearly basis, both ceilings are equally high since the maximum contribution base for workers and employees is averaged over 14 months of pay as opposed to 12 months of earnings for the self-employed.

---

[5] Social Insurance Act for Self-Employed in Industry and Craft Trades (Gewerbliches Sozialversicherungsgesetz—GSVG), BGBl 1978/560.

[6] Social Insurance Act for Self-Employed in Agriculture and Forestry (Bauern-Sozialversicherungsgesetz—BSVG), BGBl 1978/559.

[7] Social Insurance Act for Self-Employed in Liberal Professions (Freiberuflichen Sozialversicherungsgesetz—FSVG), BGBl 1978/624.

[8] Born as of 1976 and appointed from 01.01.2005. For civil servants of the appointed before the APG, specific rules do apply, depending on the employer (federation, federal states or municipality). In the following, the manifold different pension rules for civil servants outside of the APG's scope will not be discussed.

[9] Of these, around 16.700 persons have been voluntarily insured, Austrian Social Insurance (2024) Jahresbericht, p. 44. https://www.sozialversicherung.at/cdscontent/?contentid=10007.845560&portal=svportal. (Accessed 5 May 2025).

[10] Meaning that the voice of the people concerned has to be expressed in elections in the statutory representative bodies, the chambers for workers/employees and self-employed.

[11] Esp. the Ministry of Finance and the Ministry of Social Affairs, Health, Care and Consumer Protection.

[12] "*PV*", the Austrian pension insurance being the competent institution for workers and employees, "SVS", competent for self-employed and farmers and "BVAEB", competent for public-service employees, railway and mining workers.

[13] 22.8% of the contribution base, which is the salary/income up to the maximum contribution amount.

[14] However, one can increase his/her pension by paying additional contributions (higher insurance).

Apart from contributions, pension insurance is financed by the federal budget, for instance in the sense of a default guarantee if pension payments exceed the contributions.[15]

According to the principle of equivalence, pension benefits are calculated based on the number of years worked and, the amount contributed based on the income earned during the individual's working life. Since the *APG*, a unified performance-oriented personal pension account[16] exists. The pension account shows the acquired entitlements for each individual at any time via pension account statement, which includes information on the initial credit, contribution bases, contributions paid, partial credit acquired per year, and total credit on a yearly basis. If the pension starts at the standard pensionable age, the monthly pension amount is calculated based on the total credit at the pension date divided by 14. There is a special supplementary amount in the case of voluntary higher insurance, which is tax free up to 75%. The remaining 25% are subject to income tax, as are pension benefits in general (Sect. 2.5).

1.2 Occupational Pensions

Employers may voluntarily invest in second pillar pensions for their employees in the form of e.g., occupational pension funds, life insurance schemes or defined benefit programs.[17] The benefits received from occupational pensions are based on the amount contributed and the investment performance of the pension fund.

The occupational pension schemes intend to provide better financial security in retirement, which means that a one-off payment is only possible if the existing credit balance does not exceed the current limit of 15.900 EUR (in 2025) at the end of the employment relationship or when retiring.

In comparison, according to the relevance of the different pension pillars, 2.280.468 persons received a statutory pension, 325.358 a public sector pension and 274.700 an additional occupational pension in 2023 in Austria.[18] Hence, around 10% of pensioners currently receive an occupational pension.[19]

---

[15] For more information on the Austrian pension system in English, see Bundesministerium für Soziales, Gesundheit, Pflege und Konsumentenschutz (2022) The Pensions System in Austria-an Overview p. 10.

[16] Administrated by the roof organization of Austrian social insurance institutions for insured persons born on or after 1 January 1955, starting from 1 January 2005. Those who had insurance periods before the introduction of the pension account received all entitlements acquired up to 31 December 2013 as a so-called "initial credit".

[17] Occupational Pensions Act (*Betriebspensionsgesetz-BPG*), BGBl 1990/282.

[18] Statistics Austria (2025) Pensionen. www.statistik.at/statistiken/bevoelkerung-und-soziales/sozialleistungen/pensionen/pensionen. (Accessed 12 March 2025).

[19] Besides, the "new" severance pay scheme is sometimes summarized under the notion of occupational pensions as well. Under this scheme, employers are requested to direct at least 1.53% of the monthly pay to one of the eight respective funds, instead of having to provide for a severance

2 Statutory Pensions

2.1 *Pensionable Age and Labour Market*

2.1.1 "Normal" Retirement Age or Age of Reference for Old-Age Pension

The retirement age in Austria is currently set at 65 years for men and 60 years and 6 months for women. The reason behind this age gap is the "Federal Constitutional Law on different retirement ages of men and women under Social Security" (*BVG-Altersgrenzen),*[20] which stipulates that the standard female retirement age should be adjusted every six months by six months as from 2024 starting with the 1964 age cohorts. The standard retirement age will therefore be at 65 years for female and male insured persons in 2033.[21] The legal retirement age for federal civil servants is 65 for female and male pensioners.

In general, pension take-up is voluntary. An application is needed to receive a pension, and the competent insurance institution checks whether the necessary conditions have been fulfilled. An exception exists for federal civil servants, who by law retire at the end of the month in which they reach the age of 65.[22] However, a deferral may be requested.

To be eligible for an old age pension at the "normal" retirement age, individuals have to have gained 180 insurance months, with at least 84 contribution months from gainful employment. Insurance months e.g. spent providing care for a disabled child or a close relative are considered equivalent to months of contribution through traditional employment for insurance purposes.

When receiving an old-age pension at the "normal" retirement age, the pensioners may earn unlimited additional income. As an incentive to take up gainful employment while being an old-age pensioner at the "normal" retirement age, the federal government takes over the part of the pension insurance contribution which is attributable to the insured person up to a ceiling of double the marginal income threshold (112,98 EUR/month in 2025).

---

payment individually at the end of an employment relationship. See Employee and Self-Employed Income Provision Act (*Betriebliche Mitarbeiter- und Selbstständigenvorsorgegesetz—BMSVG*), BGBl 2002/100.

[20] *BVG-Altersgrenzen*, BGBl 1992/832.

[21] More information can be found at PV (2025) Pension für Frauen: Pensionsalter und Vorsorge. www.pv.at/web/pension/pension-fuer-frauen. Accessed 12 March 2025.

[22] § 13 *Beamten-Dienstrechtsgesetz* 1979—*BDG* 1979, BGBl 1979/333.

2.1.2 Early Retirement

Like all statutory pension insurance benefits, an early retirement pension requires an application and is therefore voluntary.[23] Taking up a pension before the "normal" retirement age will result in a deduction from the pension amount with each month before the "normal" retirement age.

There are three different types of pensions that may be summarized under the term of early retirement in Austria:

"Corridor pension": The criteria for taking up a "corridor pension" include a minimum age of 62 and a minimum of 480 insurance months (40 years).[24] In addition, insured persons may not be included in compulsory pension insurance or performing gainful activity above the marginal earnings threshold. Due to the age requirements and the current standard retirement age for women, the "corridor pension" will become relevant for female pensioners as of 2028.

The pension reductions when taking-up an early "corridor pension" are in line with the bonus for pension deferral and amount to 0,425% (monthly), which equals 5,1% per year. Hence, there is a ceiling of a maximum of 15,3% of reduction, if the corridor pension is taken up at the earliest possible age (62 years).[25]

The "Heavy work pension" for persons in arduous and hazardous jobs will be discussed at the respective subchapter (see in this chapter, Sect. 2.3).

The pension for "long-term insured persons" requires—for women—a minimum age resembling "normal" retirement age until it reaches 62 years.[26] For male insured persons, the minimum age is set at 62 years already. Next to the age requirements, an insurance record of 540 months of compulsory insurance from gainful employment is a prerequisite.

For long-time insured persons, the pension is reduced by 0,35% for every month (4,2% yearly, to a maximum of 12,6%).

Early retirement pensions will be suspended, in case income above the so-called "marginal income threshold" is earned (i.e. EUR 551,10 per month in 2025).[27] To allow for more flexibility, as from 2024, the early retirement pension is only discontinued in the month in which additional income exceeds the monthly threshold of marginal income by more than 40%.[28] Besides more flexibility for pensioners, the

---

[23] There are regulations for civil servants that are modelled after the early retirement provisions of the statutory pension insurance system.

[24] The age condition will be adjusted gradually to 63 years of age and 504 months/42 years of insurance as from 2026.

[25] Sozialrechts-Änderungsgesetz 2023 (SRÄG 2023), BGBl I 2023/189.

[26] Raised step by step for women born before 30 June 1965 (§ 617 para 13 *ASVG)*, meaning that it is more favourable for female insured persons to apply for the standard retirement pension at the moment.

[27] However, the interruption in pension payment leads to a subsequent pension increase by taking the contributions earned during the time of suspension into account.

[28] More generous rules apply for pensions due to incapacity to work. If the total monthly gross income exceeds € 1557.93 (2025) the invalidity or occupational disability pension is payable as partial pension and reduced by up to 50%.

main objective is to cut down on red tape in terms of suspending and continuing the pension payment in case of varying income or several subsequent short-term employment relationships.

A partial pension for old-age does not exist in the Austrian pension system up to this point, but will be introduced as from 2026, applicable to both, "normal" old-age or early retirement pensions. The legal basis is currently still under consideration, but the draft includes a reduction of working hours with continued employment and compulsory insurance in statutory pension insurance.

2.2 *Deferral of Retirement*

If the old-age pension is not claimed until after the "normal" retirement age despite the minimum insurance period and age conditions are being fulfilled, the pension will increase by 0,425% monthly (up to a maximum of 15,3%, in case of a deferral for three years) for each month of deferral.

In addition, the employee's and employer's share of the pension insurance contribution will be reduced by half while the full contribution base is accounted for the subsequent pension calculation.

For federal civil servants, the responsible Minister may defer the legally prescribed as retirement upon request. However, there is no legal entitlement to a deferral. If granted, the period of postponing pension take-up may not exceed five years.

2.3 *Retirement Regimes for Persons Considered to Be in Hazardous or Arduous Jobs*

The "heavy work pension" scheme enables those persons, performing physically and mentally demanding activities to retire at 60 years of age. The following activities are included:

- Work performed in shifts or alternating shifts, including during the night,[29]
- Work performed regularly in hot or cold conditions,
- Work performed under chemical or physical influences,
- Heavy physical work (calories burned: at least 2000 calories for men and 1400 calories for women within eight hours of working time),

[29] For night and heavy work between 10 pm and 6 am, a special contribution of 3,8% of the contribution base is payable by the employer for those calendar months in which the respective employee performs heavy night work on at least six working days. This is only relevant for a few people who may retire at 57 (male) or 52 (female) with what is called "special retirement pension" (*Sonderruhegeld*). The legal basis is provided by the "heavy night work act", (*Nachtschwerarbeitsgesetz—NSchG,* BGBl 1981/354).

- Occupational carers of people with special treatment or care needs (e.g. hospice care)
- Employment despite one's entitlement to federal care allowance of at least level three.

The Ministry of Social Affairs has issued a regulation defining the working conditions recognised as heavy work.[30] Since it is particularly difficult to determine how many calories were burned during working time and therefore, whether heavy physical work was performed, occupational lists provide for a point of reference.[31]

For receiving a "heavy work pension", the minimum age requirement is 60 for both men and women. The minimum insurance period is 540 insurance months (i.e. 45 years), whereof at least 120 months (i.e.10 years) within the past 240 calendar months (i.e. 20 years) prior to the cut-off date have to be "heavy work months".

The reduction for persons qualifying for "heavy work pension" is 0,15% per month for every month before reaching the" normal" retirement age (i.e. 1,8% yearly).

2.4 Retirement Regimes Based on Means or Income Tested Benefits

When a pensioner's income does not reach a legally defined reference rate (*Richtsatz*), the "equalisation supplement" (*Ausgleichszulage*) tops up one's pension benefit upon application.

To be eligible for the supplement, the receipt of a pension benefit (and, hence, meeting the respective age and other requirements) is required, as well as taking residence in Austria. The level of the reference rate depends on the family status. For long insurance records, the reference rate is set at a higher level. The reference rate is subject to yearly adjustment.

The "equalisation supplement" stems from federal budget instead of contributions and is therefore not to be considered as some kind of minimum pension but rather as a form of minimum income for pensioners (social assistance).

For non-pensioners, other benefits from the general social assistance scheme are applicable.

---

[30] Regulation on heavy work (*Schwerarbeitsverordnung*), BGBl II 2006/104.

[31] The lists are available at Pensionsversicherung (2025), Schwerarbeitspension: Anspruch, Berufe und Berechnung. www.pv.at/web/pension/pensionsarten/schwerarbeitspension. Accessed 20 May 2025.

2.5 *Taxation*

Contributions are deductible from income tax, in the sense that the taxable income is reduced by the amount of the contributions to social security (for pension insurance 22,8% of the income/salary up to the maximum contribution base).

Pensions are subject to income tax, after deduction of tax alleviations (e.g. "tax credit for pensioners"[32]) and health insurance contributions. Recurring bonus payments ("13th and 14th pension") are exempt from taxation up to a certain threshold and then taxed at a special lower rate. The special supplementary amount due to former higher insurance is tax free up to 75%, while the remaining 25% are subject to income tax.

Pensioners who are not subject to income tax due to a low pension[33] receive a (partial) refund of their social security contributions.[34]

If a pensioner receives more than one pension (e.g., self-employed and employee pension), the pension institution which disburses the highest amount of taxable pension benefits, is competent to pay all taxes.

3 Occupational Pensions

3.1 *"Normal" Retirement Age*

The benefit rules and conditions such as waiting periods or cut-off dates strongly depend on the specific pension plan. For instance, the covered risks may include disability and survivor benefits or be focused solely on old-age.

Usually, the cut-off date is linked to the standard statutory legal retirement age.

3.2 *Taxation*

The taxation for contributions for occupational pensions depends on who pays the occupational pension contributions: Employer contributions to the pension fund are business expenses, which reduce the employer's taxable profit. Contributions by the insured person are subject to a government premium up to a certain amount.

---

[32] Automatically taken into account by the pension insurance institution which pays the pension.

[33] Yearly income up to EUR 13.308.

[34] Bundesministerium für Finanzen (2025) Absetzbeträge bei niedrigen Einkünften (SV-Rückerstattung), https://www.bmf.gv.at/themen/steuern/arbeitnehmerveranlagung/steuertarif-steuerabsetzbetraege/absetzbetraege-niedrige-einkommen-negativsteuer.html. Accessed 20 May 2025.

Starting with the payout of the occupational pensions, the part of the occupational pension stemming from employer's contributions are subject to income tax just like statutory pensions. But they are exempt from social security contributions.

The parts of the occupational pension financed by the insured person through own contributions are tax free between 75% and 100%, depending on the plan, investment model and if the government premium was applied for by the pensioner.[35]

Joint taxation as applies to statutory pensions is relevant as well, if a statutory pension is complemented by an occupational pension. Joint taxation is carried out by the institution that pays the highest taxable income.

References

Legislation

Beamten-Dienstrechtsgesetz 1979— *BDG* 1979, BGBl 1979/333

BVG-Altersgrenzen, BGBl 1992/832

General Social Security Act, *Allgemeines Sozialversicherungsgesetz—ASVG*, BGBl 1955/189

Nachtschwerarbeitsgesetz (NSchG), BGBl 1981/354

Occupational Pensions Act (*Betriebspensionsgesetz-BPG*), BGBl 1990/282

Pension Harmonization Act 2004 (*Pensionsharmonisierungsgesetz* 2004) (BGBl 2004/142)

Schwerarbeitsverordnung BGBl II 2006/104

Social Insurance Act for Self-Employed in Agriculture and Forestry (*Bauern-Sozialversicherungsgesetz—BSVG*), BGBl 1978/559

Social Insurance Act for Self-Employed in Industry and Craft Trades (*Gewerbliches Sozialversicherungsgesetz—GSVG*), BGBl 1978/560

Social Insurance Act for Self-Employed in Liberal Professions. (*Freiberuflichen Sozialversicherungsgesetz—FSVG*), BGBl 1978/624

Sozialrechts-Änderungsgesetz (2023) (SRÄG 2023), BGBl I 2023/189

Literature

Anderwald AM Besteuerung von Alterseinkünften als konsumorientiertes Element, taxlex 2022/34, issue 5, p 155–161

Bundesministerium für Finanzen (2025) Absetzbeträge bei niedrigen Einkünften (SV-Rückerstattung)

Bundesministerium für Kunst, Kultur, öffentlichen Dienst und Sport (2024) Monitoring der Pensionen der Beamtinnen und Beamten im Bundesdienst 2024

Bundesministerium für Soziales, Gesundheit, Pflege und Konsumentenschutz (2022) The Pensions System in Austria-an Overview

Soziale Sicherheit (2023) Focus on benefits, An overview of Austrian Social Insurance 2023

Zwinger V (2020) Devolution and decentralisation in social security: the situation in Austria. In: Schoukens P, Vonk G (eds) Devolution and decentralisation in social security, the Hague, pp 57–71

[35] Anderwald, A.-M., Besteuerung von Alterseinkünften als konsumorientiertes Element, taxlex 2022/34, p. 156.

Belgium

Yves Stevens

1 Introduction to the Pension System and Its Narrative

Belgium's retirement income system comprises public, occupational, and private pension schemes. The public pension scheme is earnings-related; moreover it is underpinned by a means-tested social assistance pension.

The earnings-related public scheme consists of three different components depending on the labour situation: (1) employees (4,5 million people), (2) self-employed (1,1 million people) and (3) civil servants including teachers (0,7 million people).

Employees, self-employed, and civil servants have their own pension rights and calculation methods. Apart from these three main pension categories, there are still some special pension programs for specific categories such as such as coalmine workers, aeronautical personnel, professional journalists and commercial seafarers.[1]

Employees, self-employed, and civil servants are compulsorily insured with a seniority requirement (in theory, 45 years) and a pensionable age of 66 (2025) (gradually increased to 67 by 2030). For all three categories, the final pension income depends on previous earnings, seniority, and marital status. For employees and self-employed, the maximum pension benefit equals 60% of pensionable income (adjusted career average earnings) for singles and 75% for married individuals. For civil servants, there is a fixed income replacement rate at 75% of the last earnings, regardless of the family situation.

[1] These special categories are not further taken into account.

Y. Stevens (✉)
Faculty of Law and Criminology, Department of Social Security & Labour Law, Institute for Social Law, Catholic University of Leuven, Leuven, Belgium
e-mail: yves.stevens@kuleuven.be

E. S. van Aggelen (ed.), *Retirement and Employment*, Ius Gentium: Comparative Perspectives on Law and Justice 145, https://doi.org/10.1007/978-3-032-33561-6_3

Retirement benefits for employees and self-employed are indexed to changes in the consumer price index. The pensions for civil servants are indexed to the wage scale of their previous pay scale.

There is also a means-tested 'minimum guaranteed income for elderly people,' obtained by every person older than 66 whose pension and other income are below a certain threshold (means tested).

There are three types of occupational pension plans in the second tier: company schemes, industry-wide schemes and individual pension arrangements. Contribution rates to occupational pension plans are usually laid down in the plan rules. Most plans are predominantly employer-financed, with contribution rates ranging from 0,5% to 1% for employees with income below the social security ceiling and 4% to 5% for income above that ceiling (80.485,32 EUR in 2025). Benefits can be paid out as annuities or as lump-sum payments but the large majority is paid out as a lump-sum. The average reserves acquired amount to a sum of 24.352 EUR, but half of the affiliates has saved less than 3.459 EUR (March 2024). This means that the occupational pension plans are still rather low.[2]

Private pension schemes are individual savings accounts or individual life insurance products offered by both insurance companies and banks. They are fiscally subsidized to a certain fixed ceiling for all Belgian Citizens.

In general public pension schemes have two major goals.[3] The first goal is to reduce poverty among the elderly. This is the dimension of poverty relief of the pension scheme (In Belgium, this is mainly guaranteed by the social assistance pension scheme and the minimum pension benefits in the pension insurances). The second goal is to replace an adequate proportion of wages after retirement. This is mainly guaranteed by the insurance dimension of pensions. These two dimensions are commonly believed to be at the origin of the two basic worldwide philosophies in pension design: the assistance design covering everyone and the insurance design covering those who paid premiums related to their profession.

---

[2] https://www.pensionstat.be/nl/kerncijfers/aanvullend-pensioen/hoogte-reserves. Accessed 30 May 2025.

[3] This double aim of income replacement and poverty alleviation is present in most pension schemes in the EU. The idea that pensions should do more than only poverty alleviation is as a policy principles supported by the European Union and its member States. The 2018 Pension Adequacy Report prepared jointly by the Social Protection Committee and the European Commission is clear: it analyses the adequacy of current and future pensions, that is: how they help maintain the income of men and women for the duration of their retirement and prevent old-age poverty (European Commission, The 2018 pension adequacy report: Current and future income adequacy in old age in the EU, Brussels, 2018, 188 p.). The double aim is often rephrased by economists as poverty relief and consumption smoothing. See for example: F. CHYBALSKI, 'Poverty Alleviation and Consumption Smoothing in European Pension Systems: Convergence or Divergence?' Argumenta Oeconomica, 2018, 40(1): 181–202.

The Belgian public pension schemes are largely based on the social insurance dimension for the professional categories of employees, self-employed, and civil servants. This is commonly known as the so-called Bismarckian approach and allows for categorial diversification based on the social premiums paid. Hence the traditional forms of paid labour play a very important role in the development of the Belgian social security. Labour and social security are traditionally very much intertwined. The payment of social contributions is based on the salary (or professional income at large) which an employee, a self-employed person or a civil servant receives. This is the basis of the Belgian welfare state. In terms of insurance, there is a form of economic profitability calculus (equivalence between professional income and level of benefit). This means that it is stated that something must be given in order to get something. However, this is under pressure. Moreover there is an element of proportionality: the longer the work record (or insurance record) the higher the benefit). These principles are growingly challenged by alternative work forms, such as domestic labour or all forms of non-economic labour, and more recently by new work forms in the platform economy and the growing popularity of part-time and fixed term work (as emanation of the flexible work forms, resulting in a reduction of working hours). This necessitates policy makers to rethink the relationship between labour and social insurance in the work related pension scheme as the underlying principles of equivalence and proportionality are being questioned. Especially when it comes to minimum pensions, there is growing concern that new and alternative work forms are not well enough protected by these minimum benefits. They aim mainly at poverty prevention and this is independent of any economic profitability calculus. Furthermore there are ceilings to the pensions (so-called maxima) but there are no maxima on the contributions.

The means-tested "minimum guaranteed income for elderly people" or *Inkomensgaratie voor ouderen* is a social assistance program. It is Beveridgian in approach as it addresses all residents (universal protection) by guaranteeing a (basic) benefit. However, the scheme is essentially of social assistance nature (and not social insurance) characterized by a means test and benefit levels guaranteeing minimum subsistence; it offers universal basic protection for all in need irrespective of (social) premiums.[4] As in most of the rest of the world, the poverty reduction amongst the elderly is financed via direct taxes.

[4] In 2002, Robin Blackburn has described the essential division as being from 'two distinct traditions, the puritan notion of industry, prudence and individual responsibility, on the one hand, and the baroque idea of a well-ordered public space and beneficent, universal power, on the other'. Robin Blackburn, Banking on Death (Verso 2002) 34.

2 Statutory Pensions[5]

2.1 *"Normal" Retirement Age*

The pensionable age is 66 in 2025 and is the same for the three main categories (employees, self-employed and civil servants).[6] From 2030 it will be 67. This increase will be incremental.[7]

No rule in the pension law obliges an employee or a self-employed to retire. There is no so-called pension obligation. In practice, most employees stop working at the (early) retirement age, and most self-employed persons continue to work longer. Employers in the private sector don't have to formally approve the prolongment of the career. A common agreement is silently in place when the employee continues to work after reaching retirement age.

However, civil servants are obligated to stop. Civil servants have the right to demand postponement in some fields of work (but not all), and the public authority can grant the right to prolong for a maximum of two years.

A limited number of civil servants are recognized to have so-called hazardous jobs and their retirement age can be lower. Military personnel can retire at the age of 56, 59 or 61 depending on the length of career and the type of career. Police can retire at the age of 56 or 58 depending on the type of work done and the length of the career. Train conductors can retire at the age of 55 with 30 years of career.

In principle, a worker (i.e., employee, self-employed, or civil servant) must cease his professional activities if he wants to enjoy a retirement pension.[8] However, a lot has changed in the last decade. Although the principle is still embedded in the law, important exceptions are created:

- Regardless of career, retirees are allowed unlimited additional earnings from retirement age 66–67.
- Regardless of age, a retiree may earn unrestricted additional earnings with a career of 45 years.

This means that under the age of 66 or without a 45-year career, limits on the cumulation of work with a pension apply. If the pensioner's professional income exceeds these allowable amounts, the pension is reduced or even suspended during the year of the excess. The reduction or suspension of the pension depends on the percentage of

[5] For a detailed overview: Y. STEVENS, Pensioenen werknemers met inbegrip van de aanvullende pensioenen, in J. PUT, V. VERDEYEN en Y. STEVENS (ed.), Praktijkboek Sociale Zekerheid, Kluwer, 2025, 613-724.

[6] The retirement pension commences on the first day of the month following that during which the interested party applies for it, and at the earliest on the first day of the month following the month in which he or she reaches the age of 65.

[7] Royal Decree of 23 December 1996 implementing Articles 15, 16 and 17 of the Law of 26 July 1996 on the modernisation of social security and on safeguarding the viability of statutory pensions.

[8] Art. 39 Royal decree nr. 50 of 24 October 1967 and Art. 64 en 64bis Royal decree of 12 December 1967.

the excess. If the retiree exceeds the limit amount by less than 100% then the pension is reduced by an equal percentage (for example, 27% excess means that the retiree must repay that amount in the amount of that 27% in the following year. However, if there is an excess of more than 100%, then the pension is suspended for the entire calendar year, and the pension already paid must be repaid in full the following year).

Table 1 gives an overview of the ceilings (in 2025).

If the authorized limits are exceeded, the pensioner cannot apply for an additional pension for the periods of the excess. In other words, the pension amount does not grow further based on the exceeded limits. This is even the case when the pensioner pays social contributions. Once the pension is in the pay-out phase there is no further accrual.

Pensioners are not allowed to earn in the "grey or black economy" any more than other people. The legislator has provided for a special penalty device for retirees and their employers caught committing this type of fraud. Apart from possible recoveries of the pensioner's statutory pension, a lump-sum compensation equal to 6 times the guaranteed average minimum monthly income is due. This must be paid by the employer to the Federal Pension Service (*FPS*). In addition to this lump-sum penalty and recovery, the *FPS* may proceed to suspend the pension for a period of six months. The *FPS* can only do this if the violation on the part of the pensioner can be called "serious" or if there is a repetition. This sanction also applies to the pensioner who is engaged in such activity as a self-employed person.

Table 1 Work after retirement under the age of 66 or without a 45-year career: ceilings (in 2025)

	Retirement pension or Retirement and survivor's pension younger than the statutory retirement age		Retirement pension or Retirement and survivor's pension from the statutory retirement age or a career of 45 years	Survivor's pension after the age of 66		Survivor's pension before the age of 66	
nature of the activity carried out:	without dependent child	with dependent child		without dependent child	with dependent child	without dependent child	with dependent child
employee	gross professional income (EUR)						
	10.117,00	15.175,00	unlimited	29.221,00	35.544,00	23.555,00	35.333,00
self-employed	net professional income (EUR)						
	8.039,00	12.140,00	unlimited	23.377,00	28.435,00	18.844,00	28.206,00

Reference Art. 64 en 64bis Royal decree of 12 December 1967

2.2 Early Retirement Age

Early retirement is always voluntary in Belgium. The eligibility rules for early retirement have been tightened since 2013. The minimum age for early retirement was 60 (in 2013) to 63. With long careers, one can still retire early at a younger age. In 2012, 35 career years were still sufficient to retire early. In 2025 it is 42 years.

Overall structure for all categories (employees, self-employed, and civil servants):

- 60 years, with career of 44 years
- 61 years, with career of 43 years
- 63 years, with career of 42 years

In the Belgian statutory pension system, no malus will apply if you retire earlier.

If one combines early retirement with employment, the same rules apply as with the normal retirement age.

2.3 Deferral of Retirement

Deferral is in Belgium always voluntary. The Belgian government has implemented retirement bonuses on several occasions to promote working longer. These bonuses were discarded each time because of either limited impact or uncertain effects. For example, it was assumed that the bonuses would mainly go to those people who would continue working anyway, regardless of the existence of a bonus. Anno 2024, another pension bonus is on the governmental table. This time, workers who work beyond retirement age would receive a lump sum.

2.4 Partial Retirement

In the last decade several legislative attempts have been tried to install schemes for partial retirement. All have failed. Belgium doesn't permit the partial pay-out of pensions.

2.5 Retirement Regimes for Persons Considered to Be in Hazardous or Arduous Jobs

A limited number of civil servants are recognized to have so-called hazardous jobs and their retirement age can be lower. Military personnel can retire at the age of 56, 59 or 61 depending on the length of career and the type of career. Police can retire at the age of 56 or 58 depending on the type of work done and the length of the career. Train conductors can retire at the age of 55 with 30 years of career.

2.6 Retirement Regimes Based on Means or Income Tested Benefits

The means-tested system has the same age limits as the statutory and occupational pension system: 66 (2025–2029), and 67 from 2030 onwards.

2.7 Taxation

In principle, pensions are taxed. Statutory pensions have a triple approach. First, there is a special deduction intended for the pension sector itself. This tax is called the solidarity levy and amounts to maximum two percent of the pension income. The idea was to strengthen the mutual solidarity among pensioners with a progressive deduction from the overall pension income. By "pension" is meant any legal, regulatory or statutory retirement, seniority or survivor's pension, as well as any "additional benefit", even if the latter is not acquired or granted by virtue of legal, statutory or regulatory provisions or by virtue of a company regulation, employment contract, collective or sectoral agreement.

Secondly, there is a special levy for the health care sector. This deduction is made from the pension for health care equal to 3.55% of the total pension amount.[9] The pension amount is equal to the total pension income, including additional benefits granted either by application of legal, regulatory or statutory provisions, or by application of the employment contract, a company regulation, a collective company or sectoral agreement, but excluding vacation pay and additional supplement.

The remaining pension amount may be subject to personal income tax. The withholding tax is a provisional advance payment on the final personal income tax due. The calculation of this withholding tax is done using the official scales of withholding tax. Withholding tax is due only from a certain monthly amount: 2.221,50 EUR for the married pensioner whose spouse has no own income, or only a limited own pension, and 1.460,53 EUR for the other pensioners. Various further reductions apply to the withholding tax (e.g., in case the partner has only limited income or in case of child burden).

There is no difference in the tax regime on early retirement or deferral of retirement for statutory pensions.

[9] Art. 191, §1, 7° Health Care Act and art. 3 Royal decree 15 September 1980.

3 Occupational Pensions

3.1 *"Normal" Retirement Age*

Since 2015 the normal retirement age for occupational pension is the same as for the statutory pensions. The pensionable age is 66 in 2025 and is the same for the three main categories (employees, self-employed, and civil servants).[10] From 2030, the retirement age will be 67.

3.2 *Early Retirement*

There are no specific rules on occupational pensions and early retirement because all the age limits are linked to the statutory pensions.

There are no bonusses or maluses in occupational pensions as such. There is, however, a fiscal effect on early retirement. Lump sums taken up at early retirement are taxed 6,5% more heavy than at normal retirement age.

3.3 *Taxation*

Occupational pensions are taxed. Virtually all people take up a lump sum. This is taxed at a rate ranging from 10% (at age 66) to 16,5% (before age 66). In addition, there is the health care deduction of 3,55% and the solidarity contribution of up to 2% and municipal surcharges. Since the municipal surcharges can vary thoroughly between municipalities or cities, some so-called "shopping" does take place in tax practice, with beneficiaries opting for tax-friendly solutions by purchasing property in tax-favorable places. The tax regime of occupational pensions remains the same at deferral. Occupational pensions are taxed 6,5% more at early retirement than at the normal retirement age.

It's interesting to note that statutory and occupational pensions are not only linked with the age. The health care deduction of 3,55% and the solidarity contribution of up to 2% and municipal surcharges apply similarly to occupational and statutory pensions. Hence, there is a strong tax interconnectivity, although statutory pensions are annuities and occupational pensions are lump sums.

[10] The retirement pension commences on the first day of the month following that during which the interested party applies for it, and at the earliest on the first day of the month following the month in which he or she reaches the age of 66.

References

Legislation

Koninklijk Besluit nr. 50 van 24 oktober 1967 betreffende het rust- en overlevingspensioen voor werknemers (**Pensioenwet Werknemers**).

Koninklijk Besluit van 21 december 1967 tot vaststelling van het algemeen reglement betreffende het rust- en overlevingspensioen voor werknemers (**Pensioenbesluit Werknemers**).

Wet van 20 juli 1990 tot instelling van een flexibele pensioenleeftijd voor werknemers en tot aanpassing van de werknemerspensioenen aan de evolutie van het algemeen welzijn (**Wet Flexibele Pensioenleeftijd**).

Koninklijk Besluit van 4 december 1990 tot uitvoering van de Wet van 20 juli 1990 tot instelling van een flexibele pensioenleeftijd voor werknemers en tot aanpassing van de werknemerspensioenen aan de evolutie van het algemeen welzijn, en tot wijziging van sommige bepalingen inzake werknemerspensioenen (**Besluit Flexibele Pensioenleeftijd**).

Koninklijk Besluit van 23 december 1996 tot uitvoering van de artikelen 15, 16 en 17 van de Wet van 26 juli 1996 tot modernisering van de sociale zekerheid en tot vrijwaring van de leefbaarheid van de wettelijke pensioenen (**Wet Modernisering Werknemerspensioenen**).

Koninklijk Besluit nr. 72 van 10 november 1967 betreffende het rust- en overlevingspensioen der zelfstandigen (**Pensioenwet Zelfstandigen**).

Koninklijk Besluit van 22 december 1967 houdende algemeen reglement betreffende het rust- en overlevingspensioen der zelfstandigen (**Pensioenbesluit Zelfstandigen**).

Artikel 118 tot 154 van de Wet van 15 mei 1984 houdende maatregelen tot harmonisering in de pensioenregelingen (**Wet Harmonisering Pensioenregelingen**).

Koninklijk Besluit van 30 januari 1997 betreffende het pensioenstelsel der zelfstandigen met toepassing van de artikelen 15 en 27 van de Wet van 26 juli 1996 tot modernisering van de sociale zekerheid en tot vrijwaring van de leefbaarheid van de wettelijke pensioenstelsels en van artikel 3, § 1, 4° van de Wet van 26 juli 1996 strekkende tot realisatie van de budgettaire voorwaarden tot deelname van België aan de Europese en Monetaire Unie (**Wet Modernisering Zelfstandigenpensioenen**).

Literature

Y. STEVENS, Pensioenen werknemers met inbegrip van de aanvullende pensioenen, in J. PUT, V. VERDEYEN en Y. STEVENS (ed.), Praktijkboek Sociale Zekerheid, Kluwer, 2025, 613–724.

Y. STEVENS, Pensioenen zelfstandigen met inbegrip van de aanvullende pensioenen, in J. PUT, V. VERDEYEN en Y. STEVENS (ed.), Praktijkboek Sociale Zekerheid, Kluwer, 2025, 811–866.

Croatia

Ivana Vukorepa

1 Introduction to the Pension System and Its Narrative

The origins of Croatian pension system date back to the end of nineteenth century when various disability and old-age insurance schemes have been adopted within the Austro-Hungarian monarchy, followed by the adoption of the Act on the Mandatory Insurance for Workers in 1922 based on Bismarck's tradition. Throughout its existence it has undergone many significant changes. Until 2002, Croatian pension system was a single pillar system: public pay-as-you-go (PAYG) with defined benefit (DB) characterized by a very low retirement age and adherence to Bismarckian tradition. The transitional economy and wartime sufferings caused social instability and financial pressure, thereby bringing the need for reforms to the fore. The World Bank and the International Monetary Fund also advocated the necessity for the system's restructuring. In 1998, the first significant parametric reform focused on rationalization and the control of pension costs. In 2002, a structural reform followed and turned the Croatian pension system into a multi-scheme system (also referred to in the national and international literature as a three-pillar system).

Hence, since 2002, the Croatian pension system has been a public-private mix consisting of three schemes, popularly referred to as 3 pillars. The pension legislative framework has been amended and changed on too many occasions.[1] Currently, it

[1] For more see: Vukorepa (2015) Lost between Sustainability and Adequacy: Critical Analysis of the Croatian Pension System's Parametric Reform. Revija za socijalnu politiku, 22 (3): 279–308; Potočnjak Ž, Vukorepa I (2018) Drugi mirovinski stup: prijepori i moguća poboljšanja (Second pension pillar: debates and possible improvments). In: Miladin, P, Guinio, M (eds) Zbornik 56. susreta pravnika, Hrvatski savez udruga pravnika u gospodarstvu, Zagreb, p. 231–271. For overview in a comparative perspective with a status in 2020 see: Vukorepa (2021) Croatia. In: / Schneider, Simone M, Petrova, T, Becker, U (eds) Pension Maps: Visualising the Institutional Structure of Old Age Security in Europe and Beyond, 2nd edn, Max Planck Institute for Social Law and Social Policy, München, p. 71–84.

I. Vukorepa (✉)
Department for Labour and Social Security Law, Faculty of Law, University of Zagreb, Zagreb, Croatia
e-mail: ivana.vukorepa@pravo.unizg.hr

E. S. van Aggelen (ed.), *Retirement and Employment*, Ius Gentium: Comparative Perspectives on Law and Justice 145, https://doi.org/10.1007/978-3-032-33561-6_4

consists of four basic laws[2] and many other special laws and by-laws.[3] Here are presented main features based on the legislation in force by June 1, 2025.

The first pillar is the statutory earnings-related mandatory pay-as-you-go (PAYG) defined benefits (DB) scheme financed by contributions, while the deficit is financed from the State Budget, thus indirectly by taxes and other Government transfers. Within the first mandatory pillar (PAYG DB pillar), all economically active persons are compulsory insured (workers, self-employed, farmers, etc.). Optionally, there is the possibility of so-called “extended insurance” for persons outside work (e.g., unemployed persons or during the suspension of the employment relationship) provided they apply for it within 1 year after termination of compulsory insurance and pay pension insurance contributions themselves as to accrue insurance period. The pension system’s dependency ratio has had an increasing trend since the 1980’s, reaching its peak in 2014 at 87,57%. Since then, there has been a slow decreasing trend, reaching 74,31% at the end of 2023 and 71.82% at the end of 2024 (equivalent to the system support ratio of 1,35 and 1.39 respectively).[4]

The second pillar is a statutory mandatory fully funded defined contribution (DC) scheme based on individual retirement accounts financed by contributions and investment returns. Persons insured under the first pillar are normally also insured under the second mandatory pillar (funded DC scheme)[5] and pension benefits are drawn simultaneously.[6]

Contributions for mandatory pension pillars are earmarked. The total pension contribution rate for mandatory pension insurance is 20%. Persons covered only by a PAYG DB scheme pay all contributions only to the first pillar, while persons with mandatory insurance under both pillars pay 15% to the first pillar and 5%

---

[2] Pension Insurance Act, Act on Compulsory Pension Funds, Act on Voluntary Pension Funds, and Act on Pension Insurance Companies.

[3] Other important laws regulating mandatory PAYGO DB scheme (so called first pillar) are e.g.: (1) Maximum Pension Act, (2) Act on Pension Supplement for Pensions Earned under the Pension Insurance Act, and (3) Act on the Insurance Periods Counted with Extended Duration. Other laws (all together 18 of them), relate to contribution payment, taxation, and regulation of more favorable pension conditions for 19 special groups of insured persons (police, army, war veterans, arduous and hazardous jobs, as well as person with certain disabilities such as blind and deaf persons, person suffering from dystrophy and related muscular and neuromuscular diseases, paraplegia, multiple sclerosis etc.). For mandatory and voluntary funded DC schemes there are many by-laws (list available via Croatian Financial Services Supervisory Agency—HANFA): https://www.hanfa.hr/regulativa/mirovinski-sustav/).

[4] Author’s calculations based on historical data available from Croatian Pension Insurance Institute, Statistical information series, https://www.mirovinsko.hr/hr/statistika/860.

[5] Regarding participation in a multi-pillar system there have been three situations that should be differentiated: (1) all persons under the age of 40 (either at the time of the reform or at the time of becoming an insuree) have to participate within the two-tier mandatory system with double coverage; (2) persons aged between 40 and 50 at the time of the reform could choose between staying within the PAYGO scheme only or joining the new two-tier mandatory system with the second pillar funded part, and (3) persons over 50 had to remain within the first pillar only.

[6] Since 2019 all participants to a two-pillar mandatory system were given right to choose before retirement (pay-out phase), to return to single pillar system, if their pension from the single pillar would be more favorable than from the two-pillar mandatory system.

to the second pillar.[7] For persons employed in hazardous and physically strenuous jobs, there are additional contributions.[8] The pension contribution is paid from gross employee wages or from the "pension insurance base" (which is set in different amounts for various types of self-employed persons and some other categories like company board members).[9] Pension contributions are tax-exempt and represent cost for the employer.

Further on, it is important to note that within the mandatory part of the pension system, there is no separate scheme for special categories or occupations, but there have been special laws under the general system that afford more favourable pension conditions to numerous categories of the so-called "privileged pensioners" (e.g. active military personnel, police, war veterans, members of the parliament, workers in arduous and hazardous jobs, and person with certain disabilities such as blind and deaf persons, person suffering from dystrophy and related muscular and neuromuscular diseases, paraplegia, multiple sclerosis etc).

The mandatory part of the pension system covers the traditional risks of old age, including early retirement (but also other risks such as death, disability, and physical injury, including higher rights if the risks of death and disability were caused by accidents at work and occupational diseases). Hence, the benefits in terms of pensions under the mandatory schemes comprise old-age pensions (including several early retirement pension options), survivors' pensions and disability pensions.[10]

---

[7] Exceptionally, for some categories of persons pension contribution rates are reduced by half, e.g. for self-employed in agriculture and forestry and for so called other income recipients (those working based on contract for service or author's contract), while for student work there are no pension contributions (based on the analysis of the provisions of the Act on Contributions, see also: Grgurev and Vukorepa (2018) Flexible and New Forms of Employment in Croatia and their Pension Entitlement Aspects. In: Sander Gerald G, Tomljenovic V, Bodiroga-Vukobrat, N (eds) Transnational, European, and National Labour Relations. Europeanization and Globalization, vol. 4, Springer, Cham, p. 241–262).

[8] Art. 13. of the Act on Contributions.

[9] E.g. for liberal professions it amounts to 110% of average wage, for board members it is 100% of average wage, for registered self-employed activity it is 65% of average wage while for craftsperson registered for lump sum income it is only 40% of average wage (Arts. 66, 68, 82 of the Act on Contributions).

[10] The calculation of pension benefits within the mandatory PAYGO DB scheme (first pillar) is based on a personal points system, primarily based on average contributory earnings throughout working career and related to the length of the insurance period. Maximum pension is capped at 380% of the person's average earnings for the whole contribution period compared to economy-wide average earnings over the same period. Minimum pension is neither means tested nor set as absolute amount; it depends on the number of qualifying years multiplied by the "minimum actual pension value", which since 2023 amounts to 103% of the "actual pension value" (i.e. the value of one personal point for regular pensions). The pension benefit from mandatory funded DC scheme (second pillar) is drawn simultaneously with a pension from mandatory DB PAYGO scheme. However, due to the funded DC character of the scheme, the pension benefit from this part depends on the accumulated capital through contribution payments and investment yields, minus administrative costs and costs/fees of pension provider. Pensions are paid as monthly life-time benefit calculated based on unisex mortality tables and by considering other optional factors (e.g. guaranteed period of benefit payment to the named beneficiary in the case of pensioner's death).

The third pillar is a voluntarily funded DC pension scheme with individual retirement accounts aimed at toppling up mandatory pensions. It consists of two types of voluntary pension funds: (1) "open-ended pension funds" (open to all citizens) and (2) "closed-ended pension funds," which are special occupational retirement funds sponsored by employers, trade unions, or other professional associations, hence participation is only allowed to employees or members respectively. Third pillar voluntary schemes are financed by voluntary contributions and investment returns. They are additionally incentivised by state subsidy and tax reliefs (regarding employer's contributions to voluntary individual retirement accounts, both within open or closed funds). Occupational DB schemes cannot be offered in Croatia.[11]

2 Statutory Pensions

2.1 "Normal" Retirement Age

Retirement at "normal" retirement age (legal retirement reference age) is voluntary, since no rule in the pension law obliges an employee or a self-employed to retire. In practice, most employees stop working at the retirement age (especially due to provisions on combining work with retirement without pension reduction), while self-employed persons tend to continue working longer.

However, it is important to note that although there is no pension obligation within the pension law, labour law provisions play a significant role. Namely, Labour Act links *ex-lege* termination of employment contract to 65 with a possibility of its prolongation without limitations.[12] In the public sector rules are stricter. For example, civil servants need to stop working at the age of 65 (with a limited prolongation possibility, maximum until 67).[13] Similarly, doctors within the public healthcare network need to stop working at the age of 65 (since 2023, there is a work prolongation possibility to 68 with the employer's consent and exceptionally even above that age if there is additional consent of the Ministry of Health).[14] Nevertheless, due to lack of general practitioners, it has been prescribed that health workers in the public health service network may perform private practice until they reach the age of 68, while in the event of a threat to the provision of health care, the Minister of Healthcare may grant health workers the extension of private practice until they reach the age of 70.[15] Similar rules exist for other occupations in the public sector (e.g., pharmacists, teachers, scientists, and university professor). These labour law rules do not force a person to a pension since a person can take up employment in the private sector.

[11] This is expressly stated in the law: Art. 266 of the Act on Voluntary Pension Funds.

[12] Art. 112 of the Labour Act.

[13] Arts. 83 and 152 of the Act on Civil Servants.

[14] Art. 155, paras. 5 and 6 of the Health Care Act.

[15] Art. 67, paras. 2 and 3 of the Health Care Act.

Table 1 Statutory retirement age

Year	Standard old age for women
2025	63 years and 9 months
2026	64 years
2027	64 years and 3 months
2028	64 years and 6 months
2029	64 years and 9 months
2030	65 years

Reference Author based on legal provisions (Art. 33 and 180 of the Pension Insurance Acts)

However, these rules, in combination with a pension law rule allowing a person to combine part-time work with old-age or early retirement pension with no benefit cutback, stimulate retirement (see in more detail in this chapter, Sect. 2.4).

Within the statutory mandatory scheme, retirement age differs according to specific pension types and retiree groups.

For a "normal" old age pension, the statutory retirement age is set at 65 with a minimum insurance period of 15 years. However, this retirement age has been applicable for men since 2010, while for women a gradual transition period of slow increase (3 months per calendar year) is in force, reaching 65 by 2030 (see Table 1).[16]

Legislative increases of standard retirement age to 67 by 2033 (enacted in 2018)[17] were abandoned in 2019 after trade union protests and a referendum initiative.[18]

There is also a more favourable old age pension for long-term insured persons in place (in effect, it is early retirement for long-term insured persons with a right to full benefit without pension decrement, i.e., without malus): retirement age 60, minimum insurance period: 41 years.[19]

Some categories of persons enjoy special reductions in retirement age for old-age pension benefit based on special laws. These are the following groups:

- active military personnel, police officers, and authorized officials (e.g. in state security intelligence bodies) who have the right to old age pension based on the decision of the competent minister on termination of their service, regardless of age, if the person has accumulated minimum 30 years of insurance period, of which at least 15 years of insurance period in those special jobs or in Homeland War)[20];
- Veterans of Croatian Homeland War who have the right to a reduction of normal retirement age depending on the length of participation in the defence of Croatian sovereignty (the normal retirement age is lowered by 4 months total if the person

[16] Art. 33 and 180 of the Pension Insurance Act.

[17] Amendments to the Pension Insurance Act (NN 115/18).

[18] Amendments to the Pension Insurance Act (NN 102/19).

[19] Ibid, Art. 35.

[20] Regulated by the Act on Pension Insurance Rights of Active Military Personnel, Police Officers, and Authorized Officials.

participated in the defence from 100 days to five months, while by 1 month for each month of participation in the defence if person participated for more than five months)[21];

- persons with disabilities defined by special law (such as blind and deaf persons, persons suffering from dystrophy and related muscular and neuromuscular diseases, paraplegia, multiple sclerosis etc.) have the right to an insurance period with an extended duration (12 months is counted as 15), hence also a right to decrease in retirement age by one year for every five years of work.[22]
- persons in arduous and hazardous jobs (see in this chapter, Sect. 2.5).

The possibility of combining work with retirement was introduced in 2014 and has since been enlarged. Currently all old-age, early retirement pension receivers and survivor's pension receivers are allowed to work (as employees) part-time up to 20 hours per week, with a parallel right to full pension benefit in payment. Longer working hours lead to pension payment suspension. For working pensioners, the employer must pay pension contributions for mandatory schemes.[23]

Regarding the form of permitted work, only work in an employment relationship is allowed, as well as earnings through the so-called other income (e.g. occasional income based on a contract for service or author's contract, or receipts based on the activities in supervisory company boards). Independent work, i.e. work in the form of self-employment (e.g. tradesmen, registered professional activity) is not allowed, in which case the pension payment will be suspended.[24]

However, in May 2025 Government proposed the new Pension Insurance Act, which will significantly expand the possibility to combine work with retirement. Namely, from January 2026 pensioners older than 65 will be allowed to full-time employment or continuation of craft or independent professional activities with the right to 50% of pension amount. Furthermore, it is proposed that beneficiaries of total disability pension due to complete loss of working capacity may nevertheless be employed for less than 3.5 hours a day without pension suspension or reduction.[25]

2.2 *Early Retirement Age*

Early retirement is voluntary in Croatia. It is available up to 5 years prior to reaching normal retirement age. General early retirement qualifying conditions are as follows: statutory early retirement age of 60 and 35 years of insurance period (these retirement conditions have been applicable for men since 2010, while for women from 2030

[21] Art. 26 Act on Croatian Veterans from the Homeland War and their Family Members.

[22] Art. 26 and 27, para. 3. of Act on the Insurance Periods Counted with Extended Duration.

[23] For more see: Vukorepa (2023) Hrvatski model djelomičnog umirovljenja: kritički osvrt (The Croatian Model of Partial Retirement: A Critical Review). Zbornik Pravnog fakulteta u Zagrebu, 73 (2–3): 423–456, specifically pp. 433–438.

[24] Ibid.

[25] Arts 85 and 100, paras 2, 3 and 6 of the Proposal of the new Pension Insurance Act (May 2025).

Table 2 Standard early retirement for women

Standard early retirement for women		
Year	Age	Insurance period
2025	58 years and 9 months	33 years and 9 months
2026	59 years	34 years
2027	59 years and 3 months	34 years and 3 months
2028	59 years and 6 months	34 years and 6 months
2029	59 years and 9 months	34 years and 9 months
2030	60 years	35 years

Reference Author based on legal provisions (Art. 34 and 182 of the Pension Insurance Act)

onwards, until then, a transitional period of slow increase applies, i.e. increase of 3 months per calendar year (see Table 2).[26]

Legislative increases of early retirement age to 62 by 2033 (enacted in 2018)[27] were abandoned in 2019 after trade union protests and a referendum initiative.[28]

The reduction of benefits for early retirement has existed since 1999. However, the amount of malus has changed on many occasions.[29] Since 2020, pension decrement amounts to 0,2% multiplied by the number of months of early retirement[30] (i.e., max. Pension decrement amounts to 12% since maximum early retirement window is 5 years, hence max. 60 months). This amount of malus is low and not actuarially fair, but result of political compromise. Government proposal of the new Pension Insurance Act from May 2025 previews abolition of pension decrements (malus) for pensioners once they reach the age of 70.[31]

It is worth mentioning that there are two forms of early retirement without malus. The first is "old age pension for long-term insured person" (conditions: 60 years of age and minimum 41 years of insurance period).[32] The second is "early retirement pension due to bankruptcy" for persons fulfilling regular early retirement conditions, but whose pension insurance status was terminated due to their employer's

[26] Art. 34 and 182 of the Pension Insurance Act.

[27] Amendments to the Pension Insurance Act (NN 115/18).

[28] Amendments to the Pension Insurance Act (NN 102/19).

[29] Until the end of 2007, the early retirement decrement was 0.34% per month (hence 4.08% per year of early retirement, 20.40% for maximum 5 years of early retirement). This amount was considered to be close to actuarially neutral correction due to longer period of payments. During election year 2007 malus has been decreased to only 0.15% per month (thus to 1.8% per year; 9% for 5 years), and such situation was applicable from 2008 to 2010. From 2011 malus depended not only on the months of early retirement, but also on the years of insurance period (amounting from min. 9% to max. 20.4% for 5 years early retirement). In 2019, malus was raised to 0.3% and in 2020 reduced again to 0.2% per months of early retirement.

[30] Art. 85, para 2 of the Pension Insurance Act.

[31] Art. 83, para 9 of the Proposal of the new Pension Insurance Act (May 2025).

[32] Art. 35 of the Pension Insurance Act.

bankruptcy, provided they have been unemployed for at least 2 years continuously prior to retirement.[33]

Work during early retirement has been allowed since 2019. If a pensioner works part-time up to 20 hours per week, s/he keeps a parallel right to full pension benefit in payment. Longer working hours lead to pension payment suspension. Regarding the form of permitted work, only work in an employment relationship is allowed, as well as earnings through the so-called other income (e.g. occasional income). However, in May 2025 Government proposed expansion of the right to combine early retirement and work so that from January 2026 early retirement pensioners upon reaching the age of 65 would be allowed to full-time employment or continuation of craft or independent professional activities with the right to reduced pension, i.e. 50% of pension amount.[34]

2.3 *Deferral of Retirement*

Deferral of retirement in pension law is voluntary and without limit. However, labour law provisions, especially in the public sector, together with the right to part-time work might stimulate people to retire instead of deferring their retirement (see in this chapter, Sect. 2.4).

Bonus for retirement deferral was introduced in 2011, amounting to 0,15% per month of late retirement. Since 2023, it amounts to 0,45% per month of later retirement; it is limited to a maximum of 5 years (i.e., permanent pension increment is limited in total to a maximum of 27%).[35]

2.4 *Partial Retirement*

As indicated already in sect. 2.1. of this chapter, since 2014 Croatia adopted a model of partial retirement in the form of the right to full pension benefits in payment combined with part-time work. It was enlarged since. Currently all old-age, early retirement pension receivers and survivor's pension receivers are allowed to work (as employees) part-time up to 20 hours per week, with a parallel right to full pension benefit in payment. Longer working hours lead to pension payment suspension. For working pensioners employer must pay pension contributions for mandatory schemes. Hence, such work may lead to increases of pension benefits due to two facts: (1) pension insurance period is being accrued (which is one of the elements in the benefit formula within the mandatory PAYGO DB scheme), and (2) contributions are paid (which

[33] Art. 36 of the Pension Insurance Act.

[34] Art. 85, para 1 (11) of the Proposal of the new Pension Insurance Act (May 2025).

[35] Art. 85, para 3 of the Pension Insurance Act. Government proposal of the new Pension Insurance Act from May 2025 previews abolition of 5-year pension increment limitation.

due to personal points DB formula can affect the level of benefit within mandatory PAYGO DB scheme (I pillar), while definitely increases pension from mandatory funded DC part (second pillar). Regarding the form of permitted work, only work in an employment relationship is allowed, as well as earnings through the so-called other income (e.g. occasional income based on a contract for service or author's contract, or receipts based on the activities in supervisory company boards). Independent work, i.e. work in the form of self-employment (e.g. tradesmen, registered professional activity) is not allowed, in which case the pension payment will be suspended.[36] However, in May 2025 the Government proposed the new Pension Insurance Act, which from January 2026 significantly expands the possibility to combine work with retirement: (1) pensioners older than 65 will be allowed to full-time employment or continuation of craft or independent professional activities with the right to 50% of pension amount, and (2) total disability pensioners will be allowed to work for less than 3.5 hours a day without pension suspension or reduction.[37]

Partial retirement in the sense that there is reduced working activity combined with partial pension pay-out exists only in two cases[38]:

1. for partial disability pensioners who continue working from 70% to 100% working time in adapted jobs, in which case their pension benefit amounts to 50% (exceptionally to 66,7% if the disability was caused by an accident at work of occupational disease), and
2. for old-age police and military pensioners who retired under preferential age treatment (if they continue working full-time, then they have the right to 50% of their pension; however, if they work part-time up to 20 hours per week, then they have the right to full pension).

2.5 *Retirement Regimes for Persons Considered to Be in Hazardous or Arduous Jobs*

Deviation from "normal" retirement conditions for workers in arduous and hazardous jobs is regulated by the 2018 Act on Insurance Period Counted with Extended Duration. Despite this relatively new law, the system had existed for a long time and, in essence, did not change at all.[39] Retirement age for this group of workers depends on two elements: (1) the years worked in hazardous jobs and arduous occupations, and

[36] For more see: Vukorepa (2023) Hrvatski model djelomičnog umirovljenja: kritički osvrt (The Croatian Model of Partial Retirement: A Critical Review). Zbornik Pravnog fakulteta u Zagrebu, 73 (2–3): 423–456, specifically pp. 433–456.

[37] Arts 85 and 100, paras 2, 3 and 6 of the Proposal of the new Pension Insurance Act (May 2025).

[38] Arts 87 and 99 of the Pension Insurance Act.

[39] Hence all the elaboration and remarks related to the previous law are still valid. See: Vukorepa (2017) Retirement Policy Changes for Workers in Arduous and Hazardous Jobs: Comparative Overview and Lessons for Croatia. Zbornik Pravnog fakulteta u Zagrebu, 67 (1): 5–28.

(2) the degree of insurance period extension for each of these occupations. Hence, the pension age is reduced as follows[40]:

- by one year for every six years of work in jobs or professions in which the insurance period of 12 months is counted as 14 months,
- by one year for every five years of work in jobs or occupations in which the insurance period of 12 months is counted as 15 months,
- by one year for every four years of work in jobs or professions in which the insurance period of 12 months is counted as 16 months, and
- by one year for every three years of work in jobs or professions in which the insurance period of 12 months is counted as 18 months.

2.6 Retirement Regimes Based on Means or Income-Tested Benefits

Poverty alleviation is targeted within the mandatory PAYG DB scheme (first pillar) through a so-called minimum pension that is neither means-tested nor income-tested.[41]

Outside the pension system, there is a special social assistance measure for persons over 65 with no right to pension benefits: It is called "national allowance for elderly" and was introduced in 2021. Conditions were relaxed, and the amount has increased since 2024, so currently, this national allowance amounts to 150 EUR (monthly). The main conditions are the following: Croatian nationality, 65 years of age, 10 years of continuous residence record in the territory of Croatia immediately before submitting an application for the allowance, no right to pension benefit, no other income per household member exceeding 300 EUR (twice the amount of the national benefit for the elderly).[42]

2.7 Taxation

Regarding tax policy, contributions paid for mandatory pension schemes are tax-exempt. The employer pays them on behalf of his/her employees from the gross wage, while the gross wage represents cost on the employer side.

Pensions in payment from the mandatory schemes (first and second pillar) are taxed progressively in the same way as wage income; however, under a preferential regime due to the fact that since 2017, tax obligations based on pensions have been

---

[40] Art. 27. of the 2018 Act on the Insurance Periods Counted with Extended Duration.

[41] Minimum pension is not set as absolute amount; it depends on the number of qualifying years multiplied by the "minimum actual pension value", that since 2023 amounts to 103% of the "actual pension value" (i.e. the value of one personal point for regular pensions).

[42] Arts 4 and 5 of the Act on National Allowance for the Elderly.

reduced by 50%.[43] This rule is applicable in the same way, regardless if the pension is taken at normal retirement age, early retirement, partial retirement, or deferred retirement.

3 Occupational Pensions

As indicated above in this chapter, Sect. 1, occupational pensions in Croatia exist only within voluntary funded DC schemes (the so called third pillar that covers both private individual and occupational schemes).

3.1 "Normal" Retirement Age

Within voluntary funded DC schemes (third pillar) pension benefits can be withdrawn at a much earlier age than from mandatory schemes: at the age of 55 for temporary pensions (i.e. pensions paid out for a limited period, e.g. from 5 to 20 years), while for life-time pensions minimum pension age is set at 60 years of age.[44]

There are no limitations to the possibility of receiving an occupational pension and continuing working. Namely, retirement from the voluntary schemes in Croatia (be it occupational or individual) can be combined with work and other earnings.

3.2 Early Retirement

There are no rules on early retirement within voluntary (occupational or individual) schemes since the age for drawing benefits from these schemes is very low, only 55 for temporary pension and 60 for life-time annuities.

Since occupational and individual pensions are provided within voluntary funded DC scheme there is no direct legally prescribed malus. However, there can be only indirect malus if a person agrees on life-time payment, because in that case pension benefits are calculated based on life-expectancy at the retirement age. Hence, age at the time of retirement plays a role in the amount of monthly annuity amount for life-time pensions. However, in practice, majority of persons take up so called temporary pensions (i.e., pensions paid out for a limited period, e.g., from 5 to 20 years) where there is no longevity risk.

Retirement from the voluntary schemes in Croatia (be it occupational or individual) can be combined with work and other earnings.

[43] Art. 24, para. 5. of the Income Tax Act.

[44] Art. 115 of the Act on Pension Insurance Companies.

3.3 Taxation

Personal individual contributions to voluntary pension schemes (be it occupational or individual) are paid from taxed income. However, employers matching contributions to the voluntary individual accounts are partially tax-exempt: they are not subject to income tax up to 67 EUR (monthly) or 804 EUR (yearly).[45]

Additionally, to encourage savings within voluntary schemes (occupational or individual), the state is subsidizing voluntary contributions by 15% of the amount of the contributions actually paid (incentive can be awarded for contributions in the maximum amount of 663,61 EUR (yearly); hence, maximum state incentive amounts to 99,54 EUR (yearly).[46]

Third pillar pension benefits (occupational and individual) are fully tax-exempted (since 2018, also for tax reliefs awarded during the accumulation phase).[47]

There are no taxation specificities regarding the age at which voluntary pensions (occupational or individual) are taken.

References

Legislation

Act on Civil Servants (*Zakon o državnim službenicima*, NN 155/23, 85/24)

Act on Compulsory Pension Funds (*Zakon o obveznim mirovinskim fondovima*, NN 19/14, 93/15, 64/18, 115/18, 58/20, 156/23)

Act on Contributions (*Zakon o doprinosima*, NN 84/08, 152/08, 94/09, 18/11, 22/12, 144/12, 148/13, 41/14, 143/14, 115/16, 106/18, 33/23, 114/23, 152/24)

Act on Croatian Veterans from the Homeland War and their Family Members (*Zakon o hrvatskim braniteljima iz Domovinskog rata i članovima njihovih obitelji*, NN 121/17, 98/19, 84/21, 156/23)

Act on National Allowance for the Elderly (Zakon o nacionalnoj naknadi za starije, NN 62/20, 156/23)

Act on Pension Insurance Companies (*Zakon o mirovinskim osiguravajućim društvima*, NN 22/14, 29/18, 115/18, 156/23, 52/25)

Act on Pension Insurance Rights of Active Military Personnel, Police Officers, and Authorized Officials (*Zakon o pravima iz mirovinskog osiguranja djelatnih vojnih osoba, policijskih službenika i ovlaštenih službenih osoba*, NN 128/99, 16/01, 22/02, 41/08, 97/12, 118/12)

Act on Pension Supplement for Pensions Earned under the Pension Insurance Act (*Zakon o dodatku na mirovine ostvarene prema Zakonu o mirovinskom osiguranju*, NN 79/07, 114/11, 115/18, 156/23)

Act on the Insurance Periods Counted with Extended Duration (*Zakon o stažu osiguranja s povećanim trajanjem*, NN 115/18, 34/21)

---

[45] Art. 9, para. 1, item 18. of the Income Tax Act.

[46] Art. 135, para. 4. Act on Voluntary Pension Funds.

[47] Art. 8, para. 3. of the Income Tax Act (NN 115/16, 106/18, 121/19, 32/20, 138/20, 151/22, 114/23).

Act on Voluntary Pension Funds (*Zakon o dobrovoljnim mirovinskim fondovima*, NN 19/14, 29/18, 115/18, 156/23, 52/25)
Health Care Act (*Zakon o zdravstvenoj zaštiti*, NN 100/18, 125/19, 133/20, 147/20, 136/21, 119/22, 156/22, 33/23, 145/23, 36/24)
Income Tax Act (*Zakon o porezu na dohodak*, NN 115/16, 106/18, 121/19, 32/20, 138/20, 151/22, 114/23, 152/24)
Labour Act (*Zakon o radu*, NN 93/14, 127/17, 98/19, 151/22, 46/23, 64/23)
Maximum Pension Act (*Zakon o najvišoj mirovini*, NN 162/98, 82/01)
Pension Insurance Act (*Zakon o mirovinskom osiguranju*, NN 157/13, 151/14, 33/15, 93/15, 120/16, 18/18, 62/18, 115/18, 102/19, 84/21, 119/22)
Proposal of the new Pension Insurance Act from May 2025 (Prijedlog novog Zakona o mirovinskom osiguranju iz svibnja 2025), https://sabor.hr/hr/sjednice-sabora/prijedlog-zakona-o-mirovinskom-osiguranju-prvo-citanje-pze-br-155-predlagateljica?t=154604&tid=213615

Literature

Grgurev I, Vukorepa I (2018) Flexible and new forms of employment in Croatia and their pension entitlement aspects. In: Sander GG, Tomljenovic V, Bodiroga VN (eds) Transnational, European, and National Labour Relations. Europeanization and globalization, vol 4. Springer, Cham, pp 241–262. https://doi.org/10.1007/978-3-319-02219-2_13
HANFA (Croatian Financial Services Supervisory Agency), legislation https://www.hanfa.hr/regulativa/mirovinski-sustav/
HZMO (Croatian Pension Insurance Institute), Statistical information series., https://www.mirovinsko.hr/hr/statistika/860
Potočnjak Ž, Vukorepa I (2018) Drugi mirovinski stup: prijepori i moguća poboljšanja (Second pension pillar: debates and possible improvements). In: Miladin, P, Giunio, M (eds) Zbornik 56. susreta pravnika, Hrvatski savez udruga pravnika u gospodarstvu, Zagreb, p. 231–271, https://www.bib.irb.hr/938890;
REGOS (Central Registry of Affiliates), https://regos.hr/
Vukorepa I (2015) Lost between sustainability and adequacy: critical analysis of the Croatian pension System's parametric reform. Revija za socijalnu politiku 22(3):279–308. https://doi.org/10.3935/rsp.v22i3.1307
Vukorepa I (2017) Retirement policy changes for Workers in Arduous and Hazardous Jobs: comparative overview and lessons for Croatia. Zbornik Pravnog fakulteta u Zagrebu 67(1):5–28. https://hrcak.srce.hr/176827
Vukorepa I (2021) Croatia. In: Schneider SM, Petrova T, Becker U (eds) Pension maps: visualising the institutional structure of old age security in Europe and beyond, 2nd edn. Max Planck Institute for Social Law and Social Policy, München, pp 71–84. https://doi.org/10.17617/2.3359088
Vukorepa I (2023) Hrvatski model djelomičnog umirovljenja: kritički osvrt (The Croatian Model of Partial Retirement: a critical review). Zbornik Pravnog fakulteta u Zagrebu 73(2–3):423–456. https://doi.org/10.3935/zpfz.73.23.10

Finland

Toomas Kotkas

1 Introduction to the Pension System and Its Narrative

The Finnish old-age pension system consists of three distinguishable levels. The first level is comprised of national pension (*kansaneläke*)[1] and guarantee pension (*takuueläke*).[2] Both are a pension income-tested social assistance type of pensions. If a person's earnings-related pension income is below a certain threshold, they are first entitled to a national pension. Anybody who has lived in Finland for a minimum of three years after having turned 16 is eligible for a national pension. However, the number of years lived in Finland affects the amount of the national pension. Guarantee pension, in turn, is paid for those whose aggregate pension income (e.g., earning-related and national pension) remains below a certain threshold. A full guarantee pension is paid if a person has no other pension income.[3]

The second level consists of statutory earnings-related pensions. This level is the most important because 66% of all pensioners receive only earning-related pensions (in 2023). Almost 30% receive both statutory pensions and the national pension (in 2023). The rest receive only national pension or guarantee pension. There are three principal earnings-related pension schemes with separate acts regulating them:

[1] National Pension Act (568/ 2007, KEL).

[2] Act on Guarantee Pension (703/ 2010, TakEL).

[3] In 2025, full guarantee pension was 986.30 EUR per month.

T. Kotkas (✉)
University of Helsinki, Helsinki, Finland
e-mail: toomas.kotkas@helsinki.fi

E. S. van Aggelen (ed.), *Retirement and Employment*, Ius Gentium: Comparative Perspectives on Law and Justice 145, https://doi.org/10.1007/978-3-032-33561-6_5

- employees' pensions[4]
- self-employed persons' pensions[5]
- farmers' pensions.[6]

Finally, the third level comprises voluntary pensions acquired either by (1) employers for their employees collectively (*ryhmäeläkevakuutus*) or individually, or (2) voluntary individual pensions acquired by employees/self-employed themselves. However, the significance of voluntary pensions is quite little in Finland because they only comprise about 5% of all pensions when measured in pension contributions.

2 Statutory Pensions

2.1 "Normal" Retirement Age

In Finland, the normal retirement age is called the "minimum old-age pension age" (*alin vanhuuseläkeikä*)[7]; in what follows, this will be called "minimum retirement age". Before 2017, the minimum retirement age was 63 years within the earnings-related schemes and 65 years within the national pension and the guarantee pension schemes. From the beginning of 2017 onwards, the minimum retirement age in both income-tested pension schemes as well as earnings-related pension schemes has been bound to the life expectancy of each age cohort. This fully applies to those who have been born in 1965 or later. For instance, for a person born in 1990, the minimum retirement age is (according to life expectancy in 2025) 67 years and 7 months. There are still gradually rising fixed minimum retirement ages for persons born between 1955 and 1964.[8]

When a person reaches the minimum retirement age, they have a right to retire. In other words, retirement is not obligatory. One can defer retirement basically indefinitely, as will be explained below. However, the obligation to take a pension insurance for an employee and for a self-employed ceases after they turn 70 years. A person can still, of course, continue working as an employee or a self-employed after this

[4] Although there are separate pension acts on private sector employees, public sector employees and seafarers, the pension benefits are basically the same. The acts are the Employees' Pensions Act (395/2006, TyEL), the Public Sector Pensions Act (81/ 2016, JuEL), and the Seafarers' Pensions Act (1290/ 2006).

[5] Self-employed Persons' Pensions Act (1272/ 2006, YEL).

[6] Farmers' Pensions Act (1280/ 2006). Persons doing research on grants are also insured through the farmers' pension scheme.

[7] See e.g., TyEL 11 § and JuEL 10 §.

[8] The minimum retirement age is 63, 25 years for persons born 1955, 63, 5 years for persons born 1956, and so on.

age but the work no longer accrues old-age pension. Furthermore, the employment contract terminates automatically when the employee reaches the age of 70.

In regard to the earnings-related pension schemes of public employees, there are some exceptions to the general minimum retirement age. Namely, career soldiers' minimum retirement ages are significantly lower than the general minimum retirement age, although they, too, are bound to the life expectancy of each age cohort.[9] The same applies to border guards. The seafarers have also had lower minimum retirement ages, but they will be gradually made congruent with the general minimum retirement age.

Apart from the minimum retirement age, the earnings-related schemes do not set any particular conditions for retirement, i.e., conditions related to the length of the career or the amount of wage earnings. This is because in the Finnish earnings-related pensions schemes the level of pension benefit is variable and defined by the number of working years and the earned wage income. From the age of 17, one's earnings-related pension benefit accrues annually at a rate of 1.5% of one's gross annual earnings—this applies to employees, civil servants, and the self-employed.[10]

Regarding the statutory minimum pension schemes, there are conditions related to the length of residence and to the amount of other pension income, among others. First, in order to be eligible for the national pension, a person has to have lived in Finland for at least three years after having turned 16.[11] Secondly, because the national pension is pension income-tested, one's earnings-related pension income affects the amount of the national pension. A person is entitled to a national pension if their earnings-related (and other) pension income is below a certain threshold.[12] Thirdly, the number of years lived in Finland affects the amount of the national pension.[13]

In regard to the guarantee pension, the conditions are a bit different. In order to be eligible for the guarantee pension, a person needs, first, to receive an earnings-related and/or national pension.[14] Secondly, a person has to have lived in Finland for at least three years after having turned 16.[15] Thirdly, all other pension income must stay below a certain threshold. The amount of the guarantee pension is the difference between the threshold and the person's actual pension income.[16]

---

[9] See, JuEL Ch. 5. For instance, the minimum retirement age is 57 years for a career soldier born in 1972 and 45 years for a military pilot born in the same year.

[10] TyEL 65 § and JuEL 81 §. During the transition period from 2017 to 2025, the pension accrual rate is 1.7% for those between the ages of 53 and 62. For the self-employed, the accrual starts only at the age of 18 (YEL 62 §).

[11] KEL 9.1 §.

[12] KEL 20 §. In 2025, the threshold was 1617.13 EUR per month for a single person. If a person received earnings-related pension 65.62 EUR per month or less, they were entitled to full national pension which was 775.70 EUR.

[13] KEL 21 §. If one has lived in Finland less than 80% of the time between the age of 17 and the minimum pension age, the amount of national pension will be reduced.

[14] TakEL 7 §.

[15] TakEL 4.1 §.

[16] TakEL 8–9 §. In 2024, this threshold was 968, 69 EUR per month.

Working is allowed without any limitations while a person is on a full old-age pension—be it a minimum pension or an earnings-related pension. According to a recent study, the employment rate increased 1.7-fold between 2013 and 2020 as a result of the raised minimum retirement age. The three-month increase in the old-age retirement age of the age cohort of 1955 raised the average employment exit age by 0.6 months, and a six-month increase in the old-age retirement age of the age cohort of 1956 postponed the exit age by 1.3 months.[17]

Furthermore, according to another survey, 34% of respondents who retired between 2019 and 2021 said that they were working or had worked during their retirement. Of the respondents 16% informed that they had not worked although they would have liked to, whereas 50% informed that they had not worked and had no wish to work either.[18]

2.2 *Early Retirement*

The earnings-related pension schemes incorporate the possibility to retire early.[19] This pension is called the "partial early old-age pension" (*osittainen varhennettu vanhuuseläke*). The retirement age of the partial early old-age pension is also bound to the life expectancy of each age cohort, so that early retirement is possible three years before the minimum retirement age at the earliest. As the name indicates, the partial early old-age pension is actually a combination of a partial pension and an early retirement pension. The amount of the partial early old-age pension is either 25% or 50% of the accrued pension depending on the choice of the pensioner.[20]

Retiring early is, of course, voluntary, and there are no special conditions for partial early retirement. If one decides to retire before one's life expectancy-bound minimum retirement age, each month reduces the pension benefit by 0.4% (*varhennusvähennys*).[21] In other words, if one retires, for example, two years prior to their minimum retirement age, the partial pension is 9.6% lower than it would have been without early retirement.

The partial early old-age pension does not prevent a person from working during the said pension, and there are no restrictions concerning working hours or the amount of wage. Working during the partial early old-age pension accrues the final old-age pension.

Early retirement is not possible for groups such as career soldiers whose minimum retirement age is already lower than the normal minimum retirement age.[22] Early

---

[17] Nivalainen and Ilmakunnas (2023).

[18] Polvinen et al. (2023).

[19] Within the statutory minimum pension schemes (i.e., national pension and guarantee pension) early retirement is only possible for persons born in 1961 or before.

[20] TyEL 15–18 §, JuEL 15–18 §, YEL 12–15 §.

[21] TyEL 16.2 §, JuEL 16.2 §, YEL 13.2 §.

[22] JuEL 102.9 §.

retirement is not possible either within the national pension scheme. However, a guarantee pension can be paid for a person receiving an earnings-related partial early old-age pension. In this case, also the guarantee pension is reduced by 0.4% for each month preceding the minimum retirement age.[23]

2.3 *Deferral of Retirement*

As indicated above, retirement is not obligatory when the minimum retirement age is reached. Each deferred month increases the pension benefit by 0.4%; the so-called "increment for deferred retirement" (*lykkäyskorotus*).[24] There is no time limit for the deferral. A person can—in principle—defer their retirement for several years, increasing their pension by 4.8% per year. This also applies after an employee or a self-employed person reaches 70 which is the maximum age for statutory pension insurance. There are no conditions for deferral of retirement. However, once a person has retired (partially or fully), it is not possible to suspend and re-defer the claimed pension again.

By postponing one's retirement beyond the minimum retirement age, one can 'neutralize' the negative effect that the life expectancy coefficient has on one's pension benefit. The life expectancy coefficient is determined by the life expectancy rate of each age cohort. If the life expectancy of the population increases, the coefficient decreases reducing thus pension benefits. A "target retirement age" (*tavoite-eläkeikä*), which is higher than the minimum retirement age, is determined for each age cohort. This means that if a person postpones their retirement until the target retirement age, the negative effect of the life expectancy coefficient is fully neutralized.[25]

According to a recent survey, some 60% of the respondents informed that they had postponed their retirement despite reaching their minimum retirement age—almost 27% by less than a year, 16% by less than two years, 8% by less than three years, and 10% by three years or more. Some 30% of those whose told that they had postponed their retirement informed that the increment for deferred retirement had influenced on their decision to postpone retirement.[26]

2.4 *Partial Retirement*

As already indicated above, partial retirement is possible within earnings-related schemes in Finland. A person wishing to retire before their minimum retirement age

[23] TakEL 8.2 §.

[24] TyEL 16.3 §, JuEL 16.3 §, YEL 13.3 §.

[25] TyEL 75 c §, JuEL 115 §, YEL 69 c §.

[26] Nivalainen and Tenhunen (2024).

can choose a partial pension pay-out of either 25% or 50%. Each month of early retirement reduces the partial old-age pension benefit by 0.4%. The partial early retirement continues until the beneficiary applies for full old-age pension. So, in principle a person can stay on a partial old-age pension indefinitely.

Even though the name of the benefit is "partial early old-age pension", it does not mean that partial retirement is only possible before the minimum retirement age. Indeed, earnings-related old-age pension can also be drawn out partially after the minimum retirement age is reached. Partial retirement can therefore be combined with deferred full retirement also. If a person partially retires only after having reached their minimum retirement age, each deferred month increases the part of the pensions benefit that is not yet drawn by 0.4%.

There are no restrictions concerning work or income while in receipt of a partial old-age pension. According to a recent study, roughly 60% of persons who chose a partial early old-age pension between March 2020 and January 2022 kept receiving wage income despite partial early retirement. With some 20%, the wage income decreased. Finally, some 15% stopped receiving wage income altogether. The last group chose the 50% pay-out in particular.[27]

2.5 *Retirement Regimes for Persons Considered to be in Hazardous or Arduous Jobs*

In Finland, the earnings-related schemes include an early retirement regime for persons who have worked in arduous jobs. Currently, a person has a right to the "years-of-service pension" (*työuraeläke*) at the age of 63 if: (1) they have done mentally or physically strenuous and consuming work for at least 38 years, (2) their ability to work is permanently reduced but they are not eligible for a work disability pension, and (3) they are born in 1955 or later.[28]

The years-of-service pension benefit is the amount that the pensioner has accrued by the end of the month preceding the pension. A person on years-of-service pension is allowed to work but if the monthly wage income exceeds 986.30 EUR (in 2025), it starts gradually reducing the pension benefit. The years-of-service pension turns into regular old-age pension when the person reaches minimum retirement age.[29]

The years-of-service pension is not possible for groups such as career soldiers whose minimum retirement age is already lower than the normal minimum retirement age.

According to a recent study covering the period between 2018 and 2023, the years-of-service pension seems to work as it was designed to. Almost 75% of those

---

[27] Ilmakunnas and Sten-Gahmberg (2024).

[28] TyEL 53 a–b §, JuEL 51–52 §, YEL 50 a–b §. The age limit of the years-of-service pension will be raised in the future so that for those who are born in 1965 or later, the age limit will be two years lower than the life expectancy-bound minimum retirement age (see e.g., TyEL 82.1 §).

[29] TyEL 53 c–h §, JuEL 53–56 §, YEL 50 c–h §.

receiving this pension had been diagnosed with a musculoskeletal disorder. Years-of-service pension recipients are relatively low educated, and they have entered the job market at a young age. However, the study also suggests some potential causes for concern. Namely, 90.6% of the recipients are men. Even though the majority (80%) of applicants also are men, the rejection rate for women is nevertheless higher.[30] It may be that the system does not recognize jobs within predominantly female-dominated industries as arduous as within male-dominated industries.

2.6 Retirement Regimes Based on Means or Income-Tested Benefits

In Finland there is at least one income-tested benefit for pensioners whose pension and other income remains low. This is due to the interconnectivity between the pension pillars in Finland. It is the "housing allowance for pensioners" (*eläkkeensaajan asumistuki*).[31] A person is eligible for housing allowance for pensioners if they are living permanently in Finland, they receive a pension that qualifies for housing allowance for pensioners, and their total income is low. The housing allowance for pensioners is in some regards more beneficial than the "general housing allowance" (*yleinen asumistuki*). Firstly, the housing allowance for pensioners is higher than the general housing allowance. Secondly, the housing allowance for pensioners is available for both rental and owner-occupied homes whereas general housing allowance can only be paid for persons living in rental homes.

Of course, a pensioner can also have a right to general income support if their income is low.[32] However, the income support system does not include any special rules concerning pensioners.

2.7 Taxation

Here, I will first address the taxation of pension contributions and then the taxation of pension benefits. In regard to statutory earnings-related pensions, the total pension contribution per each employee was 24.40% of the employee's gross wage income in 2025. The employer pays some two-thirds of the contribution and the employee some one-third.[33] The employee's share of the contribution is withheld by the employer from the employee's monthly wage. The contribution thus reduces the employee's

---

[30] Riekhoff and Polvinen (2025).

[31] Act on Housing Allowance for Pensioners (571/ 2007).

[32] Act on Income Support (1412/ 1997).

[33] In 2025, the emploee's share was 7.15% if the employee was under 53 years or over 62 years, and 8.65% if the employee was between 53 and 62.

taxable income.[34] The employer's share of the contribution is considered as expenses in the company's balance sheet, and it therefore reduces the employer's taxable revenue respectively. However, if the employer also pays the employee's share of the contribution, it will be considered as salary and taxed accordingly in the employee's personal income taxation. The pensions contribution of the self-employed is about the same as with employees (24.10% in 2025), and it can be deducted in the self-employed person's or their spouse's personal income taxation or, alternatively, in the enterprise's taxation.

Statutory income-tested pensions, i.e., the national pension and the guarantee pension, are financed through general taxes—and not by pension contributions.

In regard to actual pension benefits, they are taxed basically in the same way as wage income—both are subject to progressive income tax. This applies both to statutory earnings-related pensions as well as to statutory minimum pensions. However, there are a few important differences. First, pension income is subject to pension income deduction (*eläketulovähennys*) which means that a person's pension income is taxed lighter than wage income.[35] In 2025, if a person's annual pension income remained below 13,756 EUR, they did not pay any taxes on their pension income because of the deduction. Secondly, pensioners do not pay any pension insurance contribution, unemployment insurance contribution nor daily allowance contribution for health insurance of their pension income. An old-age pensioner who is also working needs separate tax deduction cards for pension income and for wage income. These rules also apply to partial pensions.

There is no difference in taxation between normal pension benefits, early pension benefits, partial pension benefits, or deferred pension benefits.

3 Occupational Pensions

3.1 "Normal" Retirement Age

As already indicated above, the significance of voluntary pensions is very little in Finland; they only comprise about 5% of all pensions when measured in pension contributions. Because the occupational pension schemes in Finland are voluntary, the pension legislation does not set limits to retirement age. Therefore, the notions of "normal retirement age", "early retirement", "deferred retirement", and "partial retirement" do not really apply to voluntary pension schemes. However, the tax legislation sets certain age limits to the drawing out of voluntary occupational pension benefits and voluntary individual pensions.

---

[34] TyEL 152 §, YEL 114 §.

[35] Income Tax Act (1535/ 1992) 100 §.

3.2 Taxation

Regarding pensions taken by the employer for employees collectively, the insurance contributions paid by the employer are considered tax-free benefits for the employee, i.e., not taxable salary. The pension age can be defined freely within these collective occupational pension schemes. However, if the employee pays a share of the contributions of the voluntary collective pension insurance taken out by the employer, these contributions are then considered the employee's taxable earned income, i.e., salary, unless the pension benefit is only paid at the age of 70 at the earliest. If this is the case, the employees' share can be deducted from the employee's wage earnings up to 5% of the salary paid by the employer in question, but no more than 5000 EUR (yearly).

As far as voluntary pension insurance taken out by the employer for an individual employee is concerned, the regulation on pension age is stricter. The insurance contributions of voluntary pension insurance taken out by the employer for an individual employee are also considered a tax-free benefit for the employee if the total annual amount of contributions does not exceed 8500 EUR and if the insurance fulfils additional conditions laid down in the Income Tax Act. These conditions are, among others, that the pension benefit can be paid earliest at the age of 70 (for persons born in 1962 or later) and it is paid within a minimum of 10 years and with equal annual amounts. So, in this case, the tax legislation sets an age limit for the paying of voluntary occupational pension benefits.[36]

Finally, there are two forms of voluntary individual pensions taken by the individual themselves: (1) voluntary individual pension insurance and (2) a long-term savings agreement. Regarding both forms, the pension contribution is tax-deductible from capital income (up to 5000 EUR yearly) if the pension is paid or savings drawn out earliest at the age of 70 (for persons born in 1962 or later) and the pension benefits are paid or savings drawn out within a period of a minimum of 10 years. The pension benefits and drawn-out savings are taxed as capital income.[37]

A person receiving any type of voluntary pension is allowed to work without limitations.

References

Legislation

Act on Guarantee Pension (*laki takuueläkkeestä* 703/2010, TakEL)
Act on Housing Allowance for Pensioners (*laki eläkkeensaajan asumistuesta* 571/2007)
Act on Income Support (*laki toimeentulotuesta* 1412/1997)

[36] Income Tax Act (1535/ 1992) 68 §.

[37] Income Tax Act (1535/ 1992) 54d §. The tax-deductibility of voluntary individual pension contributions will no longer apply from the beginning of 2027 onwards.

Employees' Pensions Act (*työntekijän eläkelaki* 395/2006, TyEL)
Farmers' Pensions Act (*maatalousyrittäjän eläkelaki* 1280/2006)
Income Tax Act (*tuloverolaki* 1535/1992)
National Pension Act (*kansaeläkelaki* 568/2007, KEL)
Public Sector Pensions Act (*julkisten alojen eläkelaki* 81/2016, JuEL)
Seafarers' Pensions Act (*merimieseläkelaki* 1290/2006)
Self-employed Persons' Pensions Act (*yrittäjän eläkelaki* 1272/2006, YEL)

Literature

Ilmakunnas I, Sten-Gahmberg S (2024) Wage income before and after taking out a partial old-age pension, Summary. Finnish Centre for Pensions, Studies 01/2024. https://urn.fi/URN:ISBN:978-951-691-366-0

Nivalainen S, Ilmakunnas I (2023) Pension reform 2017: Impact of rising old-age pension age on employment and other labour market states, Summary. Finnish Centre for Pensions, Studies 02/2023. https://urn.fi/URN:ISBN:978-951-691-362-2

Nivalainen S, Tenhunen S (2024) Financial incentives or working conditions—What would keep people working longer? Survey of persons retiring from work on an old-age pension in 2019–2021, Summary. Finnish Centre for Pensions, Studies 02/2024. https://urn.fi/URN:ISBN:978-951-691-367-7

Polvinen A, Tenhunen S, Jarnefelt N, Kivelä M, Kuivalainen S, Nivalainen S (2023) Working in retirement Survey of persons retiring from work on an old-age pension in 2019–2021, Summary. Finnish Centre for Pensions, Studies 04/2023. https://urn.fi/URN:ISBN:978-951-691-364-6

Riekhoff A-J, Polvinen A (2025) Arduous careers in times of longer working lives: The role of the years-of-service pension and other early exit routes. Finnish Centre for Pensions, Studies 01/2025. https://urn.fi/URN:ISBN:978-951-691-387-5

Germany

Stamatia Devetzi

1 Introduction to the German Social Security System—the Bismarckian Narrative

The German social security system has often been described as the "Bismarckian" type of social security. Introduced in the late 1880s, the German social insurances (the sickness insurance was established in 1883, the job accidents' insurance in 1884, and the pension insurance in 1889) were primarily addressed to blue-collar workers. The implementation of a social security system, especially for this group, had to do with Bismarck's assumption that the emerging workers' movement was a political hazard. Hence, he considered social security as an appropriate tool to reduce the influence of and ban left-wing political parties and trade unions.[1]

The Bismarckian concept still dominates the German social security system. In fact, the branches of social *insurance* are still being primarily addressed to employees—for example civil servants are not covered by social insurance.[2] Regarding the self-employed, only specific groups of self-employed are (compulsorily) covered.

Regarding the pension system, the majority of the German workforce is mandatorily insured in the statutory old-age pension scheme. Pensions can be supplemented through (voluntary) occupational pension schemes and voluntary private pension schemes.

---

[1] These institutions had since the 1850s created insurance systems based on the objective of providing mutual assistance to workers in need and their families and they were gaining increasing political influence: Reinhard, H.-J., The New Basic Pension Supplement in Germany, in Devetzi S (Ed). (2023), Minimum Income in Old Age; Eichenhofer E. (2021) Sozialrecht, 12. Edition, Tübingen: Mohr Siebeck, pp. 21–23.

[2] A special system (*Beamtenversorgung*) exists for them instead.

S. Devetzi (✉)
Fulda University of Applied Sciences, Fulda, Germany
e-mail: stamatia.devetzi@sk.hs-fulda.de

E. S. van Aggelen (ed.), *Retirement and Employment*, Ius Gentium: Comparative Perspectives on Law and Justice 145, https://doi.org/10.1007/978-3-032-33561-6_6

2 Statutory Pensions

The statutory old age pension scheme, which is codified in Book VI of the German Social Code,[3] covers 85 percent of the population, the majority of them employees.[4] As mentioned, civil servants are not included,[5] neither are the majority of self-employed persons. Only certain vulnerable groups of self-employed are compulsorily insured: these are self-employed lecturers, nursery teachers, nursing carers and midwives. Self-employed artists and members of the publishing professions are insured under the Artists' Social Insurance Act.[6] Since 1999, self-employed persons working primarily for a single client without having employees of their own ("solo self-employed") are also compulsorily insured.[7]

Farmers and their families are mandatorily insured in the (heavily subsidized) farmers' old age security scheme (*Landwirtschaftliche Altersvorsorge*).

Self-employed persons in so-called "liberal professions" can opt out of insurance in the statutory old-age pension scheme, substituted by mandatory insurance in the *liberal professions pensions* schemes (*Berufständische Versorgungswerke*). Pension schemes for the liberal professions are mandatory for lawyers, notaries, physicians, architects, engineers, pharmacists, dentists, veterinaries, accountants, tax consultants, etc.[8] There are more than 90 autonomous and mostly fully funded pension schemes for the liberal professions. All other self-employed persons are *not* compulsorily insured by the statutory old age pension scheme—this means that they have to make old-age provisions on their own.[9]

The German statutory pension insurance institution is a corporation under public law that operates according to the principle of self-administration. "Social self-administration" means that insured persons and employers jointly "govern" their pension insurance organisation.[10]

The statutory old age pension scheme is a pay-as-you-go-financed insurance scheme with benefits being linked to contributions paid throughout a person's career. Despite the pay-as-you-go based financing principle, a significant part of the costs of the statutory pension scheme—about 23%[11]—is tax-financed. The contribution

---

[3] *German Social Code in German*: *SGB–Sozialgesetzbuch.*

[4] §1 Book VI *German Social Code–SGB VI*.

[5] The civil servants' old age pension scheme (*Beamtenversorgung*) provides privileged treatment for civil servants, judges and soldiers.

[6] Under the *German Artists' Social Insurance Act* they pay only half the contributions themselves.

[7] §2 (1) No. 9 Book VI *German Social Code.*

[8] This means that these professions are not insured in the statutory old age pension scheme.

[9] Devetzi S (2023b), Non-standard work in Germany: Self-employed and Mini-Jobs, e-RIPS, pp. 147–158, p. 149.

[10] § 44 SGB IV–Book IV German Social Code.

[11] https://rentenupdate.drv-bund.de/DE/1_Archiv/Archiv/2023/01_Bundesmittel_und_zuschuesse.html.

rates are a fixed share of the monthly gross earnings (18.6%)[12]; a contribution assessment ceiling exists (7.550 EUR monthly in 2024).[13] The contributions are shared in parity[14] between employer and employee.

There is also a possibility of *voluntary* insurance within the German pension insurance scheme: it exists for anyone who lives in Germany or for a German citizen living abroad, being at least 16 years old, and who is not yet drawing a full old-age pension, and is not subject to compulsory insurance in the statutory pension scheme. This applies, for example, to the self-employed, freelancers, or adults who are not gainfully employed, such as housewives.

The "pension formula" (*Rentenformel*) determines the amount of the monthly pension. The monthly pension amount is calculated by multiplying the "personal earnings points", the "pension type factor" and the "current pension value". The "personal earnings points" relate to the insured income for each calendar year, divided by the average income of all insured persons. In case of early or deferred retirement, this result is multiplied by an additional factor ("access factor") to adjust for early or deferred pension claiming. The "pension type factor" determines the type of pension: it expresses whether it is an old-age, reduced earning capacity, widow's or orphan's pension, for example. The "current pension value" is the monthly pension that an average earner would receive after paying contributions for one year. Pensions are adjusted yearly; the adjustment of the pension value takes into account changes in the earnings of the insured population and a "sustainability factor".

From their 27th birthday, all insured persons receive every year their personal pension information with the current status of their accrued pension entitlements. There is also a projection of the amount of the expected old-age pension and the pension entitlements in the event of a possible reduction in earnings capacity.

2.1 "Normal"Retirement Age

For insured persons (both sexes) born in or after 1964, the regular retirement age is 67 years. For those born between 1951 and 1963, the regular retirement age is gradually increasing from 65 to 67 years (see Table 1). The minimum insurance period ("waiting period") is 5 years.

---

[12] Earmarked for the pension insurance.

[13] https://www.deutsche-rentenversicherung.de/RheinlandPfalz/DE/Presse/Pressemitteilungen/2023/2023-12-07_neue_werte_2024.html.

[14] However, this is not the case for all jobs/earnings: For the so-called "mini-jobs" (up to EUR 556/month in 2025), the employer pays only a flat-rate contribution: for jobs with earnings between EUR 556 and EUR 2000/month ("midi-jobs"), different shares between employer and employee apply (roughly described: more for the employer, less for the employee): Deutsche Rentenversicherung (2025), "Minijob-Midijob: Bausteine für die Rente, https://www.deutsche-rentenversicherung.de/SharedDocs/Downloads/DE/Broschueren/national/minijobs_midijobs_bausteine_fuer_die_rente.html (update 13 March 2025).

Table 1 Overview of the "normal" retirement age

Year of birth	Retirement age
1958	66
1959	66 and 2 months
1960	66 and 4 months
1961	66 and 6 months
1962	66 and 8 months
1963	66 and 10 months
1964	67

Reference § 235 para 2 Book VI German Social Code (SGB VI)

Special conditions apply for old age pensions for long service[15] (35 years; age 67 with option of early retirement), exceptionally long service[16] (45 years; age 65), for severe disability[17] (35 years; age 65 with option of early retirement) and long-service miners[18] (25 years; age 62).

Retirement is voluntary; pensions can be taken up only after application by the person (and are not given automatically). Work after retirement is possible.

2.2 *Early Retirement*

Eligibility for early retirement is foreseen for recipients of long-service old age pensions (at age 63) and severe disability old age pensions (at age 62). However, this is only possible with negative (permanent) adjustments to pension benefits ("malus)" (−0.3% monthly or −3.6% per year). These deductions can amount to a maximum of 14.4% of the pension.[19]

Until the standard retirement age is reached, pension reductions resulting from early claiming of an old-age pension can be offset by paying contributions.[20]

As mentioned above, for pensioners with an exceptionally long service of 45 years, the retirement age is 65 (and not 67).

[15] § 236 para 1 *Book VI German Social Code (SGB VI).*

[16] § 236b *Book VI German Social Code (SGB VI).*

[17] § 236a *Book VI German Social Code (SGB VI).*

[18] §§ 40 and 238 *Book VI German Social Code (SGB VI).*

[19] Since the regular retirement age is 67 and early retirement is possible at the age of 63 at the earliest, the maximum is 4 years.

[20] § 187 a Book VI *German Social Code (SGB VI).*

2.3 Deferral of Retirement

Retirement can be deferred with positive (permanent) adjustments to pension benefits (0.5% monthly).[21] This means that the pension is increased by 6% for each year that retirement is deferred beyond the standard retirement age.

2.4 Partial Retirement

Old-age pensions can be paid as a full pension or as a *partial pension*.[22] The proportion of the partial pension can be chosen at will as long as it is at least 10% or at most 99.99% of the full pension.

The partial pension is intended to ease the transition to retirement. Insured persons can decide to what extent they still want to work or retire. Earnings points acquired during a partial pension or a full old-age pension have the effect of increasing the pension at the end of the calendar month in which the standard retirement age is reached.

The possibility of partial retirement has existed for many years in Germany[23]; however, partial pensions were quite unpopular in the past: In 2015, only 4.042 partial pensions were paid in Germany; in 2021, 7.449 partial pensions were reported. This number represents 0.9% of all pensions.

One of the main reasons for this has been the strict income ceilings. These applied to retired persons below standard statutory retirement age who made use of the options for partial old-age pensions. Also provisions in labour law were unattractive: There was no possibility of temporary employment for persons who had reached the pension age.

On the eighth December 2016—with effect from January first 2017—a new law was introduced: The "Act on the flexibilisation of the transition from working life to retirement and to strengthen prevention and rehabilitation in working life" ("Flexible Pensions Act"). It intended to encourage elderly persons to remain in employment as long as possible. The reasoning has been that older employees are indispensable because they make a valuable contribution to combating the shortage of skilled workers with their experience and potential.

With the act, persons who reduce their working hours and apply for a partial pension before reaching the statutory pension age can flexibly and individually combine partial pension and income from work.

---

[21] § 77 para 2 No 2b Book VI *German Social Code (SGB VI)*.

[22] § 42 Book VI *German Social Code (SGB VI)*.

[23] Since 1992.

Till 2022, a ceiling applied on these earnings; it increased during the Corona pandemic (up to 46.060 EUR yearly) and was completely abolished[24] from 1. January 2023.[25]

The "flexi pension" gives insured persons the opportunity to pay additional contributions into the statutory pension scheme earlier and flexibly in order to compensate for pension reductions. Early retirement can thus be better planned and secured.

Continuing to work as a pensioner pays off: Those who reach retirement age and continue to work increase their pension entitlement. Before 2017, the employer had also already paid pension insurance contributions for a pensioner who continued to work, but this would no longer have changed their pension entitlement.[26] After the Flexible Pensions Act, employees can declare to their employer that they wish to waive the exemption from insurance and continue to pay their own pension insurance contributions.[27]

Until now, relative few insured persons have made use of the options provided by the Act. It is considered that it is the low level of awareness of the opportunities offered by the Flexi Pensions Act that contributes to their relatively low usage.[28] It remains to be seen if the options will be used more in the future—especially after the abolishment of the earnings ceiling from 2023.

2.5 *Retirement Regimes for Persons Considered to be in Hazardous or Arduous Jobs*

Special conditions apply for old age pensions for *long-service miners* (25 years; age 62). Insured persons are entitled to an old-age pension for miners who have worked underground for many years if they have reached the age of 62 and have fulfilled the qualifying period of 25 years.[29]

---

[24] The abolition of all earnings limits, which is a measure to increase individual flexibility, had been in the past opposed by some German political actors, such as the trade unions, as this would, in their eyes, undermine the wage-subsituting function of pensions: Scherger S (2021), Flexibilizing the retirement transition: Why, How and for Whom?, Frontiers in Sociology, p. 6.

[25] Rittweger St and Zieglmeier C, (2023) Das neue "Doppelverdiener-Modell–Rentnerbeschäftigung und Teilrente 99.99%, NZA, pp.1560–1563; Bomm D (2023) Die Abschaffung der Hinzuverdienstgrenzen in der Rentenversicherung, SGb pp. 485–488.

[26] The reason for this is that persons who reach retirement age are not compulsorily insured any more—this means that they are generally exempt from social insurance—and pension—contributions.

[27] § 5 para 4, No 1 *Book VI German Social Code (SGB VI).*

[28] Meyer, I/Walprecht S/Petersen M/Kühnhenrich D (2022), Wie wirksam ist das Flexirentengesetz bisher? Statistisches Bundesamt, WISTA, 5/2022.

[29] § 40 *Book VI German Social Code (SGB VI).*

2.6 Retirement Regimes Based on Means or Income Tested Benefits

A "basic income support scheme in old age" *(Grundsicherung im Alter und bei Erwerbsminderung)* aiming at poverty alleviation among elderly exists in Germany.[30] The scheme is entirely tax-financed out of the general federal budget. Persons who have reached the "standard" retirement age of the statutory old age pension scheme (i.e. age 67 for persons born after 1963) and their income or assets are below subsistence level can apply for it. The benefit is only payable to elderly persons who permanently reside in Germany. It is means-tested. The means-test is based on the monthly net incomes and assets of the elderly persons and his/her spouse or cohabiting civil partner. Excluded from the test are assets of 10.000 EUR for a single person (20.000 EUR for married couples or cohabiting civil partners),[31] pension benefits from occupational or private schemes up to a certain level[32] and self-used housing. No maintenance claims against children with an annual gross income of less than 100.000 EUR are made.[33]

2.7 Taxation

Statutory old age pensions are generally taxable. However, they are currently only partially included in taxation; a transitional phase is in place.[34]

Pensioners who have been drawing a pension since 2012 have to pay tax on 64% of their pension at their individual tax rate. This percentage increases gradually for each new pensioner cohort until it reaches 100% in 2040. However, due to the tax-free allowances ("tax-free minimum subsistence level" or "basic tax-free allowance"—*Grundfreibetrag*), many pensioners will continue to pay no tax in practice. In 2025, a total annual amount of 12.096 EUR is exempted from income tax as a tax-free minimum subsistence level.[35]

---

[30] Book XII, Chap. 4 of the *German Social Code (SGB XII)*.

[31] § 90 *Book XII German Social Code (SGB XII)*.

[32] The first 100 Euro, 30% of the pension thereafter, up to max. 50% of benefit rate for basic needs.

[33] § 94 para 1a *Book XII German Social Code (SGB XII)*.

[34] § 22 Nr. 1 *EStG (Income Tax Act)*.

[35] § 32a Sec. 1 No. 1 *EStG (Income Tax Act)*.

3 Occupational Pensions and Private Pension Schemes

3.1 "Normal" Retirement Age

Occupational pension schemes are (mostly) fully funded and provided by the employer; participation is voluntary.[36] Occupational pension plans are either implemented internally by the employer in the form of "book reserves" ("*Direktzusage*") or support funds ("*Unterstützungskasse*")—or externally in the form of direct insurance ("*Direktversicherung*"), a (private) pension institution ("*Pensionskasse*"—this is a special form of a life insurance company) or pension funds ("*Pensionsfonds*").[37]

In 2002, a voluntary, state-subsidised, fully-funded private pension scheme, the "*Riester-Rente*", was introduced. It is open for all persons mandatorily insured in the statutory old age pension scheme and their spouses.[38] Participation in the scheme is financially supported by the state by granted allowances and tax refunds on contributions paid into approved/certified pension plans. In 2005, another voluntary, fully-funded private pension scheme, the "*Rürup*-pension" was created. Originally designed for self-employed persons,[39] it was extended to all persons with taxable income residing in Germany. Participation in the scheme is supported via tax reductions for approved pension plans.

Regarding age, employees are entitled to occupational pension benefits when claiming a full old age pension from the statutory old age pension scheme. There is no minimum retirement age specified in the laws. Other qualifying conditions are regulated in pension regulations at company or collective level.

> An employee who claims the retirement pension from the statutory pension insurance scheme as a full pension shall be granted company pension benefits at his request after fulfilment of the waiting period and other benefit requirements. If the retirement pension from the statutory pension insurance scheme is limited to a partial amount, the benefits from the company pension scheme may be discontinued. The retired employee is obliged to notify the employer or other pension provider immediately of any restriction of the retirement pension from the statutory pension insurance scheme.[40]

---

[36] With the exception of very specific supplementary pension schemes that are mandatory for some groups, like the supplementary pension scheme for employees of the public service.

[37] Schneider, S, The German old age security system in 2020, in: Schneider/Petrova/Becker (Eds.), Pension Maps, second edition, 2021, Max-Planck-Institute for Social Law and Social Policy, p. 185, p. 195.

[38] Also for civil servants, pensions covered by the farmers old age security scheme and recipients of pensions for reduced earnings capacity.

[39] Who are not mandatorily insured in the statutory pension scheme (and therefore without access to the "Riester-Rente").

[40] § 6 *BetrAVG (Occupational Pensions Act).*

3.2 Taxation

The taxation of occupational pensions depends—in addition to factors such as the type of company pension scheme—on the employee's/pensioner's individual tax rate. Company pensions are subject to income tax and are generally taxed according to the so-called "deferred taxation principle" (*nachgelagerte Besteuerung*). This means that the contributions to the company pension scheme are generally tax exempt[41] during the savings phase, but the capital payments in the pension are subject to tax.

References

Legislation

Einkommenssteuergesetz (EstG) (Income Tax Act)
Gesetz zur Verbesserung der betrieblichen Altersversorgung (BetrAVG) (Occupational Pensions Act)
Sozialgesetzbuch (SGB) (German Social Code)

Literature

Bomm D (2023) Die Abschaffung der Hinzuverdienstgrenzen in der Rentenversicherung, SGb (Die Sozialgerichtsbarkeit), pp. 485–488
Deutsche Rentenversicherung (2025), Minijob-Midijob: Bausteine für die Rente. https://www.deutsche-rentenversicherung.de/SharedDocs/Downloads/DE/Broschueren/national/minijobs_midijobs_bausteine_fuer_die_rente.html (update 13 March 2025)
Devetzi S (ed) (2023a) Minimum income in old age. Sakkoulas, Athens/Thessaloniki
Devetzi S (2023b) *Non-standard work in Germany: Self-employed and Mini-Jobs, e-RIPS* (E-Revista Internacional de la Protección Social). pp 147–158
Eichenhofer E (2021) Sozialrecht, 12. Edition. Mohr Siebeck, Tübingen
Meyer I, Walprecht S, Petersen M, Kühnhenrich D (2022) Wie wirksam ist das Flexirentengesetz bisher? Statistisches Bundesamt, WISTA, 5/2022
Reinhard H-J (2023) The new basic pension supplement in Germany. In: Devetzi S (ed) Minimum income in old age. Sakkoulas

[41] § 3 No 63 *EStG* (*Income Tax Act*). Contributions to a company pension scheme are not subject to income tax if they do not exceed 8.00% of the contribution assessment ceiling for the statutory pension insurance. The contributions that employees pay into their company pension are deducted directly from their gross income; this reduces the taxable income. Up to €604 per month can be paid into a company pension without having to pay tax on the money during the savings phase.

Rittweger Stephan and Zieglmeier Christian (2023) Das neue "Doppelverdiener-Modell–Rentnerbeschäftigung und Teilrente 99.99%, NZA (Neue Zeitschrift für Arbeitsrecht). pp. 1560–1563

Scherger S (2021) Flexibilizing the retirement transition: Why, How and for Whom? Conceptual Clarifications, Institutional Arrangements and Potential Consequences. Frontiers in Sociology 6:1–14. https://doi.org/10.3389/fsoc.2021.734985

Schneider S (2021) The German old age security system in 2020. In: Schneider S, Petrova T, Becker U (eds) Pension Maps, 2nd edn. Max-Planck-Institute for Social Law and Social Policy, pp 183–202. https://doi.org/10.17617/2.3359088

Switzerland

Jacques-André Schneider

1 Introduction to the Pension System and its Narrative

1.1 AVS

The federal old-age and survivors insurance law (*LAVS*) embodies Beveridgian universal national solidarity between incomes, with budgetary support. *AVS's* aim is alleviation of poverty by national solidarity. Benefits are therefore capped, whereas contributions are based on uncapped gainful activity income. *AVS* is completed later by the later federal disability insurance law (*LAI*), along the same general principles. Equality of *AVS/AI* pensions between women and men is achieved. A thirteenth *AVS* monthly pension will come into force in 2026, as a result of a constitutional initiative launched by the Swiss labour unions and approved on the third March 2024 by the people's and cantonal majority votes.[1].

Table 1 shows the average monthly AVS pension (in 2023).

Total *AVS/AI* paritarian contributions for employees are 9,4% of salary, with a specific contribution scale for self-employed. The maximum yearly *AVS* pension of CHF 30′240, after a full insurance career, necessitates an annual reference salary or gainful income for self-employed of CHF 90′720. All contributions paid on any amount above consecrates solidarity between higher and lower incomes. 92% of AVS pensioners thus receive total benefits that are higher than paid contributions.

AVS and *AI* are organized as a separate insurance institutions with yearly accounts. *AVS* receives federal state subsidies equal to 20,2% of its yearly expenses, financed partly by the VAT, with a funded reserve covering a year's benefits.

Table 2 show the AVS 2023 financial results.

[1] https://www.bsv.admin.ch/de/umsetzung-13-ahv-rente

J.-A. Schneider (✉)
Jacques-André Schneider, University of Lausanne, Lausanne, Switzerland
e-mail: jas@jaschneider.ch

E. S. van Aggelen (ed.), *Retirement and Employment*, Ius Gentium: Comparative Perspectives on Law and Justice 145, https://doi.org/10.1007/978-3-032-33561-6_7

Table 1 Average monthly AVS pension (in 2023)

Average monthly AVS pension (in 2024)		
For each married partner	Single	Widow/-er
Men CHF 1′776 Women CHF 1′719	Men CHF 1′926 Women CHF 1′956	Men CHF 2′294 Women CHF 2′246

Reference Confédération suisse, Office fédéral des assurances sociales: Statistiques de l'AVS 2024

Table 2 AVS 2023 financial results

AVS 2024 financial results		
Contributions and subsidies	Benefits	Return on reserve fund
CHF 53,719 billion	CHF 50,941 billion	CHF 2,8 billion

Reference Confédération suisse, Office fédéral des assurances sociales: Statistique de l'AVS 2024

Means-tested supplementary benefits, detailed further below, are provided in case of other benefits and income insufficiency.

1.2 Occupational Pensions

The mandatory federal law on occupational old-age, survivors and disability pensions (*LPP*) is a funded and Bismarckian social insurance, covering employees for a yearly salary between CHF 22.050 and CHF 88.200, entailing lower coverage for part-timers, particularly women. Mandatory paritarian retirement savings contributions on the insured salary are scaled from 7% between ages 25–34, 10% for ages 35–44, 15% for ages 45–54 and 18% for ages 55–65. Ongoing reform discussions aim to reduce this scale to avoid the cost disadvantage for older employees. Voluntary supplementary collective efforts represent 80% of total benefits and assets, i.e. the mandatory *LPP* covers only 20% of vested benefits. The mandatory and voluntary supplementary occupational pension plans include all measures taken on a collective basis to enable the elderly, survivors and disabled, together with the benefits provided by the federal old-age, survivors' and disability insurance scheme (*AVS/AI*), to maintain their standard of living in an appropriate manner in the event of an insured event such as old age, death or disability.

The federal law on vested benefits in occupational old-age, survivors' and disability pension plans federal (*LFLP*) prescribes the mandatory full and immediate vesting of retirement savings accounts and their transfer to the new occupational pension scheme in case of employment mobility. For high-level salary components,

Table 3 Median monthly retirement annuity (men-women), median lump sum payment (men-women), total assets and total benefit liabilities in 2023

Median monthly annuity men	Median monthly annuity women
CHF 2′058	CHF 1′198
Median lump sum payment men	Median lump sum payment women
CHF 190′000	CHF 76′365
Total assets	Total benefit liabilities
CHF 1′12,966 billion	CHF 1′033 billion

References Confédération suisse Office federal de la statistique (2024), *Statistique des nouvelles rentes 2023* https://www.bfs.admin.ch/news/fr/2024-0449; Confédération suisse, Office federal de la statistique (2024), *Statistique des caisses de pensions 2021–2023*, https://www.bfs.admin.ch/bfs/fr/home/actualites/quoi-de-neuf.assetdetail.33553951.html

Table 4 demographic split in 2023

Demographic split	
Insured actives: 4′736’943	Pensioners: 1′342’487

Reference Confédération suisse, Office fédéral de la statistique (2024), Statistique des caisses de pensions 2021–2023

art. 19a *LFLP* allows pension schemes to introduce the choice of an individual asset allocation for retirement savings.[2].

Occupational pension law allows for a choice between an annuity and/or a lump-sum benefit.

Table 3 refers to the median monthly retirement annuity (men-women), median lump sum payment (men-women), total assets and total benefit liabilities in 2023.

Table 4 presents the demographic split in 2023.

The favourable demographic ratio of pensioners to actives is biased by the significant proportion of the beneficiaries choosing a lump sum payment instead of an annuity. In 2023, only 40% of new retirees chose an annuity, whilst 41% preferred a lump-sum payment, the 19% remaining a mix of both.[3]

Table 5 shows the annual premiums and contributions.

For employees, the total of premiums to occupational pensions is on average around 13% of income which, added to *AVS/AI*, represents a total of 23′4%. The average split between employer and employee premiums in occupational pensions is 60%/40% on average, whereas the legal minimal standard is 50%/50%. Employee tax-exempted additional voluntary contributions represent about 25% of their total payments.

[2] Art. 19a LFLP

[3] Confédération suisse, Office federal de la statistique (2024), *Nouveaux bénéficiaires de la prévoyance professionnelle: moins de rentes et plus de retraits en capital.* The reasons for this evolution are the decreasing conversion rates of the retirement savings into an annuity resulting from much lower risk-free market interest rates as well as increased longevity.

Table 5 Annual premiums and contributions

Annual premiums and contributions	
Employer	Employee
Ordinary premiums	Ordinary premiums
CHF 32′635 million	CHF 23′345 million
Additional voluntary contributions	Additional voluntary contributions
CHF 681 million	CHF 7′545 million

Reference Confédération Suisse, Office fédéral de la Statistique ((2024), *Statistiques Des* Caisses *de Pensions. Chiffres clés 2021–2023, T3*

It is also estimated that the mandatory minimal occupational pension coverage (BVG) is now supplemented by a higher voluntary coverage level for more than 80% of all insured persons.

1.3 Individual Tax-Exempt Retirement Accounts

Individual tax-exempt savings for retirement, albeit survivors and disability benefits are allowed by *OPP3* for employees and self-employed within certain revenue limits. Their benefits cannot be paid before retirement, albeit death or disability.

2 AVS Retirement Age and Conditions

2.1 The Reference Retirement Age

At its inception in 1948, *AVS* prescribed a voluntary normal retirement age of 65 for men and women. The retirement age for women was then progressively brought down to 62, taking into account the 3 year difference in age between married men and women. The degraded pensions system dependency ratio, as well as gender equality, induced a rise to 64 of this retirement age, with several important gender equalization measures.

AVS' continuing degraded financial situation led to a paradigmatic change, through the so-called 2024 *AVS21* reform.[4] The general concept of a flexible retirement age between ages of 63 to 70 was introduced, the reference retirement age being 65 for men and women, with compensatory measures for women born between 1961 and 1969. The reference retirement age is defined by the maximum of 44 insurance years allowing for a full pension amount.

[4] https://www.bsv.admin.ch/fr/avs-21

The reform also introduced the possibility for partial and gradual retirement, allowing insured persons to freely decide when retiring at any month. It also allows bringing forward or deferring part of the pension in a gradual transition. The minimum amount for deferring or bringing forward part of the pension is 20%, the maximum amount 80%, with a maximum of three steps until full retirement. Early and deferred pensions are reduced, respectively increased actuarially, with smaller reductions for lower incomes, along rates fixed by the government that shall be adapted to changes in longevity.

An *AVS* retirement pension is paid on the condition of a prior minimum 11 month insurance period, the total insurance period of 44 years providing for a full pension, with a guaranteed minimum of CHF 1.260 per month and a maximum of CHF 2.520 depending on the reference career contributing income. The *AVS* pension is voluntary as it must be claimed by the beneficiary. *AVS* does not provide any special regimes.

AVS does not forbid the pursuit of gainful activity after the opening of an old-age pension. The income is subject to AVS contributions till the reference retirement age. After this age every specific income is allowed to benefit from a monthly CHF 1.400 contribution-free rebate.

2.2 *Early Retirement Age*

The voluntary early retirement age in AVS is any month from the age of 63[5] till the reference retirement age of 65, with compensatory transitional measures for women born from 1961 till 1969. The reduction is scaled from 0,6% for one month to 13,6% for 24 months of early retirement.[6] The reduction is also calculated on the lower pension resulting from an incomplete insurance and contribution career. All other conditions are equal to the AVS pension at the reference retirement age.

2.3 *Deferral of Retirement*

The *AVS* pension can be voluntarily deferred to any month till age 70,[7] but with a minimum initial deferral period of one year till age 66. Deferral gives rise to a pension accrual from 5,2% to 31,5%.[8] All other conditions are equal to the *AVS* pension at the reference retirement age.

[5] Art. 39 LAVS.

[6] Art. 56bis RAVS.

[7] Art. 40 LAVS.

[8] Art. 55ter RAVS.

2.4 Partial Retirement

The flexibility introduced by the *AVS21* reform includes the possibility for a gradual, step-by step retirement till the full pension benefit. It is now possible to bring forward or defer only part of the pension. Working hours can thus be reduced, compensating the lost income with a partial *AVS* pension. The minimum amount for deferring or bringing forward part of the pension is 20%, the maximum 80%.[9] Women in the transitional generation will continue to be able to bring forward their pension to age 62. The early pension percentage may be increased once, after which the remaining part of the pension must be taken in full. In other words, it is possible to choose a three step process from partial to full retirement. The situation is the same in the case of deferral: the percentage of the pension received may be increased once, after which the remainder of the pension must be taken in full. It is also possible to combine early retirement and deferral, to take part of the pension early and defer the remainder till after the reference retirement age. A change of percentage is thus only permitted once between the ages of 63 and 70.

2.5 Retirement Regimes for Persons Considered to Be in Hazardous or Arduous Jobs

There are no specific rules or benefits for persons in hazardous or arduous jobs.

2.6 Retirement Regimes Based on Means or Income Tested Benefits

AVS/AI pensions are reinforced by non-contributory means-tested additional AVS/AI benefits (*PC AVS*) for poverty alleviation of residents. These are non-contributory and are financed by state budgets. The means test is based on income and savings including real estate, necessitating a comprehensive investigation. Combined *AVS* and *PC AVS* benefits statistics show that single retired pensioners lacking sufficient occupational pension benefits can receive cumulative monthly benefits of up to CHF 3′173 (60% of the Swiss median income). These benefits are only paid from the start of a full or partial *AVS* pension.

Besides that, persons at the end of their unemployment insurance benefits can receive non-contributory means-tested transitional retirement benefits from the

[9] Art. 39 § 1 and 40 § 1 LAVS.

month in which they reach their 60th birthday (*LPtra*) till the AVS reference retirement age of 65. Beneficiaries must have been insured for at least 20 years in Switzerland by *AVS*, including at least five years after their 50th birthday. The annual transitional benefit and reimbursement of sickness and disability costs are paid up to a maximum annual amount of CHF 45,225 (single persons) or CHF 67,838 (couples).

2.7 *Taxation*

AVS pensions are taxed as normal income at all ages, whereas the non-contributory means-tested *PC AVS* and *LPtra* benefits are tax-exempt.

3 Occupational Pensions

3.1 *Normal Retirement Age*

AVS21 increased the reference retirement age for occupational pensions to 65 for men and women,[10] with a nine year transitional period from age 64 to 65 for women. Pensions schemes are, however, allowed to introduce a lower reference retirement from age 58,[11] and even lower in case of corporate restructurings or for reasons of public safety.[12]

Lower reference albeit obligatory retirement ages still occur however for certain professions, e.g. the federal tribunal judges, military, police, fire services, aircraft pilots and air-controllers. Elected Federal government members, some cantonal or local government members receive specific retirement benefits at the end of their governmental functions, often independently of age and service periods.

Self-employed have the choice of joining an occupational pension plan, in which case the same rules apply. Self-employed can otherwise be voluntarily covered by tax-exempted individual pension arrangements which allow early retirement five years before the reference retirement age of 65.

3.2 *Early and Deferred Retirement*

Voluntary early retirement is legally possible from age 63 and at any month, as in *AVS*, or even lower from age 58, if so provided by the applicable pension fund rules, and

[10] Art. 13 § 1 LPP.

[11] Art. 1i § 1 OPP2.

[12] Art. 1i § 2 OPP2.

deferral is possible till age 70. An early retirement age below 58 is allowed in case of company restructurings and for reasons of public security.[13] The existing range of flexible retirement options is therefor in practice extremely varied.

The *LPP* does not provide any specific provisions regarding early retirement for arduous and hazardous activities. In the construction industry, there are, however, collective agreements on early retirement schemes due to generally recognized arduous activities with specific early retirement ages (starting from 60 to 62). These schemes offer a temporary bridging pension as well the payment of occupational pensions retirement savings contributions till the reference retirement age of 65. Certain public-service schemes provide specific added benefits for periods of arduous or hazardous work.

Swiss occupational pensions impose actuarial reductions on early retirement annuities. However, there is a difference in the reduction between the annuities of the mandatory *BVG/LPP* scheme and in the supplementary schemes. The minimal *BVG/LPP* annuity is calculated along actuarial factors set by law, with a component of generational solidarity, whereas supplementary schemes set less generous actuarial factors, which are applied if the supplementary benefits englobe the mandatory benefits. The actuarial reductions will thus vary for the pensioners of purely mandatory plans or those benefitting from voluntary supplementary plans that offer higher retirement annuities. Deferral of pension annuities are rewarded by their actuarial increase.

3.3 Partial and Gradual Retirement

Pension scheme regulations shall, mirroring the *AVS* rules, allow partial early retirement from ages of at least 63 or by specific internal regulations even lower from age 58 to 65.[14] The pension scheme rules require the payment of the retirement pension annuity and/or lump-sum benefits from age 65 or their further deferral, starting any month, provided the beneficiary continues working and, for employees, continues to be employed by the same employer.

3.4 Combining Work and Full or Partial Retirement

In general, there are no limits to combining work with retirement in occupational pensions. However, in the existing pension scheme, the partial early retirement

[13] Art. 13 § 2 LPP, Art. 1i § 1 OPP2.

[14] Art. 13 LPP.

benefit shall not exceed the salary reduction amount[15] and deferral requires continued work.[16]

3.5 *Specific Protections for Unemployed Persons*

The Federal law on compulsory unemployment insurance and compensation in the event of insolvency (Unemployment Insurance Act, *LACI*) maintains mandatory *LPP* survivors and disability benefit expectations for unemployed,[17] who can also choose to maintain and further accrue their retirement benefits with the Substitute institution.[18] It is a possibility that is seldom used. Insureds who, after reaching the age of 58, cease to be subject to compulsory insurance as a result of their employer terminating their employment relationship may maintain their insurance cover partially or to the same extent as previously with the same pension fund.[19]

3.6 *Recent Rejection by Popular Vote of an Occupational Pension Reform*

On 22 September 2024, the Swiss electorate rejected the reform of their occupational pension scheme (BVG reform). The rejected proposal was to strengthen the financing of the second pillar, maintain overall pension levels and improve cover for part-time workers and low-income earners.[20]

The aim of the reform of occupational pension provision (BVG) was to lower the minimum conversion rate. The minimum conversion rate is the parameter used to determine the retirement pension under the second pillar. It is expressed as a percentage of the pension assets available at the time of retirement. Current legislation sets the conversion rate at 6.8% at age 65. For a retirement savings capital of CHF 100,000, for example, the conversion rate of 6.8% gives an annual pension of CHF 6800. The two key parameters for setting the conversion rate are life expectancy and the average return expected by pension funds over the coming years. To be able to guarantee the current 6.8% in compulsory pension provision, a return of around 5% a year is needed. Such a return cannot be achieved over the long term because of the situation on the financial markets. What's more, as life expectancy rises, pensions will have to be paid out for longer. As a result, BVG pensions (in the compulsory

[15] Art. 13b § 1 LPP.

[16] Art. 13b § 2 LPP.

[17] Art. 22a § 3 LACI.

[18] Art, 60 LPP.

[19] Art. 47a LPP.

[20] Office federal des assurances sociales: Réforme de la prévoyance professionnelle (Réforme LPP). https://www.bsv.admin.ch/de/aktuelle-reformen

part of occupational pension provision) are underfunded. To be able to pay current pensions, the pension funds affected by this situation have to use the capital income of their active members. An adjustment of the conversion rate was therefore deemed necessary to ensure the financing of the pension scheme.

Compensation measures were provided, with a transition period as well as a rise in mandatory savings contributions.[21] Besides that, special measures were included in the reform to improve the occupational pension coverage for part-time workers and lower wage earners, i.e. to improve coverage for women.[22]

3.7 *Taxation*

3.7.1 Normal Retirement Age, Early Retirement, Partial Retirement, and Deferral of Retirement

AVS and occupational pension scheme annuities are taxed as regular income. Occupational lump-sum benefits are generally taxed at 1/fifth of the individual's tax rate.

With regard to early retirement, there are no differences with taxation at the normal retirement age. However, in case of early *AVS* retirement and if the beneficiary ceases all gainful activity, *AVS* contributions shall continue to be due, calculated along a table cumulating annuities and personal assets with no further accrual of the AVS pension amount.[23] This is a very clear disincentive to an *AVS* early retirement with discontinuation of gainful activity.

AVS and occupational pension scheme partial annuities are taxed as regular income. Occupational partial lump-sum benefits are generally taxed at about 1/fifth of the individual's tax rate. Continuation of gainful activity before age 65 leads to an obligation to pay further *AVS* contributions which will, contrary to full early retirement, lead till age 65 to an accrual of the residual AVS pension amount.

In case of deferral, AVS and occupational pension scheme annuities are taxed as regular income, once the deferral ceases and benefits are paid. Occupational lump-sum benefits are taxed on payment at generally 1/fifth of the individual's tax rate.

3.7.2 Link Between Tax and Contributions

There is a strong practical link between tax and contributions. Indeed, *AVS* contributions are levied on the full gainful income, whilst the benefits are capped, i.e. there

---

[21] Office federal des assurances sociales: Les mesures de compensation https://www.bsv.admin.ch/fr/reforme-lpp-2024.

[22] Office fédéral des assurances sociales: Qu'implique la réforme de la LPP pour les personnes travaillant à temps partiel? https://www.bsv.admin.ch/fr/reforme-lpp-2024.

[23] Art. 28 RAVS

is no income ceiling on *AVS* contributions, implying significant social solidarity between income levels. Indeed, it is generally accepted that the total sum of pensions paid for 92% of AVS pensioners is lower than the total amount in contributions paid by and for them.

As a political counterpart, tax-exempt occupational pension benefits are allowed to be insured on a yearly income up to a ceiling of CHF 90′720 with tax-deductible 25% paritarian savings contributions. As *AVS* contributions are calculated on gross income, after employer occupational pension contributions, high tax-exempt occupational pension retirement savings rates have the effect of reducing the *AVS* contribution base.

There are no possibilities for additional voluntary contributions in *AVS*. However, in case of benefits deferral after the reference retirement age, paritarian *AVS* contributions on gainful income can, under certain conditions, increase the career reference income[24] and close contributory gaps.[25]

In occupational pensions, tax-exempted voluntary additional contributions calculated on the latest insured income are allowed to build up the full regulatory retirement savings account that would have accrued on such an income.[26] This constitutes an individual tax-subsidized defined benefit approach. In addition to the purchase of the full regulatory benefits on the latest insured income, the pension fund may also stipulate in its regulations that insured persons may make additional buy-backs in order to fully or partially offset the reduction in retirement benefits in the event of early retirement. Pension funds must then design their pension plans in such a way that, if the member foregoes early retirement, the benefits paid do not exceed the regulatory benefit target by more than 5%.[27]

It is also now possible to buy back existing contribution gaps in individual tax-exempt retirement savings accounts. This measure is aimed at persons who, in certain years, have not been able to make any payments into such accounts or have only been able to make partial payments.[28]

References

Legislation (Laws and their Acronyms)

Loi fédérale sur l'assurance vieillesse et survivants (LAVS), RS 831.10, 1948
Règlement sur l'assurance vieillesse et survivants (RAVS), RS 831.101, 1948
Loi fédérale sur l'assurance invalidité (LAI), RS 831.20, 1961

---

[24] Art. 29bis § 3 LAVS

[25] Art. 29bis § 4 LAVS

[26] Art. 9 § 2 LFLP and 79b LPP

[27] Art. 1b OPP2

[28] Art. 7–8 OPP3 Law reform was approved on the 6th November 2024 and in force from the 1st January 2025; https://www.admin.ch/gov/fr/accueil/documentation/communiques.msg-id-98831.html.

Loi fédérale sur les prestations complémentaires à l'AVS et l'AI (LPC), RS 831.30, 2006
Loi fédérale sur les prestations transitoires pour les chômeurs âgés (LPtra), RS 837.2, 2020
Loi fédérale sur la prévoyance professionnelle vieillesse, survivants et invalidité (LPP), RS 832.40, 1985
Ordonnance sur la prévoyance professionnelle vieillesse, survivants et invalidité (OPP2), RS 831.441.1, 1985
Loi fédérale sur le libre passage dans la prévoyance professionnelle vieillesse, survivants et invalidité (LFLP), RS 831.42, 1995
Ordonnance sur les déductions admises fiscalement pour les cotisations versées à des formes reconnues de prévoyance (OPP3), RS 831.461.3, 1985
Loi fédérale sur l'assurance-chômage obligatoire et l'indemnité en cas d'insolvabilité (Loi sur l'assurance-chômage, LACI), RS 837.0, 1982

Literature

Frey, Felix, Bollinger, Susanne, Mosimann, Hans-Jakob (2025), *AHVG/IVG/ELG Kommentar*, Orell Füssli Verlag AG
Valterio, Michel (2015), *Commentaire de la loi fédérale sur les prestations complémentaires à l'AVS/AI (LPC),* Schulthess Verlag AG
Valterio, Michel (2018), *Loi fédérale sur l'assurance-invalidité (LAI). Commentaire,* Schulthess Verlag AG
Schneider, Jacques-André (Editeur); Gächter, Thomas (Editeur); Geiser, Thomas (Editeur) (2020), *LPP et LFLP. Lois fédérales sur la prévoyance professionnelle vieillesse, survivants et invalidité et sur le libre passage dans la prévoyance professionnelle vieillesse, survivants et invalidité,* 2eme édition, Stämpfli Verlag AG
Hürzeler MM (2020) Berufliche Vorsorge. Helbing Lichtenhahn Verlag

The Netherlands

Emma Suzanne van Aggelen

1 Introduction to the Pension System and its Narrative

The statutory pension in the Netherlands is a basic state pension, also known as 'AOW' (National Old Age Pensions Act).[1]

Table 1 shows the gross amount of the AOW pension (monthly) as of 1 January 2025.

There are two types of occupational pension schemes: company pension schemes and industry-wide pension schemes. There is no legal obligation for employers to offer an occupational pension scheme to their employees. However, participation in an industry-wide pension fund can be made compulsory for a specific industry by the Minister of Social Affairs and Employment. In practice, the majority of employees participate in such an industry-wide pension scheme.[2] The majority of the self-employed, on the other hand, do not have access to an occupational pension scheme. Self-employed workers can participate in an individual pension scheme.[3]

[1] AOW stands for 'Algemene Ouderdomswet' (National Old Age Pensions Act): Wet van 31 mei 1956, inzake een algemene ouderdomsverzekering (Algemene Ouderdomswet), *Stb.* 1956, nr. 281 [National Old Age Pensions Act, published 1956, 281].

[2] van Aggelen, E.S. (2022), *Het personeel toepassingsgebied van aanvullende pensioenregelingen voor werknemers. Een rechtsvergelijkend en empirisch onderzoek naar de werking van aansluitingsregels*, Brugge, Die Keure, 27.

[3] Biesenbeek, C., de Boer, K., van Ewijk, C., van Ewijk, J., van Gooswilligen, M., Kappelle, H., Lutjens, E., Mertens, M., Muns, S., van der Schaft, H., van Soest A., (2022), "Werkenden met tekortschietend pensioen Oplossingsroutes voor de witte en grijze vlek en de pensioenopbouw van zelfstandigen", Netspar Occasional Paper 05.

E. S. van Aggelen (✉)
Faculty of Law, UHasselt, Hasselt, Belgium
e-mail: emmasuzanne.vanaggelen@uhasselt.be

Faculty of Law and Criminology, KU Leuven, Leuven, Belgium

E. S. van Aggelen (ed.), *Retirement and Employment*, Ius Gentium: Comparative Perspectives on Law and Justice 145, https://doi.org/10.1007/978-3-032-33561-6_8

Table 1 Gross amount AOW (monthly), January 1, 2025

Living alone	Married or living with another adult
1.541,53 EUR	1.047,60 EUR

Reference: Sociale verzekeringsbank (SVB), "AOW pension amounts", https://www.svb.nl/en/aow-pension/aow-pension-rates/aow-pension-rates#section_01 (accessed 9 May 2025)

Private pensions are individual banking or insurance products. Contributions are paid in for the accrual of a pension. People are encouraged to save for their private pension through a favourable tax treatment of these pension products.[4]

Recently, the Dutch pension system has been reformed. In 2019 the Dutch government and the social partners agreed on the main principles of this reform. These main principles are outlined in the so-called 'agreement in principle' ("*Principe-akkoord*"). This agreement makes clear that there are multiple goals to be reached by the pension reform. In addition to making the system more responsive to economic changes, the aim is to make the system more transparent, more personalised and better adapted to the current labour market.[5] At the same time, the social partners and the government have agreed not to change what they consider to be the strengths of the pension system. This means, e.g., that participation in an industry-wide pension fund can still be made mandatory for the entire sector. However, participation is not considered to be the only strong element. Other elements, such as lifetime payout annuity, collective risk sharing and beneficial tax treatment are also considered to be strengths of industry-wide pension funds.[6]

An important legislative element of the reform is the so-called 'New Pension Act'. This New Pension Act was approved by the Dutch Senate on May 1, 2023. The Act entered into force on July 1, 2023. There is, however, a transition period to adjust the pension schemes.[7] This new act will have a major impact not only on employees but also on employers and pension providers, as some key elements of the Dutch pension system will be changed, e.g., defined benefit pension schemes will be replaced by DC-schemes, a new pension contract will be introduced, and the minimum entry age will be lowered.[8]

---

[4] Bollen-Vandenboorn, A.H.H. (red.) (2023), *Pensioen en de belangrijkste toekomstvoorzieningen*, Den Haag, Sdu BV., 521 ev.

[5] Sociaal-Economische Raad (2019), *Naar een nieuw pensioenstelsel*, 2019, https://www.ser.nl/nl/Publicaties/naar-nieuw-pensioenstelsel (accessed 9 May 2025).

[6] Sociaal-Economische Raad (2019), *Naar een nieuw pensioenstelsel*, 2019, https://www.ser.nl/nl/Publicaties/naar-nieuw-pensioenstelsel (accessed 9 May 2025).

[7] Besluit van 22 juni 2023 tot vaststelling van het tijdstip van inwerkingtreding van de Wet toekomst pensioenen en het Besluit toekomst pensioenen, *Staatsblad* 2023, nr. 218 [Decree of 22 June 2023 establishing the date of entry into force of the Future Pensions Act and the Future Pensions Decree, published 2023, nr. 218].

[8] Wet van 3 juni 2023 tot wijziging van de Pensioenwet, de Wet inkomstenbelasting 2001 en enige andere wetten in verband met herziening van het pensioenstelsel, standaardisering van het nabestaan-denpensioen, aanpassing van de fiscale behandeling van pensioen en enige andere wijzigingen ten

As far as the pension contract is concerned, the New Pension Act is a real game changer. In the current Dutch pension system, most occupational pension schemes are defined benefit schemes.[9] The New Pension Act, however, specifies the types of occupational pension schemes that can be offered. A choice can be made between three types of defined contribution schemes: a flexible contribution scheme, a solidarity contribution scheme, and a contribution-capital scheme. This means that defined benefit schemes are no longer allowed. In accordance with the new national legislation, pension accrual must be based on a defined contribution scheme. Pension funds as well as insurance companies are obliged to implement these new rules.[10]

2 Statutory Pensions

2.1 "Normal" Retirement Age

Until 2012, everyone received their AOW pension at the age of 65. In 2012, legislation was introduced to raise the retirement age to 67 in 2023.[11] In 2015 the government even decided to raise the retirement age more quickly due to concerns about the pension system's sustainability. This resulted in new legislation raising the age to 67 in 2021.[12]

The reform of the Dutch pension system, however, had an impact on the retirement age. The social partners were concerned about the increase in the retirement age, as some older workers felt unable to continue working in good health until retirement, due to the anticipated rapid increase in the state pension age and the lack of attention to sustainable employability. Therefore, the social partners stressed that it is important that people can reach the state pension age in good health. In response, the government

---

aanzien van pensioen (Wet toekomst pensioenen), *Staatsblad* 2023, nr. 216 [Future Pensions Act, published 2023, nr. 216].

[9] van Popta, B. en Steenbeek, O. (Eds.) (2021), *Transition to a new pension contract in the Netherlands: Lessons from abroad*, Netspar Occasional Paper 03, 6.

[10] Dietvorst, G.J.B. (red.) (2024), *PensioenPocket 2024*, Deventer, Kluwer, 40–42.

[11] Wet van 12 juli 2012 tot wijziging van de Algemene Ouderdomswet, de Wet werk en bijstand, de Wet inkomstenbelasting 2001 en de Wet op de loonbelasting 1964 in verband met stapsgewijze verhoging en koppeling aan de stijging van de levensverwachting van de pensioenleeftijd (Wet verhoging AOW- en pensioenrichtleeftijd), *Staatsblad* 2012, nr. 328 [Act on the increase of the AOW- and retirement age, published 2012, nr. 328].

[12] Wet van 4 juni 2015 tot wijziging van de Algemene Ouderdomswet, de Wet op de loonbelasting 1964, de Wet verhoging AOW- en pensioenrichtleeftijd, de Pensioenwet, de Wet verplichte beroepspensioenregeling en Overige fiscale maatregelen 2013 in verband met de versnelling van de stapsgewijze verhoging van de AOW-leeftijd, *Staatsblad* 2015, nr. 218. [Act of 4 June 2015, published 2015, nr. 218].

Table 2 AOW retirement age up to 2029

Year	AOW retirement age
2025	67
2026	67
2027	67
2028	67 and 3 months
2029	67 and 3 months

Reference: Author's table, using the applicable legislation

decided to slow down the increase in the retirement age.[13] This resulted in new legislation slowing down the increase of the retirement age to 67 in 2024.[14]

In 2025 the retirement age is still 67. After 2025 the retirement age will be linked to the life expectancy estimates by Statistics Netherlands (CBS).[15] An increase in the AOW age must be announced at least 5 years in advance.[16] For the years 2026 and 2027 the government has already announced that the retirement age will be 67,[17] and for the years 2028 and 2029 the retirement age will be 67 and 3 months.[18]

Table 2 shows the AOW retirement age up to 2029.

To get an AOW pension, you must be insured under the Dutch AOW pension scheme. The criterion for being insured is residence. If you have lived in the Netherlands, you are automatically insured under the AOW scheme.[19]

---

[13] Brief van de minister van sociale zaken en werkgelegenheid: toekomst pensioenstelsel, *Eerst Kamer der Staten-Generaal*, Vergaderjaar 2018–2019, 32,043, nr. 457 [Senate of the States General, Parliamentary documents 2018–2019, 32,043, nr. 457].

[14] Wet van 3 juli 2019 tot wijziging van de Algemene Ouderdomswet, de Wet op de loonbelasting 1964, de Wet verhoging AOW- en pensioenrichtleeftijd, de Wet versnelling stapsgewijze verhoging AOW-leeftijd en de Wet tegemoetkomingen loondomein in verband met temporisering van de stapsgewijze verhoging van de AOW-leeftijd (Wet temporisering verhoging AOW-leeftijd), *Staatsblad* 2019, nr. 246 [Act to slow down the increase of AOW-age, published 2019, nr. 246].

[15] Art. 1 Wet van 2 december 2020, houdende wijziging van de Algemene Ouderdomswet en de Wet op de loonbelasting 1964 in verband met de verandering van de koppeling van de AOW- en pensioenrichtleeftijd aan de stijging van de levensverwachting (Wet verandering koppeling AOW-leeftijd), *Staatsblad* 2020, nr. 503 [Act relating to the modification of the link between the AOW-age and rising life expectancy, published 2020, nr. 503].

[16] Art. 7a Algemene Ouderdomswet [National Old Age Pensions Act].

[17] Mededeling van de Minister van Sociale Zaken en Werkgelegenheid van 4 december 2020 tot bekendmaking van de pensioengerechtigde leeftijd en de aanvangsleeftijd in 2026, *Staatscourant* 2020, nr. 65,110; Mededeling van de Staatssecretaris van Sociale Zaken en Werkgelegenheid van 5 november 2021, tot bekendmaking van de pensioengerechtigde leeftijd en de aanvangsleeftijd in 2027, *Staatscourant* 2021, nr. 46,409.

[18] Mededeling van de Minister voor Armoedebeleid, Participatie en Pensioenen van 9 november 2022 tot bekendmaking van de pensioengerechtigde leeftijd en de aanvangsleeftijd in 2028, *Staatscourant* 2022, nr. 30,748; Mededeling van de Minister voor Armoedebeleid, Participatie en Pensioenen van 13 november 2023 tot bekendmaking van de pensioengerechtigde leeftijd en de aanvangsleeftijd in 2029, *Staatscourant* 2023, nr. 31,782.

[19] Art. 6 Algemene Ouderdomswet [National Old Age Pensions Act].

To get a full AOW pension, you must have lived in the Netherlands for a sufficient period of time, i.e. for 50 years before you reach pensionable age. If you live or have lived in the Netherlands but do not have enough years of residence (i.e., less than 50 years), you will not get a full AOW pension. Your AOW pension will be reduced by 2% each year you have not lived in the Netherlands.[20] There are no special regimes for, e.g., civil servants, army, police.

Getting an AOW pension doesn't mean you have to leave the labour market. The AOW legislation does not oblige people to stop working. The amount of the AOW pension is the same for a pensioner who leaves the labour market at retirement age as it is for a pensioner who does not leave the labour market at retirement age.[21]

2.2 *Early Retirement Age*

It is not possible to receive the AOW pension before the legal retirement age. To receive AOW, people must wait until they reach the AOW retirement age as determined in the National Old Age Pensions Act.[22] Nevertheless, social partners have asked the government to take specific measures for people who are already close to their retirement age, as these people may feel overwhelmed by the new retirement age or may be concerned about how to reach the retirement age in good health (see in this Chapter, Sect. 2.5).[23]

2.3 *Deferral of Retirement*

About 4 months before a person reaches retirement age, a letter is sent by the Social Insurance Bank. After receiving this letter, it is possible to claim your AOW pension.[24] It's important to claim your AOW pension on time, otherwise you may not be able to reclaim unpaid pension payments.[25] Therefore, the non-take-up of the AOW state pension is very low.[26]

---

[20] Art. 13 Algemene Ouderdomswet [National Old Age Pensions Act].

[21] Bollen-Vandenboorn, A.H.H. (red.) (2023), *Pensioen en de belangrijkste toekomstvoorzieningen*, Den Haag, Sdu BV., 119–120.

[22] Art. 7 Algemene Ouderdomswet [National Old Age Pensions Act].

[23] Brief van de minister van sociale zaken en werkgelegenheid: toekomst pensioenstelsel, *Eerst Kamer der Staten-Generaal*, Vergaderjaar 2018–2019, 32,043, nr. 457, 12–16 [Senate of the States General, Parliamentary documents 2018–2019, 32,043, nr. 457].

[24] Sociale Verzekeringsbank (SVB), "Claiming an AOW pension if you live in the Netherlands", https://www.svb.nl/en/aow-pension/arranging-your-affairs-online/applying-for-an-aow-pension-if-you-live-in-the-netherlands (accessed 9 May 2025).

[25] Art. 16 Algemene Ouderdomswet [National Old Age Pensions Act].

[26] Algemene Rekenkamer, "Ouderdomsregeling ontleed 2019", p. 27–28. https://www.rekenkamer.nl/publicaties/rapporten/2019/11/13/ouderdomsregelingen-ontleed (accessed 5 May 2025).

2.4 *Partial Retirement*

A partial pay-out of the AOW is not possible. People who decide to take up their AOW-pension will receive the full amount.

2.5 *Retirement Regimes for Persons Considered to Be in Hazardous or Arduous Jobs*

There are no specific retirement regimes for persons considered to be in hazardous or arduous jobs. Nevertheless, with the retirement age increase, the social partners are concerned that some people may feel overwhelmed by the new retirement age or may struggle with how to reach the retirement age in good health (*supra* 2.2). Certain categories of employees are often considered, such as those in hazardous or arduous jobs.[27]

The government has taken into account this concern of the social partners. One of the measures taken is the so-called 'temporary exemption from the RVU-levy.' 'RVU' refers to early retirement arrangements. Such an arrangement allows the employee to retire before reaching AOW retirement age while being financially compensated by the employer. This financial compensation for the employee serves to bridge the period between the end of the employment and the AOW retirement age. In the past the government decided to discourage these RVU-arrangements between employers and employees. Therefore, a pseudo financial levy of 52% for the employer, also called the 'RVU levy', has been introduced.[28] It is clear that this levy makes it very unattractive for the employer to offer an early retirement arrangement.

Due to the increase of the AOW retirement age and the concerns raised about people being able to reach the AOW retirement age in good health, a temporary exemption from the financial levy of 52% for early retirement arrangements has been introduced. This exemption implies that the RVU-levy is omitted once certain conditions are met. The conditions imply that the arrangement can be offered no longer than 3 years before the AOW retirement age,[29] that the financial compensation will not exceed a certain threshold,[30] that the arrangement will be concluded no later

[27] Brief van de minister van sociale zaken en werkgelegenheid: toekomst pensioenstelsel, *Eerst Kamer der Staten-Generaal*, Vergaderjaar 2018–2019, 32,043, nr. 457 [Senate of the States General, Parliamentary documents 2018–2019, 32,043, nr. 457].

[28] Memorie van toelichting, Wet bedrag ineens, RVU en verlofsparen, *Tweede Kamer der Staten-Generaal*, Vergaderjaar 2019–2020, 35,555, nr. 3 [House of Representatives of the Netherlands, Parliamentary documents 2019–2020, 35,555, nr. 3].

[29] Art. 32ba, punt 7 Wet van 16 december 1964, houdende vervanging van het Besluit op de Loonbelasting 1940 door een nieuwe wettelijke regeling (Wet op de loonbelasting 1964), *Staatsblad* 1964, nr. 524 [Wage Tax Act 1964, published 1964, nr. 524].

[30] Art. 32ba, punt 7 Wet op de loonbelasting 1964 [Wage Tax Act 1964].

than 31 December 2025 and that the employee reaches AOW-retirement age no later than 31 December 2028.[31]

The temporary exemption of the RVU-levy is not the only measure taken by the government to help people to reach the retirement age in good health. An example of another measure is a tax-friendly leave of up to 100 weeks that can be used to retire earlier.[32]

2.6 *Retirement Regimes Based on Means or Income Tested Benefits*

Once a person reaches the AOW-retirement age, lives in the Netherlands, and doesn't get a full AOW pension, he or she may be eligible for the so-called 'AIO'. Such an AIO is meant as income support for the elderly with income below the guaranteed minimum income. The benefit is income and means-tested.[33]

2.7 *Taxation*

If you are insured under the AOW pension scheme, contributions must be paid to the Dutch Tax and Customs Administration (*Belastingdienst*). In 2025, the AOW

---

[31] Art. V, G Wet van 14 januari 2021 tot wijziging van de Pensioenwet, de Wet verplichte beroepspensioenregeling, de Wet op het financieel toezicht, de Wet inkomstenbelasting 2001 en de Wet op de loonbelasting 1964 in verband met de introductie van de mogelijkheid om een deel van de waarde van de aanspraken op ouderdomspensioen of op periodieke uitkeringen van oudedagsvoorzieningen in de derde pijler op de ingangsdatum daarvan te laten afkopen, de tijdelijke versoepeling van de pseudo-eindheffing bij regelingen voor vervroegde uittreding en de uitbreiding van de fiscale ruimte voor het sparen van bovenwettelijk verlof (Wet bedrag ineens, RVU en verlofsparen), *Staatsblad* 2021, nr. 20 [Act of 14 januari 2021, published 2021, nr. 20]; Besluit van 14 januari 2021 tot vaststelling van het tijdstip van inwerkingtreding van de Wet bedrag ineens, RVU en verlofsparen, *Staatsblad* 2021, nr. 21 [Decree of 14 January 2021, pubished 2021, nr. 21].

[32] Wet bedrag ineens, RVU en verlofsparen [Act of 14 januari 2021, published 2021, nr. 20]; Besluit van 14 januari 2021 tot vaststelling van het tijdstip van inwerkingtreding van de Wet bedrag ineens, RVU en verlofsparen, *Staatsblad* 2021, nr. 21 [Decree of 14 January 2021, published, 2021, nr. 21].

[33] Wet van 9 oktober 2003, houdende vaststelling van een wet inzake ondersteuning bij arbeidsinschakeling en verlening van bijstand door gemeenten (Wet werk en bijstand), *Staatsblad* 2003, nr. 375 [Act of 9 October 2003, published 2003, nr. 375].

contribution 17.9% of your income.[34] In some circumstances it is possible to voluntarily contribute to the AOW scheme if some years were not insured due to lack of residency.[35]

A pension under the AOW scheme is subject to wage tax and national insurance contributions such as contributions for general health insurance.[36] There are also tax credits. If the pensioner's income is less than 45.308 euros (in 2025), the basic tax credit is 2.035 euros (in 2025). An additional tax credit of 531 euros (in 2025) is available for a pensioner living in a single household.[37]

3 Occupational Pensions

3.1 Normal Retirement Age

The retirement age can be found in the pension scheme. It's possible that the retirement age specified in the pension scheme is lower than the AOW retirement age. However, certain restrictions must be taken into account as specified in national legislation (see Sect. 3.2).[38]

[34] Art. 11 Algemene Ouderdomswet [National Old Age Pensions Act]; Art. 1 Regeling van de Minister van Sociale Zaken en Werkgelegenheid van 13 november 2023, nr. 2023–0000518574, tot vaststelling van de premiepercentages werknemers- en volksverzekeringen, maximumpremieloon werknemersverzekeringen en opslag kinderopvangtoeslag 2024 (Regeling tot vaststelling premiepercentages werknemers- en volksverzekeringen, maximumpremieloon werknemersverzekeringen en opslag kinderopvangtoeslag 2024), *Staatscourant* 2023, nr. 31,686 [Regulation of 13 November 2023, nr. 31,686].

[35] Art. 34 ev. Algemene Ouderdomswet [National Old Age Pensions Act].

[36] Art. 34, lid 1 Wet op de loonbelasting 1964 [Wage Tax Act 1964]; art. 11, lid 2. Besluit van 17 mei 1965, houdende uitvoering van de Wet op de loonbelasting 1964, *Staatsblad* 1965, nr. 202 [Decree of 17 May 1965, published 1965, nr. 202]; see about national health insurance: Wet van 3 december 2014, houdende regels inzake de verzekering van zorg aan mensen die zijn aangewezen op langdurige zorg (Wet langdurige zorg), *Staatsblad* 2014, 494 [Act of 3 December 2014, published 2014, nr. 494].

[37] Art. 22 b en art. 22c Wet op de loonbelasting 1964 [Wage Tax Act 1964].

[38] Due to the Dutch pension reform, the regulation concerning the pensionable reference age for occupational pension schemes has been abolished (see also: Lutjens, E.(ed.) (2023) *Mr. C. Assers Handleiding tot de beoefening van het Nederlands Burgerlijk Recht. 7. Bijzondere overeenkomsten,* Deel XI. Pensioen, Deventer, Kluwer, nr. 92 (accessed online)).

3.2 *Early Retirement*

Occupational pension schemes may offer participants the option of retiring before or after the retirement age specified in the pension scheme.[39] However, there are some restrictions that need to be taken into account. National legislation stipulates that the earliest date from which a pension can be paid is the first day of the month in which the person reaches an age 10 years below the AOW retirement age, unless the pension scheme allows an earlier start date. The same legislation also stipulates that the pension must be paid no later than the date on which the person concerned reaches an age that is five years higher than the AOW retirement age.[40]

3.3 *Work Past Retirement (Including Partial Retirement)*

Occupational pension schemes may also offer participants the possibility of combining work and full or partial retirement. In principle, it is not required to limit additional earnings. If the occupational pension scheme offers participants the option of retiring (part-time) before the retirement age specified in the pension scheme, there is no legal obligation to establish whether the (former) employee intends to reduce his or her income-generating activities to the same extent.[41]

3.4 *Taxation*

Occupational pensions are taxed. It's not (yet) possible to take up the pension as a lump sum. The pension income is taxed as income from work and home ownership (box 1), which means that a progressive tax rate is applied. However, special tax rates will apply once you reach the AOW retirement age as the AOW contribution of 17.9% (*supra* 2.7) is not required anymore.[42]

---

[39] Art. 62, 1,b Wet van 7 december 2006 houdende regels betreffende pensioenen (Pensioenwet), *Staatsblad* 2006, nr. 705 [Pension Act, published 2006, nr. 705]; E. Lutjens (ed.) (2023), *Mr. C. Assers Handleiding tot de beoefening van het Nederlands Burgerlijk Recht. 7. Bijzondere overeenkomsten*, Deel XI. Pensioen, Deventer, Kluwer, nr. 92 (accessed online).

[40] Art. 18a, punt 4, a en b Wet op de loonbelasting 1964 [Wage Tax Act 1964]; E. Lutjens (ed.) (2023), *Mr. C. Assers Handleiding tot de beoefening van het Nederlands Burgerlijk Recht. 7. Bijzondere overeenkomsten*, Deel XI. Pensioen, Deventer, Kluwer, nr. 92 (accessed online).

[41] Belastingdienst: Centraal Aanspreekpunt Pensioenen, "V&A 23–005: Uiterste moment van vervroegde ingang ouderdomspensioen", 1 juli 2023,
https://centraalaanspreekpuntpensioenen.belastingdienst.nl/publicaties/va-23-005-v010723/ (accessed 9 May 2025).

[42] Art. 21 en art. 21b Wet op de loonbelasting 1964 [Wage Tax Act 1964]; Art. 21 Wet van 16 december 2004, houdende regels betreffende de financiering van de sociale verzekeringen (Wet

Table 3 Occupational pensions-tax rates

Taxable income from work (including pensions) and homeownership*	Tax rates (in 2025)**
0 EUR-38.441 EUR	17,92%
38.441 - € 76.817 EUR	37,48%
75.817 EUR and upwards	49,50%

* For people born before January 1, 1946 the amount of taxable income differs from the amounts as mentioned in this table. **Different tax rates may apply to taxable income between €0 and €38,098 in the year in which you reach retirement age. Reference: website of the Dutch Tax Administration (https://www.belastingdienst.nl/wps/wcm/connect/bldcontentnl/belastingdienst/prive/inkomstenbelasting/heffingskortingen_boxen_tarieven/boxen_en_tarieven/box_1/box_1 (accessed 30 May 2025))

The tax rates are shown in Table 3. There is no special tax regime for early/partial or deferred retirement.

In the Netherlands, pension pillars cannot be considered to be completely separated. Some elements interconnect with one another. To calculate the occupational/individual pension benefits, it is, for example, important to take the state pension benefit (AOW) into consideration as a part of the income is expected to be covered by the state pension, which is called the offset (franchise). Over this franchise, no additional pension entitlements are accrued. Therefore, the basic value of pensionable earnings is the gross income less the offset.[43] Also, with the Dutch pension reform, new elements of interconnectivity were implemented between occupational pension schemes and supplementary pension schemes, as the tax treatment of individual pension accrual is largely aligned with the tax treatment of occupational pension accrual, aiming to make pension saving more attractive for self-employed workers and to move towards a more 'neutral' pension system in which the type of employment is less important.[44]

References

Legislation

Brief van de minister van sociale zaken en werkgelegenheid: toekomst pensioenstelsel, *Eerst Kamer der Staten-Generaal*, Vergaderjaar 2018–2019, 32043, nr. 457

financiering sociale verzekeringen), *Staatsblad* 2004, nr. 36 [Social Insurance Financing Act, published 2005, nr. 36].

43 Art. 18a, 2 en 3 Wet op de Loonbelasting 1964 [Wage Tax Act 1964].

44 Memorie van toelichting bij de Wet toekomst Pensioenen, Tweede Kamer der Staten Generaal 2021–2022, 36,067, nr.3, p. 144 ev [House of Representatives of the Netherlands, Parliamentary documents 2021–2022, 36,067, nr. 3].

Mededeling van de Minister voor Armoedebeleid (2022) Participatie en Pensioenen van 9 november 2022 tot bekendmaking van de pensioengerechtigde leeftijd en de aanvangsleeftijd in 2028. Staatscourant nr. 30748

Mededeling van de Minister voor Armoedebeleid (2023) Participatie en Pensioenen van 13 november 2023 tot bekendmaking van de pensioengerechtigde leeftijd en de aanvangsleeftijd in 2029. Staatscourant nr. 31782

Memorie van toelichting bij de Wet toekomst Pensioenen, Tweede Kamer der Staten Generaal 2021–2022, 36067, nr. 3

Memorie van toelichting, Wet bedrag ineens, RVU en verlofsparen, Tweede Kamer der Staten-Generaal, Vergaderjaar 2019–2020, 35555, nr. 3

Regeling van de Minister van Sociale Zaken en Werkgelegenheid van 13 november 2023, nr. 2023-0000518574, tot vaststelling van de premiepercentages werknemers- en volksverzekeringen, maximumpremieloon werknemersverzekeringen en opslag kinderopvangtoeslag 2024 (Regeling tot vaststelling premiepercentages werknemers- en volksverzekeringen, maximumpremieloon werknemersverzekeringen en opslag kinderopvangtoeslag 2024), *Staatscourant* 2023, nr. 31686

Wet van 16 december 1964, houdende vervanging van het Besluit op de Loonbelasting 1940 door een nieuwe wettelijke regeling (Wet op de loonbelasting 1964), Staatsblad 1964, nr. 524

Besluit van 17 mei 1965, houdende uitvoering van de Wet op de loonbelasting 1964, Staatsblad 1965, nr. 202

Wet van 9 oktober 2003, houdende vaststelling van een wet inzake ondersteuning bij arbeidsinschakeling en verlening van bijstand door gemeenten (Wet werk en bijstand), Staatsblad 2003, nr. 375

Wet van 16 december 2004, houdende regels betreffende de financiering van de sociale verzekeringen (Wet financiering sociale verzekeringen), Staatsblad 2005, nr. 36

Wet van 3 december 2014, houdende regels inzake de verzekering van zorg aan mensen die zijn aangewezen op langdurige zorg (Wet langdurige zorg), Staatsblad 2014, nr. 494

Wet van 3 juli 2019 tot wijziging van de Algemene Ouderdomswet, de Wet op de loonbelasting 1964, de Wet verhoging AOW- en pensioenrichtleeftijd, de Wet versnelling stapsgewijze verhoging AOW-leeftijd en de Wet tegemoetkomingen loondomein in verband met temporisering van de stapsgewijze verhoging van de AOW-leeftijd (Wet temporisering verhoging AOW-leeftijd), Staatsblad 2019, nr. 246

Wet van 2 december 2020, houdende wijziging van de Algemene Ouderdomswet en de Wet op de loonbelasting 1964 in verband met de verandering van de koppeling van de AOW- en pensioenrichtleeftijd aan de stijging van de levensverwachting (Wet verandering koppeling AOW-leeftijd), Staatsblad 2020, nr. 503

Wet van 14 januari 2021 tot wijziging van de Pensioenwet, de Wet verplichte beroepspensioenregeling, de Wet op het financieel toezicht, de Wet inkomstenbelasting 2001 en de Wet op de loonbelasting 1964 in verband met de introductie van de mogelijkheid om een deel van de waarde van de aanspraken op ouderdomspensioen of op periodieke uitkeringen van oudedagsvoorzieningen in de derde pijler op de ingangsdatum daarvan te laten afkopen, de tijdelijke versoepeling van de pseudo-eindheffing bij regelingen voor vervroegde uittreding en de uitbreiding van de fiscale ruimte voor het sparen van bovenwettelijk verlof (Wet bedrag ineens, RVU en verlofsparen), Staatsblad 2021, nr. 20

Besluit van 14 januari 2021 tot vaststelling van het tijdstip van inwerkingtreding van de Wet bedrag ineens, RVU en verlofsparen, Staatsblad 2021, nr. 21

Besluit van 22 juni 2023 tot vaststelling van het tijdstip van inwerkingtreding van de Wet toekomst pensioenen en het Besluit toekomst pensioenen, Staatsblad 2023, nr. 218

Mededeling van de Minister van Sociale Zaken en Werkgelegenheid van 4 december 2020 tot bekendmaking van de pensioengerechtigde leeftijd en de aanvangsleeftijd in 2026, Staatscourant 2020, nr. 65110

Mededeling van de Staatssecretaris van Sociale Zaken en Werkgelegenheid van 5 november 2021, tot bekendmaking van de pensioengerechtigde leeftijd en de aanvangsleeftijd in 2027, Staatscourant 2021, nr. 46409

Wet van 31 mei 1956, inzake een algemene ouderdomsverzekering (Algemene Ouderdomswet), Stb 1956, nr. 281

Wet van 7 december 2006 houdende regels betreffende pensioenen (Pensioenwet), Stb. 2006, 705

Literature

Belastingdienst: centraal aanspreekpunt pensioenen, "V&A 23–005: Uiterste moment van vervroegde ingang ouderdomspensioen", 1 juli 2023., https://centraalaanspreekpuntpensioenen.belastingdienst.nl/publicaties/va-23-005-v010723/ (accessed 9 May 2025)

Biesenbeek, C., De Boer, K., Van Ewijk, C. Van Ewijk, J. Van Gooswilligen, M. Kappelle, H. Lutjens, E, Mertens, M., Muns, S. Van der Schaft, H. Van Soest, A. (2022) "Werkenden met tekortschietend pensioen Oplossingsroutes voor de witte en grijze vlek en de pensioenopbouw van zelfstandigen", Netspar Occas Pap 05

Bollen-Vandenboorn, A.H.H. (red.) (2023) *Pensioen en de belangrijkste toekomstvoorzieningen*, Den Haag, Sdu BV, 2023, 675 p

Dietvorst, G.J.B. (red.) (2024) PensioenPocket 2024, Deventer, Kluwer, 40–42

Dutch Tax Administration (https://www.belastingdienst.nl/wps/wcm/connect/bldcontentnl/belastingdienst/prive/inkomstenbelasting/heffingskortingen_boxen_tarieven/boxen_en_tarieven/box_1/box_1 (accessed 30 May 2025))

Lutjens, E. (ed.) (2023) *Mr. C. Assers Handleiding tot de beoefening van het Nederlands Burgerlijk Recht. 7. Bijzondere overeenkomsten*, Deel XI. Pensioen, Deventer, Kluwer, 1052 p

Sociaal-Economische Raad (2019) "Naar een nieuw pensioenstelsel", https://www.ser.nl/nl/Publicaties/naar-nieuw-pensioenstelsel (accessed 9 May 2025)

Algemene Rekenkamer, "Ouderdomsregeling ontleed 2019", p. 27–28. https://www.rekenkamer.nl/publicaties/rapporten/2019/11/13/ouderdomsregelingen-ontleed (accessed 4 May 2025)

Sociale verzekeringsbank (SVB), "Claiming an AOW pension if you live in the Netherlands", https://www.svb.nl/en/aow-pension/arranging-your-affairs-online/applying-for-an-aow-pension-if-you-live-in-the-netherlands (accessed 9 May 2025a)

Sociale verzekeringsbank (SVB), "AOW pension amounts", https://www.svb.nl/en/aow-pension/aow-pension-rates/aow-pension-rates#section_01 (accessed 9 May 2025b)

van Aggelen ES (2022) Het personeel toepassingsgebied van aanvullende pensioenregelingen voor werknemers. Een rechtsvergelijkend en empirisch onderzoek naar de werking van aansluitingsregels, Brugge, Die Keure, p 341

van Popta, B. en Steenbeek, O. (Eds.) (2021) Transition to a new pension contract in The Netherlands: lessons from abroad, Netspar Occasional Paper 03, 6

The United Kingdom

James Kolaczkowski

1 Introduction to the Pension System and its Narrative

The pension system in the UK[1] has been known for a history of funded occupational defined benefit pension provision and a relatively low state pension, both elements have seen significant changes. The origins of the current universal state pension that was introduced in 1948[2] come from the influential Beveridge Report in 1942,[3] after significant political consideration, the result was essentially a pay-as-you-go system designed to provide benefits at a 'subsistence' level to keep people out of poverty.[4] The system has seen the introduction of different forms of earnings related additional pensions with significant incremental changes that created a complex regime of systems running in parallel, with different rules depending upon your age of retirement.[5]

The current state pension has been simplified to remove earnings related elements for new retirees but with the promise of increases to pensions in payment in line

---

[1] The United Kingdom covers England, Wales, Scotland (that make up 'Great Britain') and Northern Ireland. This note focusses upon the position in Great Britain, where pension policy is governed by the Westminster Parliament and enacted by the Department for Work and Pensions. Devolution has meant that elements of some policies that affect pensions may differ between devolved nations, such as taxation thresholds.

[2] National Insurance Act 1946.

[3] Beveridge, *Social Insurance and Allied Services* Cmd 6404 (His Majesty's Stationery Office 1942).

[4] For a review of the early development of the system, see Bozia, Crawford, Tetlo, The History of State Pensions in the UK: 1948 to 2010, IFS Briefing Note BN105 (Institute for Fiscal Studies 1948).

[5] Pemberton (2006) Politics and Pension in Post War Britain in Pemberton, Thane, Whiteside (eds) (2006) Britain's Pension Crisis: History and Policy. Oxford University Press.

J. Kolaczkowski (✉)
James Kolaczkowski, Law School, University of Exeter, Exeter, UK
e-mail: J.Kolaczkowski@exeter.ac.uk

E. S. van Aggelen (ed.), *Retirement and Employment*, Ius Gentium: Comparative Perspectives on Law and Justice 145, https://doi.org/10.1007/978-3-032-33561-6_9

with a 'triple lock'.[6] Despite these recent changes, the narrative of pensions in the UK is still based upon a state pension that needs to be supplemented through an occupational pension or a private individual pension. The introduction of automatic enrolment in 2012 emphasised this approach, with the requirement for employers to automatically enrol qualifying employees and contribute towards their pensions. There have been significant improvements in participation through placing what could be seen as a state social responsibility to ensure that citizens are provided for in the hands of private employers,[7] emphasising the need for individual responsibility in the narrative of pension provision in the UK. It can therefore be said that individualism is an important part of the UK pensions narrative.[8] A second element of the UK pensions narrative is one of freedom, this can be seen in freedom of choice following recent changes to rules permitting more flexibility to access defined contribution pension benefits discussed below in Sect. 3, and also freedom for employers in how they choose to provide occupational pensions, albeit within a significant amount of pension, tax and employment law. This chapter identifies key elements of the legal structure within which pensions are provided in the UK and insights on individualism and freedom are included in the UK Chapter in Part III.

The political situation in the UK changed following a general election on 4 July 2024. Before coming into power, the government indicated that it would retain the 'triple lock' annual increase to the state pension but said it would review pension provision with a view to improving security in retirement and increasing investment in the UK economy.[9]

Phase one of this review focused on investment and resulted in a Pensions Bill that is currently being debated in parliament.[10] As part of Phase Two the government has established a Pensions Commission to look at adequacy that is expected to report in 2027. Additionally, the government's stated intention is to introduce welfare reform to reduce public spending.[11]

---

[6] An annual increase in line with the lower of average earnings, inflation (Consumer Price Index) or 2.5%.

[7] Kolaczkowski (2020) The Social Role of Occupational Pension Schemes. In Agnew, Davies, Mitchell (eds) Pensions: Law, Policy and Practice. Hart Publishing, pp. 195–196.

[8] See also Berry on state intervention through the National Employment Savings Trust as part of the automatic enrolment regime, in Berry (2021) The substitutive state? Neoliberal state interventionism across industrial, housing and private pension policy in the UK, Competition and Change, Vol 26(2) pp. 242–265.

[9] Labour Party Manifesto, 13 June 2024, available at: https://labour.org.uk/updates/stories/labour-manifesto-2024-sign-up/ Accessed 2 April 2025.

[10] HM Treasury, Department for Work and Pensions, Ministry of Housing Communities and Local Government, Pensions Investment Review Interim Report November 2024, https://assets.publishing.service.gov.uk/media/6736181254652d03d5161199/Pensions_Investment_Review_interim_report.pdf. Accessed 2 April 2025.

[11] Pathways to Work: Reforming Benefits and Support to Get Britain Working Green Paper (28 March 2025) https://www.gov.uk/government/consultations/pathways-to-work-reforming-benefits-and-support-to-get-britain-working-green-paper. Accessed 2 April 2025.

Total expenditure on the state pension and specific pensioner benefits[12] in 2024–2025 was estimated to be 150.7 billion GBP rising from 141.9 billion GBP in the year 2023–2024.[13] The total UK GDP in cash terms was reported to be £2848 billion GBP in 2024.[14] The Office for National Statistics issued a forecast of population size for the period between 2021 and 2036 which estimated that the UK population in 2023 was 68.4 million and estimated an increase of 6.6 million between 2021 and 2036.[15] It was also estimated that the proportion of people aged 85 and above would increase from 1.6 million (2,5% of total population) to 2.6 million (3,5% of total population) by 2036.

2 Statutory Pensions

This section considers the pension provided by the state, it does not consider pension schemes that are set up through legislation as is the case for some public sector occupational schemes such as the Local Government Pension Scheme.

2.1 "Normal" Retirement Age

The state pension is a mandatory pension that is contributed to by paying National Insurance out of income, payments can be made by employers directly to *HMRC* (His Majesty's Revenue and Customs), self-employed persons typically pay through their self-assessment tax returns.

The state pension age is currently 66 for men and women. The pension age is equal for men and women after a process of equalisation that ended in 2018. The age has been increasing since 2010 and is still increasing. According to the latest government report on the proposed timetable, the age will increase to 67 between 2026–2028 and to age 68 between 2044 and 2046.

However, legislation provides for periodic reviews of the state pension age[16] and a further review is underway that will consider whether there should be a link to life expectancy and the financial sustainability, amongst other factors.

---

[12] Pension credit, pensioner housing benefit and the winter fuel allowance.

[13] Office for Budget Responsibility, Economic and Fiscal Outlook, March 2025, CP 1289, pp. 112–113.

[14] House of Commons Economic Indicator briefing note, 16 May 2024, Number 02783.

[15] Office for National Statistics, National Population Projections: 2021-based interim released 30 January 2024 available at: https://www.ons.gov.uk/peoplepopulationandcommunity/populationandmigration/populationprojections/bulletins/nationalpopulationprojections/2021basedinterim. Accessed 20 June 2025.

[16] Pensions Act 2014 s27.

The state scheme was reformed in 2016[17] with the introduction of a single pension that replaced the previous two tier structure of a basic state pension and an additional earnings related state pension. The new state pension is paid to men born on or after 6 April 1951 and women born on or after 6 April 1953. People born before this date receive the old system of state pension that is made up of a basic flat rate amount (up to 176.45 GBP a week in 2025–2026) and an earnings related amount. Writing in 2010, the UK approach to the state pension has been described by Bozio et al. as a 'mainly flat rate, largely non-contributory system, periodically tempted by the higher replacement rate of social insurance schemes but always eventually frightened by their cost'.[18] The new state pension shows a desire to maintain a sufficient flat rate pension through the triple lock, but arguably the fear of too much state responsibility is still present through the expectation of individual savings through automatic enrolment.

The new state pension in 2025–2026 is paid at a rate of 230.25 GBP a week (or 11,973 GBP a year) and is designed to pay this full amount if you have 35 qualifying years of National Insurance payments. If you have more than 10 but less than 35 qualifying years, you will receive a state pension that is lower than the full amount. However, there is some protection for those on very low incomes. If your weekly income is below a certain amount, a UK citizen may apply for it to be topped up through a 'pension credit'. For a single person this would mean that weekly income would be topped up to 227.10 GBP, this is subject to adjustment to take into account receipt of other benefits or savings above 10,000 GBP.

The new state pension is subject to increases known as the 'triple lock', this means that each year the pension will increase at the highest of i) average earnings, ii) prices according to the Consumer Price Index (CPI) and iii) 2,5%. This is a controversial measure as it is a significant public spending commitment. The Office for Budget Responsibility reported that expenditure on welfare was expected to increase by 16.7 billion GBP in the year to March 2025, partly due to the use of CPI as an inflation measure.[19]

The state pension system does not have different forms of pension for people in particular types of work, certain jobs that may be deemed hazardous may have more generous workplace occupational pension schemes.

It is possible to continue to work beyond reaching state pension age, but if you choose to work after taking your state pension you will still need to pay tax on your income according to your marginal rate in accordance with the income tax rules.

---

[17] Pensions Act 2014, applicable to people reaching state pension age from 6 April 2016.

[18] Bozia, Crawford, Tetlo, The History of State Pensions in the UK: 1948 to 2010, IFS Briefing Note BN105 (Institute for Fiscal Studies 2010). p 69.

[19] Office for Budget Responsibility, Economic and Fiscal Outlook, March 2025, CP 1289, https://obr.uk/efo/economic-and-fiscal-outlook-march-2025. Accessed 29 April 2025 pp. 111–112.

2.2 Early Retirement Age

It is not possible to take the state pension at an age earlier than your designated state pension age, other state benefits may be available depending upon your situation, such as statutory sick pay or universal credit that was introduced in 2013 and covers benefits previously provided as six separate benefits, such as housing benefit or a job seeker's allowance.

2.3 Deferral of Retirement

The state pension is not paid directly to an individual unless they take action to claim it. They can choose to take it at their state pension age or to defer taking their pension. If the new state pension is deferred it is increased by 1% for every 9 weeks, meaning an overall annual increase of approximately 5,8%. For those receiving the old state pension, you may also defer and receive a pension (increased by 1% for every 5 weeks or 10,4% annually) or a lump sum if you have deferred for over 12 months.[20]

2.4 Partial Retirement

It is not possible under the new state pension to take part of a state pension and continue working with the intention to collect the rest at a later date.[21] It is possible to claim a full entitlement to a state pension and continue working after reaching state pension age. The government has issued guidance that encourages people considering retirement to 'take control by working differently'.[22] If someone works past state pension age they will not have to make National Insurance contributions but the pension received will count towards their income tax liability in the usual way.

However, whilst the current state pension does not permit payments of early or partial pension there are freedoms to do this within the occupational pension system.

---

[20] Department for Work and Pensions, Guidance on Deferring state Pension, www.gov.uk/deferring-state-pension. Accessed 2 April 2025.

[21] It may technically be possible to access part of a state pension if someone had reached state pension age before 6 April 2016 and deferred taking their state pension and chosen to take part of the state pension as an early lump sum.

[22] HM Government, 'Take control by working differently', www.yourpension.gov.uk/control-working-differently/. Accessed 2 April 2025.

2.5 *Retirement Regimes for Persons Considered to Be in Hazardous or Arduous Jobs*

The state pension is universal and 'flat rate', it does not provide specific pensions for those in certain types of employment. Occupational pension schemes for certain professions that may be deemed hazardous are often more generous than in other sectors.

2.6 *Retirement Regimes Based on Means or Income Tested Benefits*

There are some benefits available for pensioners on low incomes, a pensioner may apply for a pension credit, a housing benefit or a winter fuel allowance. Essentially, as a pension credit will top up a single person's pension to 227.10 GBP, to be able to apply for this you need to have an income below this amount taking into account your state pension and other benefits from pensions, earnings and most social security benefits.[23] The DWP is concerned that not enough people are applying for pension credit and issued an information campaign in September 2024 as it was estimated that up to 880,000 pensioners were missing out on a benefit worth up to £3900 a year.[24]

If you are over state pension age and meet the eligibility criteria, such as having savings below 16,000 GBP, you may also apply for housing benefit to support paying rent. The winter fuel allowance was a benefit that permitted anyone born before 22 September 1959 to apply for a one off annual payment of between 100 GBP and 300 GBP per person depending upon age and income. This is no longer available on a universal basis, since September 2024, winter fuel allowance is only available on a means tested basis. Different considerations apply for all of these benefits if you are living alone or with a partner.

2.7 *Taxation*

The state pension is funded through National Insurance payments by employers and employees. For the tax year 2025–2026, National Insurance has to be paid by anyone who is 16 and above and is either a) an employee who earns more than 242 GBP per week in one job or ii) self-employed and earns profit of more than

[23] Although income from some benefits are not included, such as child benefit or disability living allowance.

[24] Department for Work and Pensions Press release, 'You could get Pension Credit'—week of action drive take up, www.gov.uk/government/news/you-could-get-pension-credit-week-of-action-to-drive-take-up. Accessed 2 April 2025.

Table 1 National Insurance: rates for employees

Pay	Rate
242 GBP to 967 GBP per week (or 1048 GBP to 4189 GBP per month)	8%
Over 967 GBP per week	2%

Author's table, using data from HM Revenue and customs. [26]

Table 2 National Insurance: rates for self-employed

Pay	Rate
Profits between 12,570 GBP and 50,270 GBP	6%
Profits over 50,270 GBP	2%

Author's table, using data from government guidance. [27]

12,570 GBP per year. Under the previous state pension rules it was possible for an occupational pension to 'contract out' of the earnings related element of the state pension, meaning there were reduced National Insurance payments for the employee and the employer.[25]

National insurance is paid in accordance with different classes which depend on your employment status. Since 6 April 2025, employers pay National Insurance at a rate of 15% on income above the threshold of 5000 GBP, a significant increase on the previous rate of 13,8% on income above 9100 GBP. Employees pay National Insurance, usually deducted by the employer, at the rates as shown in Table 1.

Self-employed who earn profits of 6725 GBP up to 12,569 GBP in a year are given National Insurance credits, for those earning 12,570 GBP and above contributions are due at the rates as shown in Table 2.

Income tax on pension income from either the state or occupational pensions is paid by individuals in accordance with their marginal income tax rate. The tax treatment is the same for state pension that is received at state retirement age and pension amounts that have been deferred. It is not possible to receive your state pension earlier that the state pension age.

Income tax in England is paid at the rates in the financial year 2025/2026 (shown in Table 3).

---

[25] 'Contracting out' was abolished for defined contribution schemes from 6 April 2012 and for defined benefit schemes from 6 April 2016.

[26] HM revenue and Customs, Rates and thresholds for Employers, www.gov.uk/guidance/rates-and-thresholds-for-employers-2024-to-2025. Accessed 2 April 2025.

[27] HM Government, Self-employed National insurance rates, www.gov.uk/self-employed-national-insurance-rates. Accessed 2 April 2025.

Table 3 Income tax: rates (financial year 2025/2026)

Band	Taxable Income	Rate
Personal allowance	Up to 12,570 GBP	0%
Basic rate	12,571 GBP to 50,270 GBP	20%
Higher rate	50,271 GBP to 125,140 GBP	40%
Additional rate	Over 125,140 GBP	45%

Author's table using data from government guidance. [28]

3 Occupational Pensions

Occupational pensions take many forms in the UK, they may provide defined benefits, defined contribution or 'money purchase' benefits or a combination of the two. There are several large pension schemes that provide benefits for members of central or local government, statutory bodies or nationalised industries. These schemes generally provide some form of defined benefits and operate on a pay-as-you-go basis with responsibility for payment resting with the relevant sponsoring government department. One notable exception is the Local Government Pension Scheme, which is funded, meaning contributions are invested and used to pay the benefits in the same way as many private sector defined benefit occupational schemes.

3.1 Automatic Enrolment

Workers are automatically enrolled into a 'qualifying' pension scheme, this can be a defined benefit scheme but employers usually use a defined contribution scheme that must meet certain requirements, such as the total contribution rate of 8% (3% employer and 5% employee).[29] All 'eligible jobholders' must be enrolled in an automatic enrolment pension scheme from the date they meet the eligibility criteria (their automatic enrolment date), if they decline or opt out they must then be re-enrolled every 3 years.[30]

Automatic enrolment has been seen as a success by the government, with data showing that there has been an increase in workplace total annual contributions in

[28] HM Government guidance, Income Tax rates and Personal Allowances, www.gov.uk/income-tax-rates. Accessed 2 April 2025.

[29] Introduced by the Pensions Act 2008.

[30] A 'jobholder' is defined as someone who is: working in Great Britain under a contract, aged at least 16 but under 75 and paid qualifying earnings (between £6, 240 and £50,270 a year). To be an 'eligible jobholder' you must also be at least 22 years old, be under state pension age and have earnings above the earnings trigger of £10,000 in a year.

real terms from 41.5 billion GBP in 2012 to 62.3 billion GBP in 2022.[31] Further reforms may be enacted in the future to widen the reach of automatic enrolment. Following a private members' bill in 2023, the government now has the power to reduce the qualifying age for automatic enrolment and to abolish the lower earnings limit,[32] but it is uncertain whether there will be political motivation to make changes that could increase the burden on employers.

3.2 Defined Contribution Pensions

Defined contribution schemes may be provided as part of a trust based occupational pension scheme or be contract based, such as through a Group Personal Pension plan for that employer, in such a scheme the employee has a contract with an external scheme provider. The provider will receive contributions towards the scheme and invest the funds, this has minimal risk for the employer beyond paying contributions on time. Following the introduction of the 'pension freedoms' in 2015,[33] there are more options for defined contribution plans. In addition to the traditional option of buying an annuity, it is possible to either take 25% as a tax-free lump sum and then withdraw the remaining 75% whenever you choose by 'drawing down' from your pension pot as income, subject to income tax at your marginal rate, or withdraw in several lump sum payments subject to the 25% rule. Accessing funds under the new pension freedoms will reduce your annual tax allowance to 10,000 GBP, see Sect. 3.7 below.

There are a significant amount of defined contribution schemes that provide workplace pensions to fulfil the automatic enrolment requirements. The master trust[34] has been used to provide defined contribution pensions through automatic enrolment, there are currently 33 Master Trusts on the register maintained by the Pensions Regulator,[35] the government sees the master trust as a positive way of consolidating defined contribution pension scheme assets.[36]

In 2023 the Pensions Regulator authorised the first collective defined contribution (CDC) pension scheme,[37] these schemes allow an employer or group of employers

---

[31] Department for Work and Pensions (26 October 2022) Ten years of automatic enrolment in workplace pensions: statistics and analysis https://www.gov.uk/government/statistics/ten-years-of-automatic-enrolment-in-workplace-pensions/ten-years-of-automatic-enrolment-in-workplace-pensions-statistics-and-analysis. Accessed 29 April 2025.

[32] Pensions (Extension of Automatic Enrolment) Act 2023.

[33] Taxation of Pensions Act 2014.

[34] Introduced by the Pension Schemes Act 2017.

[35] Pensions Regulator Register of Master Trusts, https://www.thepensionsregulator.gov.uk/en/master-trust-pension-schemes/list-of-authorised-master-trusts. Accessed 2 April 2025.

[36] Department for Work and Pensions Evolving the regulatory approach to master trusts (November 2023) https://www.gov.uk/government/publications/evolving-the-regulatory-approach-to-master-trusts/evolving-the-regulatory-approach-to-master-trusts. Accessed 29 April 2025.

[37] Introduced by the Pensions Act 2021.

to establish a defined contribution scheme that pools longevity and investment risk and provides aspired but not guaranteed pension benefits as an alternative to defined benefit provision.

3.3 Defined Benefit Pensions

There are still a significant amount of occupational defined benefit occupational pension schemes[38] that must generally be established under trust, meaning the fund is kept separately from the employer's own finances.[39] Pollard observes that from a fundamental legal starting point, occupational pensions can be said to operate under a 'tripartite structure', involving a trust deed between employer and trustees, a contract between the employer and the pension scheme member and a trustee—beneficiary relationship between the members as beneficiaries and the trustees under the trust deed.[40] Defined benefit pensions offer a pension benefit calculated in relation to a specified formula, historically these typically related to the employee's final salary and provided a generous pension of 2/3 final salary for someone who worked for 40 years.[41] As they are now less popular amongst employers due to the costs and risks associated with managing such funds, many schemes have adopted less favourable benefit structures such as using career average earnings or a smaller percentage of final salary. Many such schemes have also closed to new members or closed the defined benefit section to future accrual and replaced it with a defined contribution scheme.

The most comprehensive annual review is conducted by the Pension Protection Fund that pays benefits following the insolvency of a pension scheme employer. In 2024, using data from 8.9 million scheme members, the report showed that 46% were pensioner members, 46% were deferred members and 8% were active members, and that 58% were no longer accruing new benefits, 33% were closed to new members with just 8% open to new members.[42] There are still a significant amount of assets under management at 1.167,1 billion GBP, with a net surplus across defined benefit schemes of 219.2 billion GBP.[43]

---

[38] The term occupational pension scheme is defined in the Pension Schemes Act 1993, s1

[39] Pensions Act 2004, s252.

[40] Pollard (2013) The Law of Pension Trusts, Oxford University Press, p. 3.

[41] Typically calculated as 1/60 x final salary x years of pensionable service.

[42] The Pension Protection Fund, The Purple Book 2024 (March 2024) an annual review which covers most members of defined benefit schemes in the UK available at: https://www.ppf.co.uk/news/Purple-Book-2024. Accessed 2 April 2025.

[43] Calculated on a s179 basis, meaning the level of funding needed to secure benefits with the Pension Protection Fund.

3.4 *"Normal" Retirement Age*

Pension schemes are free to set the age when a pension normally becomes payable, but they must be within the limits under tax laws in order to avoid a tax charge. A pension scheme that is registered with *HMRC* may only pay a pension to someone aged at least 55 years old (known as a 'normal minimum pension age') without incurring an 'unauthorised payment charge' unless they meet an ill-health condition or have a protected right to an earlier pension age.[44] Any payment of retirement benefits before this age will incur an unauthorised payment charge of 40% of the payment.[45] This normal minimum pension age is due to increase to 57 on 6 April 2028 for most pension schemes, certain uniformed public service schemes are excluded.[46]

An occupational scheme is likely to have a pension age of 60 or 65, pension ages must be the same for male and female members.[47] There are statutory minimum increases for pensions in payment,[48] but schemes may pay above these limits. There is currently no limit on pension ages set in law, however, schemes may have a limit on the age when someone may take their benefits set at 75 which was mandatory under the previous law, this requirement was removed but pension schemes have a discretion to keep this age if it is already present in the rules.

The normal pension age may be lower in certain schemes, often in the public sector and pension schemes that provide for occupations that are deemed hazardous such as the Police Force or the Fire Service. The Police Force is an example of such a scheme where certain members may have a protected pension age of 50 if they had given 25 years of service whilst being a member of the relevant police service pension scheme.[49]

It is possible to pay additional voluntary contributions if the scheme rules permit this for defined contribution and defined benefit pensions. For defined benefit schemes this is known as purchasing 'added years' that may be used to increase the benefit. Scheme rules may or may not permit this and the pension income is taxed in the same way as normal pension income.

---

[44] This applies to members with an unconditional right to a pension at an age under 55 before the tax rules in the Finance Act 2004 came into force on 6 April 2006.

[45] And potentially an additional 15% surcharge if other limits are exceeded, see Finance Act 2004 s208.

[46] Finance Act 2004 s 279.

[47] Equality Act 2010 s67 on equal pay following Case C-262/88 *Barber v Guardian Royal Exchange* [1990] ECR I-01889.

[48] For pensionable service on or after 6 April 1997 up to and including 5 April 2005 the lesser of prices (currently using the Consumer Prices Index, 'CPI') or 5% and for pensionable service on or after 6 April 2005, the lesser of prices (CPI) and 2.5%, Pensions Act 1995 s51 and associated regulations.

[49] Police Pension Scheme 1987, there is also a right to retire before 50 if you have 30 years pensionable service.

3.5 Early Retirement

An occupational pension may be taken before the pension scheme's normal pension age (but after the 'normal minimum pension age') if the scheme rules permit. In a defined benefit arrangement this will typically mean a reduction in the pension amount to take account the fact that it is being paid early.

If someone leaves employment, National Insurance contributions will no longer be paid by an employer, so the individual may want to buy additional National Insurance credits to make sure they get enough qualifying years in order to get a full state pension when they reach state retirement age.

Early leavers who do not take their pension and do not 'retire' have certain minimum statutory rights to preserve the pension that has been built up and to revalue the pension when it is in payment.[50] Occupational schemes may provide more, but as a minimum: (i) if they have defined benefits and have at least 2 years' pensionable service they are entitled to a deferred pension, for defined contribution benefits, a member needs only 30 days' pensionable service, (ii) if they have defined benefits early leavers with between three months and two years pensionable service have a right to a cash transfer to another scheme or a return of contributions, and (iii) if they have defined benefits and less than three months (or 30 days for defined contribution schemes), they have no statutory rights to receive a benefit, but schemes often provide for a return of contributions paid into the scheme. The pension amount must be revalued when it comes into payment to take account of inflation, there is a statutory minimum but the pension scheme rules may provide above this.

3.6 Working Past Retirement

If an employer has a compulsory retirement age this will be treated as direct age discrimination unless it can be objectively justified as a proportionate means of achieving a legitimate aim.[51] Despite rules against age discrimination coming into force some years earlier, this change only came in to force in 2011, as the UK initially retained a national default retirement age of 65, a policy that received criticism[52] and is an example of the legal difficulties of aligning policy goals in employment and pensions. It is still possible for a pension scheme to keep a normal pension age, such as 65,[53] which effectively means this age may still be considered as an unofficial 'target age' for retirement.

[50] Pension Schemes Act 1993 Part IV and associated regulations.

[51] Equality Act 2010, s13(2).

[52] Kilpatrick (2008) The New UK Retirement Regime, Employment Law and Pensions, Industrial Law Journal, Vol 37 No 1 March 2008.

[53] Equality Act (Age Exceptions for Pension Schemes) Order 2010/2133, Schedule 1, paragraph 11.

Pension scheme rules may allow an employee to continue to work beyond the scheme's normal pension age and defer taking their pension, for a defined benefit scheme this may involve an actuarial increase to the benefit that can be made whether or not they continue in service.[54] The Equality Act Age Exceptions Order does allow a limit to be placed on the amount of years of accrual.[55] Although there could be age discrimination issues if, without objective justification, a pension scheme ceased to allow accrual of benefits after an employee has reached their scheme's normal pension age but continued working.

The Finance Act 2004 does not prohibit someone to accrue and draw a pension at the same time, so it is possible to be an active member and also a pensioner member provided that your pension scheme rules allow you to do this. It is therefore possible for a pension scheme to allow someone to retire and take some or all of the pension benefit. The option may not be popular amongst pension schemes due to the administrative difficulties and possible risk of complaints arising from permitting only certain types of employee to have early access to benefits. To give an example, the Civil Service Pension Scheme allows partial retirement provided that the employee takes some or all of their pension and changes their role with a reduced salary by at least 20%. Equality law prohibits discrimination on grounds of age,[56] but the interaction between flexible retirement provisions and existing rules on how and when people can access benefits in occupational pension schemes have been questioned. The Department for Work and Pensions (DWP) launched a consultation in 2007 regarding whether there should be a specific exception for occupational pension schemes, but despite acknowledging 'significant uncertainty' and representation from a large trade union that not many schemes had adopted partial retirement, it did not feel there was enough evidence to make any changes in the law.[57]

3.7 *Taxation*

A pension scheme must be registered with *HMRC* to receive tax relief, that is available on all pension contributions for people up to age 75.[58] Contributions from an employer do not count towards the employee's income tax[59] and are not eligible for

[54] Equality Act (Age Exceptions for Pension Schemes) Order 2010 (SI 2010/2133), Schedule 1, paragraph 2.

[55] Equality Act (Age Exceptions for Pension Schemes) Order 2010 (SI 2010/2133), Schedule 1, paragraph 21.

[56] Employment Equality (Age) Regulations 2006.

[57] Department for Work and Pensions Flexible Retirement and Pension Provision Government Response to the Consultation on Draft Regulations' https://webarchive.nationalarchives.gov.uk/ukgwa/20130128102031/http://www.dwp.gov.uk/docs/flexible-retirement-responses.pdf. Accessed 29 April 2025, p 12.

[58] Finance Act 2004, s188(3)(a).

[59] Income Tax (Earnings and Pensions) Act 2003 s308.

National Insurance contributions.[60] Income made by the pension scheme on investments is exempt from income tax[61] and capital gains made on any investments are also exempt from capital gains tax.[62]

When someone receives a pension they can generally take a pension commencement lump sum of up to 25% of the value of their pension[63] with a total limit of 268,75 GBP as the total lump sum allowance for benefits in all pension schemes. Pension income is taxed at the marginal rate for income tax.

Pension contributions are often made on a 'net pay' basis whereby employee contributions are deducted from gross pay, before income tax is applied. Employers may also give the option to pay extra pension contributions in a 'salary sacrifice' arrangement meaning the employee receives less salary and therefore has a lower National Insurance liability. Pension tax is paid by individuals in accordance with their marginal income tax rate as set out above in Table 3, Sect. 2.7.

There are taxation limits for how much can be saved in an occupational pension, the primary piece of legislation for taxation is the Finance Act 2004 which consolidated a number of different regimes with effect from 6 April 2006. The taxation rules for workplace pensions remain complicated. There is an Annual Allowance for how much you can save in a year of 60,000 GBP, above which you must pay tax at your marginal rate of income tax.[64] The annual allowance tapers down to 10,000 GBP for higher earners who receive above 260,000 GBP a year. There is an additional 'money purchase annual allowance' that applies a tax charge to a member who accesses a defined contribution pension flexibly and continues making further contributions to that scheme in excess of 10,000 GBP.

The Lifetime Allowance (LTA) in the UK was 1,073,100 GBP in 2023/2024 tax year but it was disapplied in that year[65] and abolished for the 2024/2025 tax year,[66] it has been replaced by new tax rules meaning there are two new allowances. Firstly, a lump sum allowance of 268,275 GBP which is a cumulative limit that applies to the total amount of cash that you can take tax free. Secondly, a lump sum and death benefit allowance of 1,073,100 GBP which includes serious ill-health lump sums and death benefit lump sums, there is also a limit on transfers to overseas pension schemes set at the same rate. Above this level you must pay income tax at your marginal rate.

Early or partial retirement can result in taxation penalties when taking a pension if you retire before age 55 (unless you have an ill-health condition or a protected

---

[60] Social Security (Contributions) Regulations 2001 (SI 2001/1004).

[61] Finance Act 2004, s186.

[62] Finance Act 2004, s187.

[63] Finance Act 2004, Schedule 29 sets out the 'applicable amount' of pension than can be taken depending upon the type of benefit.

[64] Finance (No2) Act 2023s 20 set this rate for the 2023/2024 tax yar and it set to stay the same unless changed in future years.

[65] Finance (No2) Act 2023 s18, in effect the 55% tax charge for breaching the lifetime allowance was replaced by taxation at the marginal rate.

[66] Finance Act 2024, s14.

pension age) there may be three tax charges. Firstly, an unauthorised payment charge of 40% to the member, secondly an unauthorised payment surcharge of an extra 15% payable by a member that has received more than 25% of the pension value in a year (or by an employer where they have received 25% or more in value of their pension scheme). Thirdly, a scheme sanction charge payable by the pension scheme[67] that is set at 40% of the chargeable payments with some reduction to take into account amounts paid by the member for the unauthorised payment charge.

For smaller pension pots it is possible to pay defined benefits as a trivial commutation lump sum if that individual's total pension benefits in all schemes are less than 30,000 GBP.[68] There is also a scheme specific regime where pension pots up to 10,000 GBP can be paid as a lump sum.[69]

References

Legislation

Primary Legislation

Equality Act (2010a)
Finance (No 2) Act (2023)
Finance Act (2004)
Finance Act (2024)
National Insurance Act (1946)
Pension Schemes Act (1993)
Pensions Act (1995)
Pensions Act (2004)
Pensions Act (2008)
Pensions Act (2014)
Pensions Act (2017)
Pensions Act (2021)

Secondary Legislation

Equality Act (Age Exceptions for Pension Schemes) Order 2010b (SI 2010/2133)
Social Security (Contributions) Regulations 2001 (SI 2001/1004)

---

67 Finance Act 2004, s 240.

68 Finance Act 2004 Schedule 29 paragraphs 7–9.

69 Finance Act 2004, s164(1)(f) and associated regulations.

Literature

Berry (2021) The substitutive state? Neoliberal state interventionism across industrial, housing and private pension policy in the UK, Competition and Change 26(2):242–265

Kilpatrick (2008) The New UK Retirement Regime, Employment Law and Pensions, Industrial Law Journal, Vol 37 No 1 March 2008 pp 1–24

Kolaczkowski (2020) The social role of occupational pension schemes. In: Agnew, Davies, Mitchell (eds) pensions: law. Hart Publishing, Policy and Practice, pp 189–209

Pemberton (2006) Politics and pensions in post war Britian. In Pemberton, Thane, Whiteside (eds) Britain's pension crisis: history and policy. Oxford University Press, pp 39–63

Pollard (2013) The law of pension trusts. Oxford University Press

Reports and Online Sources

Beveridge (1942) *Social insurance and allied services* Cmd 6404. His Majesty's Stationery Office

Bozia, Crawford, Tetlo, the history of state pensions in the UK: 1948 to 2010, IFS briefing note BN105 (institute for fiscal studies, 2010)

Department for Work and Pensions (26 October 2022) Ten years of automatic enrolment in workplace pensions: statistics and analysis https://www.gov.uk/government/statistics/ten-years-of-automatic-enrolment-in-workplace-pensions/ten-years-of-automatic-enrolment-in-workplace-pensions-statistics-and-analysis. Accessed 29 April 2025

Department for Work and Pensions (28 March 2025a) Pathways to Work: Reforming Benefits and Support to Get Britain Working Green Paper https://www.gov.uk/government/consultations/pathways-to-work-reforming-benefits-and-support-to-get-britain-working-green-paper. Accessed 2 April 2025

Department for Work and Pensions, Guidance on Deferring state Pension, <www.gov.uk/deferring-state-pension. Accessed 2 April 2025

Department for Work and Pensions Evolving the regulatory approach to master trusts (November 2023). https://www.gov.uk/government/publications/evolving-the-regulatory-approach-to-master-trusts/evolving-the-regulatory-approach-to-master-trusts. Accessed 29 April 2025

Department for Work and Pensions Flexible Retirement and Pension Provision, 10 December 2009., https://webarchive.nationalarchives.gov.uk/ukgwa/20130128102031/http://www.dwp.gov.uk/docs/flexible-retirement-responses.pdf. Accessed 8 April 2025

Department for Work and Pensions Flexible Retirement and Pension Provision Government Response to the Consultation on Draft Regulations' https://webarchive.nationalarchives.gov.uk/ukgwa/20130128102031/http://www.dwp.gov.uk/docs/flexible-retirement-responses.pdf. Accessed 29 April 2025

Department for Work and Pensions Press release, 'You could get Pension Credit'—week of action drive take up, www.gov.uk/government/news/you-could-get-pension-credit-week-of-action-to-drive-take-up. Accessed 2 April 2025

HM Government, 'Take control by working differently', www.yourpension.gov.uk/control-working-differently/. accessed 2 April 2025

HM Government, Self-employed National insurance rates, www.gov.uk/self-employed-national-insurance-rates. Accessed 2 April 2025

HM Government guidance, Income Tax rates and Personal Allowances, www.gov.uk/income-tax-rates. Accessed 2 April 2025

Office for Budget Responsibility, Economic and Fiscal Outlook, March 20254, CP 1289027, https://obr.uk/efo/economic-and-fiscal-outlook-march-2025. Accessed 29 April 2025

Retirement and Employment

To Retire or to Work? That's the Question: Choice or Necessity!?

Yves Stevens, Emma Suzanne van Aggelen, Stamatia Devetzi, James Kolaczkowski, Toomas Kotkas, Jacques-André Schneider, Ivana Vukorepa, and Verena Zwinger

The countries examined in this book have some clear common challenges when it comes to questions related to the older workforce. It is obvious that shortages in the labour market lead to different legislation compared to when there is high unemployment. By policymakers, pension law may be seen as an instrument for labour policy. However, it remains an open question whether this is a good manner of proceeding in the welfare state. After all, for some the question whether to retire or not, is not a real question but rather a necessity. Hence, to retire or to work? That is the question.

In the sections that follow, the topic of 'work and retirement' is approached from common themes such as early retirement, part-time retirement, deferred retirement or taxing pensions. Both statutory pensions and occupational pensions are envisaged. Functional comparative law is thereby used as a method. This functional comparative law approach takes certain themes as a starting point and then examines how these

Y. Stevens (✉)
Catholic University of Leuven, Faculty of Law and Criminology, Department of Social Security & Labour Law, Institute for Social Law, Leuven, Belgium
e-mail: yves.stevens@kuleuven.be

E. S. van Aggelen
Faculty of Law, UHasselt, Hasselt, Belgium

Faculty of Law and Criminology, KU Leuven, Leuven, Belgium

E. S. van Aggelen
e-mail: emmasuzanne.vanaggelen@uhasselt.be

S. Devetzi
Department of Social and Cultural Sciences, Fulda University of Applied Sciences, Fulda, Germany
e-mail: stamatia.Devetzi@sk.hs-fulda.de

J. Kolaczkowski
Law School, University of Exeter, Exeter, UK
e-mail: J.Kolaczkowski@exeter.ac.uk

E. S. van Aggelen (ed.), *Retirement and Employment*, Ius Gentium: Comparative Perspectives on Law and Justice 145, https://doi.org/10.1007/978-3-032-33561-6_10

themes are approached in the different legal systems. Specifically, this also means that this chapter is based on the country reports from Part I.[1]

Statutory and occupational pensions are treated concurrently and together in this overarching chapter. Although the two forms of pension have different legal logics and often different rationales, the labour market in which they are implemented is the same. It is therefore the interaction between the labour market and pension provision that drives this chapter. How does pension law currently interact with labour market policies? This interaction between pension law and labour market is the common thread throughout.

1 Pensionable Age and Labour Market

Pensions have been around for a very long time. In Roman times pensions referred to a kind of property right after years of service in the Roman army.[2] And it is widely believed that the modern word pension originates from the Latin word 'Pensio', *which* means payment, recompense or compensation.[3] Also throughout the Middle Ages, various forms of pensions existed for military service, clergy and some public officials.[4] These were often ad hoc and not standardized. It's only relatively recently

T. Kotkas
Faculty of Law, University of Helsinki, Helsinki, Finland
e-mail: toomas.kotkas@helsinki.fi

J.-A. Schneider
University of Lausanne, Lausanne, Switzerland
e-mail: jas@jaschneider.ch

I. Vukorepa
Department for Labour and Social Security Law, Faculty of Law University of Zagreb, Zagreb, Croatia
e-mail: ivana.vukorepa@pravo.unizg.hr

V. Zwinger
Austrian Pension Insurance, Business Division for Legal Affairs and Research, Vienna, Austria
e-mail: verena.zwinger@pv.at

[1] All references to particular countries can be found in the country reports without always making internal references. This is inspired by optimised readability.

[2] Stevens, Y (2022), "On the origin of pensions". In Kolaczkowski, J, Maher, M. J., Werbrouck, J. and Stevens (eds)., in *The Evolution of Supplementary Pensions: 25 Years of Pension Reform*, London, Edward Elgar Publishing, 15.

[3] *Pensio, onis*, (female). For a full analysis on the origin of pensions, see: Stevens, Y. (2022), "On the origin of pensions". In Kolaczkowski, J, Maher, M. J., Werbrouck, J. and Stevens (eds)., *The Evolution of Supplementary Pensions: 25 Years of Pension Reform*, London, Edward Elgar Publishing, 2022, 10–36.

[4] van der Valk, L (1998), "Overheid en de ontwikkeling van het verzekeringswezen 1500–1815". In van Gerwen, J. en van Leeuwen, M. (ed.), *Studies over zekerheidsarrangementen*, Nederlands Economisch Historisch Archief, Amsterdam/Den Haag, 23–48.

that pensions are embedded in a structural way whereby the government is involved in its structuring. It is well known that Germany with its first state-run social insurance program in the nineteenth century was at the basis of the modern concept of pension as being a legal right to retire. This can also be seen as a kind of official start of statutory pensions.[5]

This so-called Bismarckian concept of social insurance led to a pension concept whereby the pension is based on contributions linked to wages earned. The links between labour, wage, contributions, insurance and benefits is key to understand this type of pension.[6] However, contrary to previous forms of compensation and pensions, the rise of modern old-age social insurance as well as occupational pension schemes in the 19th and early twentieth century was intrinsically linked to the new reality brought by industrialisation and the spread of market-based economies. Indeed, these new set-ups were explicitly designed to facilitate the separation with older workers whose capacities had receded without benefitting anymore from broader pre-industrial social support systems, thus preventing old-age destitution.[7]

Risk sharing and solidarity are essential within any pension system. In the so-called Beveridge social protection concept citizenship and taxation are key to understand the universal right to access pensions. In the Beveridge social protection model the risk sharing for old age is mainly defined by the concept of poverty alleviation while in the Bismarckian model income replacement is more prominent than poverty alleviation.[8]

Irrespective of the Bismarckian or the Beveridge model, the right to retire is nowadays conceived as a right to retire from the labour market, which is a remarkable change of perspective introducing a new paradigma. This idea is even more novel than the nineteenth century social insurance idea. At the origin of the so-called Bismarckian idea was the notion of insurance with a link between benefits and contributions. Pensions in the nineteenth century were mainly seen as an element of (social) insurance. This idea is still present in many existing statutory pensions but another pension concept was added after World War II: the idea that a pension also reflected some kind of "deserved rest". A rest from what? From work.[9]

Due to this idea that one could earn a kind of "resting period", a far clearer distinction between the period where somebody worked and somebody didn't work

---

[5] Stevens, Y (2022), "On the origin of pensions". In Kolaczkowski, J, Maher, M. J., Werbrouck, J. and Stevens, Y. (eds)., in *The Evolution of Supplementary Pensions: 25 Years of Pension Reform*, London, Edward Elgar Publishing, 15.

[6] Böckerman, P., Skedinger,P. and Uusitalo, R. (2018). "Seniority rules, worker mobility and wages: Evidence from multi-country linked employer-employee data". *Labour Economics* 51, 48–62, https://doi.org/10.1016/j.labeco.2017.11.006.

[7] Van Langendonck, J., Jorens, Y. and Louckx, F. (2023), *Handboek socialezekerheidsrecht* (11de editie), Intersentia, Brussel, 16–17.

[8] Van Langendonck, J., Jorens, Y. and Louckx, F. (2023), *Handboek socialezekerheidsrecht* (11de editie), Intersentia, Brussel, 16–19.

[9] For an historical overview (from a Belgian perspective) on the different pension notions: Werbrouck, J.M. (2022), *Het multidimensionale pensioenbegrip*, Boom Juridisch Antwerpen, 514p. (in Dutch).

installed itself in the minds of people and society at large. Previously, the idea to stop working after having reached the statutory retirement age wasn't common or widespread. Only those with sufficient resources after retirement could do so. Most people remained in the workforce even if they had acquired a pension. A pension was a kind of top-up in order to avoid poverty in old age. The pension amounts were just—mainly due to the low contributions—insufficient to fully retire from the labour market. Farmers kept on farming, blue collar workers kept on working but habitually at a lower alacrity and with less wages.[10]

All in all, we could argue that the idea that retirement implies leaving the labour market entirely is relatively new, and should be distinguished from the historical concept of compensation offered for the forced exit from salaried work due to old-age limitations. But then again, almost all concepts of the modern welfare state are relatively new. However, this distinction between "in" or "out" of the labour market has gained ground rather strongly from the 1970s onwards. This had to do with high youth unemployment in Europe during the 1970s. The European 1970s were marked by economic challenges, notably the oil crises of 1973 and 1979, which even led to temporary stagflation—a combination of stagnant economic growth, high inflation, and high unemployment.[11] Traditional industries such as manufacturing and mining were declining due to globalization, technological advancements, and shifts towards service-oriented economies. This transition often led to massive layoffs and increased unemployment rates. Young people were particularly affected.[12]

The solution at hand were so-called bridging pensions, also known as "bridge pensions" or "early retirement pensions".[13] All over Europe the concept developed over several decades. Bridging pensions were introduced in almost all European countries as a policy tool to mitigate the impacts of high unemployment. By providing financial support to older workers who were close to retirement age, governments and companies could encourage early retirement, thus freeing up jobs for younger workers.[14]

---

[10] Noordam, F. (1998), "Sociale verzekeringen 1890–1950" in J. van Gerwen en M. van Leeuwen (ed.), *Studies over zekerheidsarrangementen*, Nederlands Economisch Historisch Archief, Amsterdam/Den Haag, 570–604 (in Dutch).

[11] For a very interesting source on the history of these systems, see the movie, "Historique des retraites en France" (in French) at https://enseignants.lumni.fr/fiche-media/00000001741/historique-des-retraites-en-france.html.

[12] Rodrik, D. (1997), "Has Globalization Gone Too Far?". *Washington, DC: Peterson Institute for International Economics* (also known as the Institute for International Economics), 128 pages, ISBN 0–88,132-2415; International Labour Organization (ILO), "World of Work Report 2014: Developing with jobs", Geneva, 2014, https://www.ilo.org/publications/world-work-2014-developing-jobs; O'Higgins, N. (2017). *Rising to the youth employment challenge: New evidence on key policy issues*, Geneva: International Labour Organization, https://www.ilo.org/publications/major-publications/rising-youth-employment-challenge-new-evidence-key-policy-issues

[13] Please note, that other, mostly temporary, brigding mechanisms between a person's labour market exit and pension receipt are not included in this study.

[14] Ebbinghaus, B. (2006), *Reforming Early Retirement in Europe, Japan and the USA*, Oxford University Press, Oxford, 352 pg. ISBN: 978–0–19-928,611-9.

Hence bridging pensions or early retirement schemes originated as a pragmatic response to economic restructuring and high unemployment rates designed to facilitate the early exit of older workers from the labour market, thus alleviating unemployment pressures and aiding younger workers' entry into employment.[15] At least this was how it was conceived. Pensions were seen—for the first time—as an instrument of (labour) market policy. Governments believed that they could mold the labour market by using pension law instruments.

As the main theme of this book reflects on this idea of interaction between pension law and labour market policies, the first and foremost important legal notion is the "retirement or pensionable age". It is striking that quasi all countries involved in this research use a kind of legal definition referring to "a reference age" whereby is meant that retirement either can be earlier or later than this reference age. This reference age is fixed by law for all statutory pensions examined in this study. When it comes to occupational pensions, the picture is more diffuse. The pensionable age is are often mentioned in the law but it's important to check whether schemes' rules can create exemptions.

The basic legal narrative and rationale of such a reference age is of course that any pension system has some kind of age in place whereby the retirement benefit can be received. Apart from many other conditions such as length of career, number of years contributed, and citizenship, one might say that the "retirement age" is a true basic condition for all pension systems, irrespective of the statutory or occupational nature of the pensions.

From a legal point of view, this means that an individual is legally entitled to a social or occupational benefit in a later phase of life. In practice, of course, a person is likely to only retreat from the labour market if he is financially capable to do so. So, even if a person has reached the retirement age, then he or she will continue working if it is necessary to survive (and as long as no other social benefits might be claimed). We know for a fact that—in a Bismarckian pension setting—claiming a pension later usually results in a higher replacement rate at least for the same average earnings and the same career length.[16]

This legal and individual point of view is different from the macro-economic point of view whereby the pensionable age is seen as a factor defining the redistribution and risk sharing between cohorts and generations.[17] Setting a certain retirement age allows a government to manage the welfare state both by the contributions paid into the system and the benefits paid out of the system. This is valid both in PAYG

[15] See on this topic the very intriguing text: Neumark, D., Burn, I. and Button, P. (2019). "Is It Harder for Older Workers to Find Jobs? New and Improved Evidence from a Field Experiment". *Journal of Political Economy* 127 (2), https://doi.org/10.1086/701029.

[16] European Commission (2024), Directorate-General for Employment, Social Affairs and Inclusion, "The 2024 pension adequacy report—Current and future income adequacy in old age in the EU", Volume I, Publications Office of the European Union, p. 168.

[17] For an excellent introduction in these mechanisms, see Barr, N. and Diamond, P. (2008), "*Reforming pensions: principles and policy choices*". Oxford University Press, Oxford, Chap. 7, 111–126.

and funded pension schemes. A government can thus define some kind of macroeconomic equivalency between contributions and benefits by lowering or increasing the pensionable age.[18]

The pensionable age is thus without any doubt a determining factor in the sustainability of any pension system.[19] The so-called dependency ratio—the ratio of the combined total of individuals considered dependent (typically the youth and the retired) to those in the working-age group—is closely defined both by mortality and the pensionable age.[20] Raising the effective retirement age and thus prolonging working life has been at the heart of many pension and labour policies in the last decades.[21] Another similar and important rationale is life expectancy.[22] We know that the impact of life expectancy differences on pension wealth closely correlates with the remaining life expectancy at retirement age, and therefore depends on the pensionable age.[23]

However, the link between pension policy and the labour market must not be seen as too evident either. For long, there was a belief that the labour market was some kind of communicating vessel between younger and older persons. This idea, also known as "the lump of labour fallacy", still has its effects nowadays as some legislators are still struggling with the relationship between retirement and labour.[24]

---

[18] See also: OECD (2019) "Pensions at a glance 2019: OECD and G20 indicators", OECD Publishing, Paris, 224p.

[19] See for example on Belgium: Deroose, M., Melyn, W., Stinglhamber, P., and Van Parys, S. (2023). "Is public spending on pensions in Belgium sustainable? A comparison with other euro area countries". *NBB Economic Review*, 2–30.

[20] J. WOSS, "The impact of labour markets on economic dependency ratios", in J. MESZAROS (ed.), Life-cycles and Pension systems, Progress, Budapest, 2011, 63–70.

[21] Labour market projections and economic growth projections go hand in hand for example in following publication of the European Commission: European Commission (2024), Directorate-General for Employment, Social Affairs and Inclusion, "Long term projections of pension adequacy in a selection of countries: report produced in the context of the 2024 pension adequacy report", Publications Office of the European Union, 40p.; for an overview of the countries having implemented a link between life expectancy and pensions, see: OESO (2021). Pensions at a glance 2021. OECD Publishing, page 84 and European Commission (2015), "The 2015 Ageing Report. Economic and budgetary projections for the 28 EU Member States 2013–2060", European Economy 3, 397p; European Commission (2021), "The 2021 Ageing Report. Economic and budgetary projections for the EU member states (2019–2070)", Institutional Paper 148, 375p.

[22] Vermeer, N. (2016). "Age anchors and the expected retirement age: an experimental study". *De Economist* 164, 255–279, doi 10.1007/s10645-016-9276-1; Van Solinge, H. and Henkens, K. (2009). "Living longer, working longer? The impact of subjective life expectancy on retirement intentions and behaviour". *European Journal of Public Health*, 47–51.

[23] European Commission (2024), Directorate-General for Employment, Social Affairs and Inclusion, "The 2024 pension adequacy report—Current and future income adequacy in old age in the EU", Volume I, Publications Office of the European Union, p. 147.

[24] Autor, D. H. (2015). "Why Are There Still So Many Jobs? The History and Future of Workplace Automation". *Journal of Economic Perspectives*, 29(3), 3–30; OECD (2006). "Ageing and Employment Policies: Live Longer, Work Longer", OECD Publications, Paris; Van Solinge, H. and Henkens, K. (2009). "Living longer, working longer? The impact of subjective life expectancy on retirement intentions and behaviour". *European Journal of Public Health*, 47–51.

In the next sections, the link between retirement and work is looked at for statutory and occupational pensions. The following themes are considered: the flexibility in pensionable age, deferred retirement, early retirement, partial retirement, retirement regimes for persons in arduous and hazardous jobs, retirement regimes based on means or income testing and taxation.

2 "Normal" Retirement Age or Age of Reference

In this section we look at the different aspects of retirement access regarding the age at which a person can retire. It is not strange to assume that there is a link between retirement age and leaving employment.[25] After all, most people that retire also stop working in the job they did before. However, this does not have to be the case. We see in various countries that this link is superficial because people can combine work and retirement or can postpone retirement or work in another job whilst in early retirement. Understandably, such work then can affect the built-up or pay-out of statutory or occupational pensions.

It seems obvious that there is some kind of legal act stating what the retirement age is. That is to say that there is a statute prescribing when somebody is entitled to a pension on the basis of a certain age. However, not all countries included this book have such a fixed legal notion of what the "normal" pensionable age is. In fact, from a legal point of view there are several dates which can be considered "normal". But this can be both earlier or later than a certain given age. From a legal perspective, it seems more correct to talk about a reference age. This age of reference is then legally used to indicate whether retirement is advanced or postponed. This reasoning is valid for both statutory and occupational pensions studied in this book.

2.1 *Narratives of the "Normal" Retirement Age*

Looking at the eight countries in this book, there are different prevailing narratives of the pensionable age or age of reference.

A rather common narrative is that of a stable economy setting a pensionable age as a means to leave the labour market which might induce a workforce turnover and make room for other employees and promote a dynamic economy.[26] Nonetheless, a pensionable age is not a synonym for leaving the labour market. After all, in all eight countries, employment after the age of reference is possible.

---

[25] Kosonen, H., Keskinen, K., Nikander, P., and Lumme-Sandt, K. (2000), "Employment Exits Near Retirement Age: An Agency-analysis". *Nordic Journal of Working Life Studies*, 11(1), 63–83.

[26] M. WERDING, "Incentive effects of public pension schemes" in J. MESZAROS (ed.), *Life-cycles and Pension systems*, Progress, Budapest, 2011, 72–73.

Another common narrative is the link between the pensionable age and the sustainability of the system.[27] It is understood that the pensionable age has a direct effect on sustainability.[28] A very low age can lead to budgetary challenges. However, pension systems are part of cultural and historical settings meaning that uniform answers to the budgetary questions cannot be looked at in isolation from their social context. This explains the differences in, for example, pensionable ages, early retirement and pension taxation between various countries with different economic backgrounds.[29] The country reports show that countries can also be more flexible in this regard when it comes to occupational pensions in comparison to statutory pensions. This does not only have to do with the scope or ambit of statutory pensions (often much larger and more prominent than occupational pensions) but also with the more voluntary or wage-like nature of occupational pensions. There is also a certain logic to this. After all, the occupational pensions are often more embedded in the employment sphere.

Occupational pensions are usually based on funding instead of PAYG in statutory pensions. Demography, inflation and returns on investment have different effects on both pension forms. No pension form is unaffected by demography, inflation or even returns on investments but the scope and timing can differ strongly.

Another narrative is that retirement provides individuals with the opportunity to enjoy a period of leisure after work.[30] It allows for travel, hobbies, spending time with family, and other activities that contribute to overall life satisfaction and mental well-being. However, it is obvious that there are two major issues at hand. Firstly, it is not possible to enjoy a period of leisure without adequate financial means. These means can have several sources such as statutory, occupational and individual pensions or other forms of savings. Secondly, achieving a good quality of life should be seen as a lifelong aim and not as a binary option between an unpleasant working life and a pleasurable retirement. To put it in a witticism, life should not start at retirement.

When it comes to statutory pensions there is also a kind of "equality narrative" whereby a standard retirement age ensures fairness across different age cohorts,

---

[27] Weaver, R.K. (2016). "Privileging Policy Change? Sustaining Automatic Stabilizing Mechanisms in Public Pensions". *Social policy & Administration* 50(2), 148–164.

[28] Rabaté, S. (2019). "Can I stay or should I go? Mandatory retirement and the labor-force participation of older workers". *Journal of public economics* 180, 104,078, https://doi.org/10.1016/j.jpubeco.2019.104078.

[29] See also the Pension Adequacy Report of 2024 on budgetary impacts (European Commission (2024), Directorate-General for Employment, Social Affairs and Inclusion, "The 2024 pension adequacy report—Current and future income adequacy in old age in the EU", Volume I, Publications Office of the European Union, p. 105 and following).

[30] This pension concept of "resting period" is but one of many pension concepts. In 2002 Yves Stevens developed the idea of the multidimensional hypernym of pensions in his PhD (see: Stevens, Y (2002), Equality and solidarity in occupational pensions for employees: from remuneration to social protection (in Dutch), PhD, Faculty of Law, Leuven, 23–25; for a more recent reference: Stevens Y. (2019), 'The Role of the Government in Creating or Enhancing the Access to Funded or Unfunded Pensions in the Modern Welfare State'. In Da Costa Cabral, N. and Cuncha Rodrigues, N. (eds.), *The Future of Pension Plans in the EU Internal)Market*, Springer International Publishing, Cham, 61–63.

sectors and professions and prevents unequal treatment.[31] However, this narrative is unconnected with the realities of the cohorts, sectors and professions. From a legal point of view, many of the existing differences between all types of groups can be justified under discrimination law, specifically based on the rule of equality, meaning that unequal situations should be treated unequally under the equality narrative. Furthermore, the macro-economic reasoning of equality is more linked to fairness than to the legal approach of equivalence. This means that legal discriminations are based on individual situations and not on macro-economic considerations.[32]

The narrative behind the social contract views is that pensionable ages are part of the social contract, where workers contribute collectively to the system with the understanding that they will be supported in their old age through pensions and benefits.[33] The social contract is thus seen as an intergenerational contract whereby each generation is assumed to be willing to pay for the previous generation. Generation after generation, the solidarity between generations is built up. Especially in PAYG systems such theory is easy to envisage. After all, one can always refer to the necessity to pay now so that a later generation will not be able to refuse payment. However, this type of social contract is not only a legal fiction but a fiction in general. Not only is there a lack of understanding of pension rights, there is also no direct correlation between the amount of contributions and the amount of pension that is ultimately received. This lack of correlation undermines the idea of the social contract. Any generation might easily claim that their generation has to pay far more than any previous generation due to for example a higher government debt. But there is more to it. The idea of a social contract is far less easy to defend in funded pension systems. Although collective funding exists, it is almost never defined on a national intergenerational scale such as in PAYG systems. Funded schemes operate more often on a smaller scale such as within a branch of industry, a company or even on an individual level. The social contract idea in funded schemes refers more to indirect forms of financing such as tax cuts or lower social security contributions than for normal wages. These more indirect influences are hard to grasp within an idea of a social contract.[34] Funded collective schemes can however present risk sharing element if a certain level of future benefits is guaranteed in some form or another, by analogy with traditional collective insurance, or when annuity retirement benefits are paid and guaranteed, which all entail a dose of generational and collective solidarity. Funded schemes benefitting from national insolvency guarantees also present an element of generational and national solidarity.[35]

---

[31] Stevens, Y (2022), *EU pension law*, London, Edward Elgar Publishing, 52–53.

[32] Reeskens, T., and Van Oorschot, W. (2013). "Equity, equality, or need? A study of popular preferences for welfare redistribution principles across 24 European countries". *Journal of European Public Policy*, 20, 1174–1195.

[33] See: D'Agostino, F. (2024). "Contemporary Approaches to the Social Contract". *The Stanford Encyclopedia of Philosophy* (online article): https://plato.stanford.edu/archives/spr2024/entries/contractarianism-contemporary/.

[34] Ibidem.

[35] Art. 3 and 8 Directive 2008/94/EC of the European Parliament and of the Council of 22 October 2008 on the protection of employees in the event of the insolvency of their employer; jurisprudence of

All in all, we discern five main legal narratives: stable economic turnover, sustainability, leisure after work, equal treatment and upholding the social contract. Over the last decades, in all narratives a shift took place towards a more open approach of retirement and work without a clear break between these two. A certain blend of work and retirement is increasingly present and this is fitted within the legal narratives whereby it depends on the national context which narrative fits most with both a statutory and occupational pension. In the Netherlands and Switzerland for example, the idea of a social contract is clearly present in both the statutory pension system and the occupational pension system. Due to possible solidarity buffers and the mechanism behind the possible indexing of annuities, there is clearly some kind of social contract present in the Dutch and Swiss occupational systems.[36] In the UK, however, this is arguably less clear as the social solidarity element is perhaps not as evident as in pension systems in other countries. Despite the fact that the UK state pension is essentially funded based on a PAYG basis, and has seen some increase in provision in recent years, it has essentially provided a subsistence income, where an individual is expected to have pensions and savings above this level.[37]

2.2 What Is a "Normal" Retirement Age?

Not all countries in this book have a certain fixed legal notion of what a "normal" pensionable age is or could be. From a legal point of view, there are several retirement ages which can be considered "normal". After all, it is not abnormal to take early or later retirement.[38] From a legal perspective, it is more correct to talk about a legal reference age. This legal age of reference can be found in statutory and occupational pensions but the narratives behind the reference age can differ strongly based on the "role" the different pension types have in a given national context. The reference age is therefore used to delineate the moment whereby an earlier or later retirement is possible.

When looking at the statutory pensions in the eight countries, the following ages occur. Croatia and Austria have a reference age of 65 (in Austria for women 60 years and 6 months but increasing to 65, in Croatia for women transitional period, reaching 65 in 2030), the UK and Belgium have 66 and Germany together with the Netherlands have 67. Switzerland has introduced a flexible retirement age concept between ages 63 and 70. Finland has opted for a link to life expectancy not legally defining any

the European Court of Justice on insolvency protection in occupational pension schemes: decisions of 25 January 2007, Robins e.a., C-278/05; 25 April 2013, Hogan e.a., C-398/11; 24 November 2016, Webb-Sämann, C-454/15; 6 September 2018, Hampshire,C-17/17; 19 December 2019, Günther Bauer, C-168/18.

[36] See, e.g., Ponds, E. en Webers, E. (2024), "Solidarity buffer and solidarity preferences", Netspar Design Paper 238, 87p.

[37] See UK Country report.

[38] Vermeer, N. (2016). "Age anchors and the expected retirement age: an experimental study". *De Economist* 164, 255–279, doi: https://doi.org/10.1007/s10645-016-9276-1.

fixed age of reference but a true "moving" retirement age for each age cohort. In Finland, the year of birth defines the reference age. For instance, for a person born in 1990, the minimum retirement age is (according to current life expectancy) 67 years and 10 months. Such a clear link between life expectancy is rather uncommon. In the Netherlands however—after 2025—the retirement age is also linked to life expectancy.[39]

When it comes to occupational pensions the framework is often but not always linked to statutory pensions. In Belgium, the Netherlands and Germany there is a clear legal link between the reference age for statutory and occupational pensions. This means that the reference age for the occupational pension is either defined by or identical to the statutory pensions. In Belgium and Germany this meant the occupational pension can only be taken up at the same moment as the statutory pension. In the Netherlands the reference age in the occupational pension is linked to the statutory reference: access to the occupational pension depends on the pension scheme, but is must respect restrictions as it is for example not possible to retire earlier than 10 years before the statutory reference age which will be linked to life expectancy in the future. In Austria, the statutory reference age is in practice often mirrored when it comes to permanent benefits from occupational pension insurance, but there is no direct legal link. The conditions are to be determined in the agreement between the employer and the occupational pension fund. In Croatia, Switzerland and the UK a separate age of reference is used in the law. In the UK this is 55 years (i.e. the minimum age) with a clear tax link, in Switzerland is 65 and in the voluntary DC type of pension in Croatia it is 55 for temporary pensions (i.e. pensions paid out for a limited period, e.g. from 5 to 20 years), while for life-time pensions is set at 60 years of age. As stated earlier, Finland has no "proper occupational" pension and thus no real age of reference either.

All in all, it is correct to state that the occupational reference age is usually legally linked to the possibility to take up a statutory pension be it earlier or later. This link is rather surprising if one would consider occupational pensions as a method of gaining additional savings. One could think that occupational pension benefits, being additional savings, might allow workers to stop working before statutory pension benefits can be paid out. Such an idea about early labour market exit due to occupational pensions was and is however not really present in any of the countries included in our study. It is rather the opposite. The statutory retirement age defines the occupational retirement age. Of course, this can be explained by several reasons such as too low occupational benefits or tax disincentives for early retirement. Obviously, setting a retirement age for occupational pensions allows the government to safeguard (some of) the rationales for the statutory pensionable age or reference age, such as the sustainability of the system and the budgetary challenges that come with workers

[39] Such an increase in retirement age must be announced at least five years in advance. For example in 2023 the retirement age for those who can retire in 2029 was thus announced to be 67 years and three months.

leaving the labour market earlier.[40] The stricter the link is between the reference age for occupational pension and statutory pensions, the stronger the budgetary aspects are safeguarded by the pension system.

Often, mere age requirements are not sufficient to have access to retirement. Additional requirements relate for example to minimum standards regarding the length of the insurance period. In Switzerland, for example, a minimum length of insurance period of 11 months in one year is required. In Germany, the minimum insurance period (waiting period) is still 5 years and in the UK at least 10 years national insurance contributions must be paid. This is even exceeded by Austria, where 15 years of minimum insurance period (seven of which due to gainful employment) are required for statutory old age pension. Such requirements, however, can also relate to residency. In the Netherlands, for example, a 'full' state pension can in principle only be granted to residents living in the Netherlands for 50 years (in 2025: from the age of 17 until 67). Other additional conditions can be linked to age cohorts. In Germany for example the reference age is set at 66 only for insured persons born in or after 1964. In the Netherlands age cohorts are decisive condition for raising the retirement age. In Finland, life expectancy is not such a condition. It is just a way to define what the minimum retirement age means. So both countries, use life expectancy as an element of defining the pension system, but in a different legal set up.

The relationship between the age of reference (both in statutory and occupational pensions) and other conditions or requirements indicate that the underlying narratives cannot be determined solely by the reference age but also by other conditions or terms. All these specific conditions show the complex nature of pension systems that are culturally and historically embedded in different types of welfare states. The residency or citizenship condition for example in the UK and the Netherlands are far less easy to explain in Austria, Belgium or in Germany due to the financing techniques. Where in the UK and Netherlands the statutory pension is financed out of tax money, the Austrian, Belgian and German pension system is mainly based on social insurance.

Despite these differences, we see that almost all countries have taken an approach to increase the pensionable reference age over the last two decades.[41] For example the UK is currently aiming for age 68[42] and Belgium at the age of 67. The Finnish and the Dutch models of linking the retirement age to life expectancy fits into the same idea. Raising the reference age for women to 65 in Austria and Switzerland is based on a similar idea. The main obvious rationales for raising the reference ages in the countries is the stable economic turnover in combination with the sustainability of the system. Hence the classic narrative of the social contract occurs: we need to take care of each other over generations. New generations grow older than before but that

[40] See also: Whitehouse, E., D'Addio, A., Chomik, R. and Reilly, A. (2009), "Two Decades of Pension Reform: What has been Achieved and What Remains to be Done?". *The Geneva Papers on Risk and Insurance—Issues and Practice*, 34, 515–535.

[41] Hess, M. (2017) "Rising Preferred Retirement Age in Europe: Are Europe's Future Pensioners Adapting to Pension System Reforms?". *Journal of Aging & Social Policy* 29(3), 245–261, DOI: 10.1080/08959420.2016.1255082.

[42] To be phased in for people born in 1977–78 in the UK.

doesn't mean that the present young generations will not be old at a certain moment. The combination of the three rationales (stable economic turnover, sustainability and social contract) defines the legal framework. This is also partially valid for occupational pensions in the sense that young people enter into the economy at large and are the stable factor for tax income in general.

3 Deferred Retirement

Deferral of retirement allows people to leave the labour market after their pensionable reference age. When looking at deferral from a classical social insurance perspective, it seems rather obvious that deferral always is (or should be) voluntary.[43] After all, it seems logical that people living in a (relatively) free world cannot be obliged to stay in the labour market once they are entitled to a pension, if they don't want to stay in the labour market. No wonder that many European countries[44]—including those involved in this study—know deferral.

Nonetheless, there are differences in degrees of freedom. This is linked to the general approach to the welfare state. For example, the Netherlands and the UK have relatively universal Beveridge type of statutory pensions. Both in the UK and the Netherlands deferral is possible but it doesn't influence their right to a pension. In the Netherlands everybody takes up the statutory pension from the first day of the pensionable age.[45] Due to the fact that the statutory pension is a fixed amount (depending on the years of citizenship), deferral only leads to a certain loss in the Netherlands and there is no possibility to reclaim any unpaid pensions. Hence deferral in the Netherlands is a fiction. One is free to defer but it is rather implausible from a personal point of view.[46] A similar system exists in the UK. The UK state pension is not paid directly to an individual unless they take action to claim it. So, if one doesn't claim then there is a loss like in the Netherlands. However, the pension amount is not fixed in the UK like in the Netherlands. Deferral leads in the UK to an increase of the pension (1% extra for every 9 weeks of deferral or 5,8% for a year of deferral). In Switzerland, deferral with increased benefits till age 70 is also possible and monthly accrued pensions are only time-barred after five years. There is thus an inherent bonus

---

[43] Hofäcker, D. (2015). "In line or at odds with active ageing policies? Exploring patterns of retirement preferences in Europe". *Ageing & Society* 15, 1529–1556.

[44] European Social Policy Analysis Network (ESPAN) (2025), "Flexible retirement pathways. An analysis in 28 European countries", Publications Office of the European Union, 92p.

[45] The Dutch law states: "The old-age pension starts on the day on which the interested party meets the conditions for entitlement to an old-age pension." (art. 16.1. Algemene Ouderdomswet (National Old Age Pensions Act)).

[46] In 2018 the non-take of the statutory old age pension (*AOW*) was less than 0,04%. These are the following reasons for non-take up: unfamiliarity with the right to AOW pension, unfamiliarity with the forms and lack of proper guidance for dependents. Algemene Rekenkamer, "Ouderdomsregeling ontleed 2019", p. 27–28. https://www.rekenkamer.nl/publicaties/rapporten/2019/11/13/ouderdoms regelingen-ontleed (accessed 20 May 2025).

system in the UK and Switzerland for deferral that is not existing in the Netherlands. So, although there is very similar in pension typology, the freedom within the UK and Switzerland leads to a higher pension benefit.

The degree of flexibility in the Netherlands, the UK and Switzerland is of course closely linked with the set-up on occupational pensions in these countries. For example, there are significant freedoms within the occupational system in the UK and Switzerland, with the state pension as a universal minimum amount payable to all. The fact is that in the UK deferral leads to a higher amount in the statutory pension, but it is not possible to pay extra contributions into the state system that would allow a more significant increase. The deferral set up in Switzerland is similar to the UK. This is seen as rather inflexible. Although it might well be justifiable in a PAYG system based on taxes and strong income solidarity. However, the UK and Swiss system cannot be seen without their strong role for occupational pensions. It is therefore suggested that the inability to increase the state pension amount through additional contributions demonstrates the emphasis upon the role of the employer and upon the individual rather than resistance from the government to allow a flexible system. So, the statutory pension is really looked upon as a minimum system for poverty alleviation. Unsurprisingly a similar reasoning can be found in the Netherlands. The Dutch pension system allows flexibility in retirement age for occupational pensions in relation to the age that you take the statutory AOW pension. Therefore, what appears to be a stricter position does not necessarily mean that the system in the Netherlands does not support flexible working. The state provision under the AOW is a minimum level of support designed to be supplemented by other provisions such as occupational or personal pensions. In a comparable way to the UK, the role of the state pension within the design of the system reflects less options around the state pension.

An interesting point of difference in deferral beyond the age of reference is the question whether there is a maximum age of deferral. Switzerland for example has a flexible retirement age starting at age 63 and the maximum possible accrual age is at 70. But there is no automatic payment at that age. The pension still must be claimed. If not, then a pensioner loses. So, the pension remains accrued until the age of 70. But also here there is a role for occupational pensions. Swiss occupational pensions offer considerable deferral flexibilities and even tax-exempt buy-back contributions to increase retirement benefits. On the other side of the spectrum is Belgium. Belgium does not have such a maximum of 70 years like in Switzerland. As long as one doesn't claim a statutory pension and pays social contributions, the pension accrues in principle. However, once a person claims a Belgian statutory pension and receives it, then all accrual will stop even if they continue working and paying social contributions. Due to the absolute link between statutory and occupational pensions in Belgium, any choice for deferral leads to deferral for all pensions.

Croatia does not have a maximum age in statutory pensions, but it has installed a bonus system for retirement deferral limited to maximum 5 years.[47] Each month

[47] Government proposal of the new Pension Insurance Act from May 2025 previews abolition of 5-year pension bonus limitation.

of deferral amounts to 0,45% increase leading to a maximum permanent pension increment of 27%. In Croatia the bonus is integrated in the pension amount itself and thus leading to an overall higher pension. Austria does not have a maximum age either but also a kind of maximum of years of deferral for obtaining a bonus after the pensionable reference age. In Austria, the bonus for deferral ceases after three years upon fulfilling the conditions for old age pension, and equals 5,1% per year or 15,3% in total. In addition, for the period in which retirement is deferred, the pension insurance contribution rate is reduced by half for employees and employers. However, contributing further due to a gainful activity and not taking the pension will still increase the pension after the three years. So only the bonus accrual stops but the pension accrual remains after three years until the pension is claimed. In Croatia the bonus is integrated in the pension amount itself and thus leading to an overall higher pension. Belgium has a similar bonus set-up of maximum three years but with a big difference on the reference age. In Belgium the bonus accrual is already possible from the early retirement age onwards and not from the pensionable reference age like in Austria.

The legally perhaps most complicated bonus system on deferral in statutory pensions exists in Finland. By postponing one's retirement beyond the minimum retirement age, one can 'neutralize' the negative effect that the life expectancy coefficient has on one's pension benefit. The life expectancy coefficient is determined by the life expectancy rate of each age cohort. While the life expectancy of the population increases, the coefficient decreases thus reducing pension benefits. A 'target retirement age' (tavoite-eläkeikä), which is higher than the minimum retirement age, is determined for each age cohort. This means that if a person postpones retirement until the target retirement age, the negative effect of the life expectancy coefficient is fully neutralized. The intriguing idea in Finland is of course that the bonus is not actually a bonus but more a neutralization of the malus if somebody retires early. In this respect it is interesting to compare it to the Belgian system whereby there is a true bonus after early retirement by an increase in pension. So, to put it differently: in Belgium longer working leads to a reward and in Finland working longer leads to "less punishment". One could see this as a so-called carrot and stick motivation. This is a motivational approach offering a "carrot" or reward for good behaviour and a "stick" or negative consequence for poor behaviour. It must be pointed out, however, that if a person decides to defer their retirement in Finland also after reaching the "target retirement age", the 0.4% increase per each deferred month still applies. In other words: the "carrot and stick model" turns into a "carrot only model". In Finland a person can defer their retirement indefinitely, even beyond the age of 70 which is the age when employers' insurance obligation ends.

The German system of deferral and bonusses is probably the most straightforward and transparent of the countries involved in this research. Retirement can be deferred with positive (permanent) adjustments to pension benefits (0.5% per *month*).[48] This means that the pension is increased by 6% for each *year* that retirement is deferred

[48] § 77 para 2 No 2b Book VI German Social Code (*SGB VI*).

beyond the standard retirement age. Unlike the Belgian or Finnish system, the start of the bonus is the reference age.

So, all in all, there are different approaches in statutory pensions amongst the countries in this study. The basic idea could be simple: if people work longer, the pension should also be higher. After all, they also contribute to the system in paying taxes/contributions. But it turns out it is not that simple. We can see that there are more permissive systems that have more focus upon the state pension provisions which provide the possibility to both defer taking the pension and to improve the amount of that pension through increasing contributions or working longer. Prolonging the career is always possible in statutory pensions but bonusses are limited—either in terms of the amount or in duration.

When looking at the complexity of deferred retirement schemes, it is clear that some narratives prevail. We don't know whether there is a link between working longer and living longer. If there would be a correlation, then of course it would mean that mortality goes down with higher employment rates in the labour force. Hence the narrative of sustainability plays a role. However, there is no clear scientific evidence.[49] The only sure observation is that the relationship between retirement timing and longevity is complex and influenced by a multitude of factors. So far there is no strong evidence that retirement increases the mortality risk. Probably—and this is just a guess—there is some kind of common belief amongst legislators in Europe that there is actually no link between longevity and working longer.[50] This actually rather fatalistic idea means that working longer should be a desired situation for governments because people pay longer taxes and contributions without dying later. So why not promote such a system?

There are probably two main reasons. The first one is of course that it remains scientifically uncertain whether there is a correlation or not between working longer and dying later. Secondly, it goes against the narrative of equality. Not everybody is physically or mentally capable of working longer. A lot of blue-collar workers such as construction workers are simply physically incapable of working longer. So, in order to promote a system of working longer, the labour market should be far more dynamic, allowing for example, construction workers to fulfil other functions in the labour market in a later phase of life. But for as long as European labour markets are not more dynamic, the legal narrative of equal treatment between persons will prevail. In this narrative all people should be entitled to a more or less similar access to retirement. Besides this narrative there is also the narrative of the pension enabling people to leisure after work. People are entitled to some form of rest after years of work. Thereby, of course, it is quite clear that working is not an equally pleasant

[49] See on the relation between retirement age and mortality also: Wu C, Odden MC, Fisher GG, Stawski RS (2016), "Association of retirement age with mortality: a population-based longitudinal study among older adults in the USA". J Epidemiol Community Health 70(9), 917–23, https://doi.org/10.1136/jech-2015-207.097.

[50] See also the sources in: Pestieau, P. and Racionero, M. (2016). "Harsh occupations, health status and social security". *Journal of Economics* 117, 239–257; Rabaté, S. (2019). "Can I stay or should I go? Mandatory retirement and the labor-force participation of older workers". *Journal of public economics* 180, 104,078, http://doi.org/10.1016/j.jpubeco.2019.104078.

experience for everyone. For many people, work is a burden and not a pleasure. Advocating for longer working careers is easy for someone who is passionate about their work. However, if work is a necessity for survival in daily life, then working longer is really not an option. In that respect, the word 'retirement pension' really does mean a right to rest.

Deferral of the statutory retirement can have an impact on the (possibility of) retirement in the occupational scheme. As mentioned above, in some countries, the possibilities to defer retirement with regard to the statutory pensions are linked to the occupational pension system. In Belgium and Germany the retirement ages for both statutory and occupational pensions are linked. Hence there is no flexibility. A rather 'inflexible' system also exists in the Netherlands and in the UK with regard to deferral of retirement in the statutory pension system. Switzerland is a bit more open. But the counterpart is a much greater flexibility with regard to deferral of retirement in the occupational pension system. In all three countries the statutory pension is considered a minimum system for poverty alleviation complemented by occupational pension savings in order to mitigate the risk of losing the pre-retirement lifestyle. This legislative framework still shows that, compared to the statutory pension, occupational pensions have often historically developed in different legal settings as more responsibility is given to employers (or to social partners, such as in the Netherlands) to shape the occupational pensions system. Flexibility with regard to the deferral of retirement, can also be found in Switzerland, where the maximum age of deferral is the same as the maximum age of deferral for statutory pensions, i.e. 70 years. However, there is no legal obligation to take up the statutory pension benefits and the occupational pension benefits at the same time. In Belgium, on the other hand, once one retires and receives statutory pension benefits, one cannot defer his occupational pension. The Belgian government has strengthened the link between the retirement age for statutory pension and occupational pension, not only with regard to the 'normal' retirement age, but also with regard to deferral of retirement. By installing a strict link, the government in fact strengthens the narrative of safeguarding the purpose of occupational pension benefits as retirement savings additional to the statutory pensions.

4 Early Retirement

Early retirement refers to situations where countries allow individuals to retire and draw the pension benefits earlier than their reference retirement age. Early retirement exists in most of the statutory pension schemes of the analysed countries (Austria, Belgium, Croatia, Finland, Germany, Switzerland), however differing in their generosity. Interestingly, the UK state pension and the public statutory pension in the Netherlands do not allow early retirement. However, in occupational pensions it is possible in the Netherlands maximum 10 years prior to the statutory pension, in the UK from the age of 55 and in Switzerland from the age of 58. The non-existing flexibility in statutory pensions is lessened by the flexibility in occupational pensions in these three countries. Overall, the possibility of early retirement appears to be readily accepted in some countries, though not to the same extent in others.

Countries' approach to early retirement can be differentiated according to several criteria, such as:

- Existence or non-existence of early retirement rules both in legislation and schemes' rules;
- General rules or special rules for certain groups (self-employed, civil servants, police, army etc.);
- Voluntary or mandatory take up of early retirement[51];
- Specific conditions for early retirement (e.g. age, insurance or career record etc.);
- Effects on benefit calculation (e.g. through malus), etcetera.
- Size of the early retirement window compared to normal/reference retirement age; and.

Historically, the initial surge of early retirement in the 1970s was due to several factors. Firstly, in most OECD countries gross pension replacement rates had increased since the early 1960s. Employees were more inclined to withdraw from the labour market as soon as they had reached a pensionable age if the income replacement rate was sufficiently high. Secondly, pension systems whereby pension accrual was higher at older ages had failed. Systems whereby for example the average wage of the last 10 years of the career determined the amount of the pension were reduced in scope. Hence there was less economic reason to stay longer in employment and postpone retirement. However, this must be nuanced. Depending on the way the pension system is built, it might well be that longer calculation periods can have a similar effect. For example, instead of the last 10 best year, a 40 years insurance period can lead to lower pensions and therefore the will to stay in the labour market can rise. Thirdly, and more importantly, early labour market exits were in late 1970s and early 1980s induced by rising (youth) unemployment which caused changes in parallel social security schemes such as "bridging pensions". Namely, the unemployment insurances offered longer indemnification periods often until the retirement age and several types of disability benefits were distributed more generously. These schemes were not originally intended to support people in retirement. However, changes in eligibility conditions have effectively turned them into early retirement programs.[52]

Based on these three or similar evolutions, numerous countries also introduced or expanded the early retirement options in their old-age statutory systems. These often generous early retirement provisions in social security systems also induced employers to encourage more employees to retire early. In particular, early retirement was used as an instrument to facilitate staff reductions during economic recessions. In some countries it was even a method to circumvent loopholes regarding termination

---

[51] Hakola, T. and Uusitalo,R. (2005). "Not so voluntary retirement decisions? Evidence from a pension reform". *Journal of Public Economics* 89, 2121–2136.

[52] Butler, M., Huguenin, O., Teppa, F. (2004), "What Triggers Early Retirement? Results from Swiss Pension Funds", Center for research on pensions and welfare policies, Working paper 35/04, April 13, 2004.

rules. Hence, there was a possible erosion of the employment protection legislation.[53] Pension legislation can rarely be read irrespective of the employment law.

More recently the trend of expanding early retirement has shifted. Noticeable is the trend that countries are more inclined to tighten early retirement rules while at the same time orientating towards flexible and partial retirement due to new challenges in the retirement systems, especially system dependency ratio problems due to increased longevity, lower fertility rates and emigration issues.[54] Hence a less permissive era is at hand, and this is reflected in the legislation on both statutory and occupational pensions. Since the reference ages of both statutory and occupational pensions are often linked (supra), there is no doubt that the shift to more stringent rules for early retirement can be found in both types of pension systems.

4.1 Narratives for Early Retirement

Countries often implement forms of early retirement for various reasons.[55] A primary factor is labour market conditions such as surpluses in the labour market, a decreased form of employability of older workers or high unemployment rates. Whether these rationales are economically valid or not, is a question for socio-economists (e.g. the debate on the lump of labour fallacy (see supra)).[56] Legally these reasons are used to justify, true or not, the early retirement conditions. In periods to strengthen the conditions for early retirement, the opposite reasoning is used: labour market shortages, an increased employability of older workers and low unemployment rates.[57]

Linked to the labour market conditions are of course general economic conditions such as economic (financial) crises necessitating early retirement schemes to alleviate economic strain.[58] In practice, early retirement schemes are used by employers for restructuring business and cost-cutting measures including (mass) layoffs. Older employees are often more wage-costly and thus early retirement offers a flexible and

[53] Dorn, D. and Sousa-Poza, A. (2005), "Early Retirement: Free Choice or Forced Decision?", CESifo Working Paper Series No. 1542.

[54] OECD, Pensions at a Glance series, especially 2021, 2019 (OECD (2019) "Pensions at a glance 2019: OECD and G20 indicators", OECD Publishing, Paris, 224p; OECD (2021), "Pensions at a Glance 2021: OECD and G20 Indicators", OECD Publishing, Paris, 222p).

[55] Engels, B., Geyer, J. and Haan, P. (2017). "Pension incentives and early retirement". *Labour economics* 47, 216–231.

[56] An interesting paper on this topic is written by Axel H. Börsch-Supan in 1998 (Borsch-Supan, A. (1998), "Incentive Effects of Social Security on Labor Force Participation: Evidence in Germany and Across Europe", NBER Working Paper 6780, https://doi.org/10.3386/w6780.

[57] Staubli, S. and Zweimuller, J. (2013). "Does raising the early retirement age increase employment among older worker?". *Journal of public economics* 108, 17–32, doi.org/10.1016/j.jpubeco.2013.09.003.

[58] See: Mastrobuoni, G. (2009). "Labor supply effects of the recent social security benefit cuts: Empirical estimates using cohort discontinuities". *Journal of Public Economics* 93(11–12), 1224–1233.

low-cost way out. In some countries cheaper labour, like students, platform workers and on-call workers are then readily at hand for some employers.

Another narrative is health.[59] On an individual level, health-related conditions can play a significant role. Where individuals may experience reduced working ability due to age or illnesses but do not (yet) qualify for disability pensions, governments will tend to alleviate this with earlier access to retirement.[60] But there is more to it. Health conditions also play a more general role in the overall narrative of (early) access to retirement. It is not uncommon that hazardous or arduous jobs give access to earlier retirement. The reasoning there is that a person having worked in this type of job is entitled to have a least some years in retirement in good health.

This kind of reasoning whereby the right to a period of healthy retirement should be granted links with another rationale. That is that personal preferences and lifestyle choices regarding work-life balance should be taken into account.[61] Often this has to do with family conditions which can prompt early retirement as well. For example, when persons choose or need to become caregivers for grandchildren or frail (older) family members. This can be due to insufficient formal state care or can be based on personal preferences. Whatever the reasons, early statutory retirement schemes can alleviate these needs of caregiving or personal preferences. This rationale is obviously linked with the most common reason for partial retirement whereby people start working part time with or without a partial retirement benefit. Additional interesting issues linked to early retirement are the connections with the economic situation and statistical longevity of the beneficiaries, in particular the advantages for the more privileged persons in terms of personal wealth and life-expectancy linked to past careers. It is thus considered that these categories are more likely to retire early, while less privileged categories are more likely to stop working due to ill health (especially when not qualifying for disability pension). Regarding middle income earners, it can be argued that they are most likely to remain in paid work until normal/reference pension age.[62]

When early retirement also means a stop on gaining income via labour, early retirement often requires sufficient financial resources. To put it bluntly: early retirement might not always be an option for all if it means living in (quasi) poverty. Or in other words: early retirement is not always a possible choice on an individual level.[63]

---

[59] French, E. and Jones, J.B. (2017). "Health, health insurance and retirement: a survey". *Annual Review of Economics* 9, 383–409, doi.org/10.1146/annurev-economics-063016-103616.

[60] The relations between healthcare and early retirement is a very intriguing topic. A good analysis on this topic can be found in Clark, R.L. and Mitchell, O.S., "The Changing Retirement Paradigm". In Clark, R.L. and Mitchell, O.S., *Reinventing the Retirement Paradigm*, Oxford University Press, 2005, 3–13.

[61] Anderson, A., Markussen, S. and Roed, K. (2021). "Pension reform and the efficiency equity tradeoff: impacts of removing the early retirement subsidy". *Labour economics* 72, 102,050.

[62] Künzler, G. and Knöpfel, C. (2002), *Les pauvres vivent moins longtemps. Couche sociale, mortalité et politique de l'âge de la retraite en Suisse*, Lucerne, Caritas Suisse, 100p.

[63] Dolls, M. and Krolage, C. (2023). "Earned, not given'? The effect of lowering the full retirement age on retirement decisions". *Journal of Public Economics* 223, 104,909, doi.org/10.1016/j.jpubeco.2023.104909.

Both occupational and individual pensions can play a role here in the narrative behind early retirement. Early retirement can be seen as a narrative of "bought free time". At this point, the more income-like nature of occupational and individual pensions becomes relevant. Retiring from the labour market only makes sense if sufficient resources exist. If resources are limited, workers are more or less forced to stay on the labour market. Also, even though one could retire, one would probably be less tempted if the gap between his (final) salary and the pension benefits is too big. In other words, retaining the pre-retirement lifestyle can be a determining factor in the decision whether or not to retire. Occupational pension benefits can help to keep the standard of living by saving for retirement in addition to the retirement income from statutory pension schemes.[64]

4.2 Prerequisites

4.2.1 Voluntary or Involuntary Take Up of Early Retirement?

In all the countries that allow early retirement within their statutory pension system, the actual take up of early retirement is voluntary (Austria, Belgium, Croatia, Finland, Germany, Switzerland). This is a logical solution, since early retirement exits are designed as an exemption and not a rule. So, there is no narrative for a country to force early retirement that can burden the long-term sustainability of a pension system.

When contemplating the voluntariness of early retirement, one should also consider other measures existent within the pension law, taxation law or labour law that can have discouraging or encouraging effects on the actual take up of early retirement. In this sense, measures within pension law (e.g. in the form of malus) can play a role. Also, taxation rules (e.g. taxation disadvantages), as well as a combination of pension law and labour law rules can be decisive for personal choice whether to stop working and retire early, or to continue working while retired (fully or partially) if the system allows combining pensions with work.

The voluntary take up of early retirement is predominantly based on the narrative of personal preferences and lifestyle choices of the individual. Depending on the personal situation, a person will choose to retire early or not. This may involve very different reasons such as health, family situation, financial capability or personal development.

[64] See e.g.: Gierusz, A., Kowalczyk-Rólczyńska, P., Pobłocka, A., and Rutecka-Góra, J. (2022), "Changes in approach to risk sharing in supplementary pension schemes". In Kolaczkowski, J., Maher, M., Stevens, Y., and Werbrouck, J.M. (eds.), *The Evolution of Supplementary Pensions*, Edward Elgar, 410–438.

4.2.2 For Whom?

Most of the countries in this study that have an early retirement possibility have general rules covering all potential pensioners, be it employees, self-employed or civil servants (Austria,[65] Belgium, Finland, Croatia, Switzerland). However, such a wide-ranging opinion may give a false impression. There are, in fact, two other important underlying mechanisms at play. First, there is the general social or labour law framework that sometimes facilitates other forms of early exit from the labour market for a number of occupational groups. Secondly, and even more importantly, quite a few countries have special pension regimes for so-called arduous and hazardous work[66] Often these specific regimes are linked to some form of civil service such as police, army, fire brigade and so on. But also people with so called demanding and onerous jobs such as miners[67] are entitled to earlier retirement ages. Such preferential treatment for access to old-age retirement is legally mainly prescribed by lower old-age retirement conditions, e.g. in the form of lower retirement age than normal/reference age and/or lower insurance/career/residence periods. This observation is valid for several countries.

The specific prerequisites or conditions for early retirement show that some narratives play a very important role. When it comes to early retirement for hazardous and arduous jobs it is clear that the health narrative plays an important role. Miners and soldiers, for example, are known to have physically comparatively hard work. People who work in security jobs such as police officers, for instance, are more often than average confronted with situations where psychological stress can arise.

4.2.3 At What Age after how Long?

It might seem a rather odd question: from what age onwards is early retirement possible? After all the answer depends on what the reference retirement age is. It should be "some time" before the reference age. But given the fact that it is rather

---

[65] Austria had special rules for civil servants until 2005. Since then, legislation changed in the direction of applying general rules also to civil servants, designated commonly as "new" civil servants (meaning those born as from 1976, appointed as of 2005). However, due to historic reasons and previously existent different arrangements, in Austria still has some special rules for "older" civil servants (i.e. born before 1976 and appointed until 2004, if they were federal civil servants or working for one of the municipalities/states).

[66] For example Finland knows this category of arduous and hazardous jobs. But it also applies to Finish career soldiers. In Croatia this list is longer. Are for example included: active military personnel, police officers and authorized officials in state security intelligence bodies, as well as for persons in arduous and hazardous jobs and persons with disabilities due to specifically enumerated illnesses or health status (e.g. blind and deaf persons, person suffering from dystrophy and related muscular and neuromuscular diseases, paraplegia, multiple sclerosis etc.).

[67] For example in Germany, special conditions apply to long-service miners (retirement is possible at the age 62 after at least 25 years of work/insurance) and in Austria employees in miners' companies are under certain conditions eligible to an earlier exit of the labour market.

complicated to define this "normal" or reference age, it is plain that formulating an answer is not that straightforward.

We discern the following in our study:

- The definition of the early retirement is defined by a fixed period defined as a "window" prior to the "normal" or reference age. This is the case in Finland (3 years before normal/reference retirement age—which is life expectancy bound) for statutory pensions. But it is also the case for the Netherlands when it comes to occupational pensions: maximum 10 years prior to the statutory pension age.
- The early retirement is a fixed age. The UK has no real early retirement for the statutory pension but it allows voluntary early retirement within occupational schemes for employees from the earliest age of 55, depending on the particular rules of the pension scheme (which will increase to 57 in 2028). In Switzerland—with its flexible age regime—it can be set at the age of 63. This is also valid for occupational pensions. The rules of the pension fund may, however, provide for a lower age up to 58. Occupational pension schemes have considerable leeway in drawing up their regulations. The existing range of flexible retirement options is extremely varied.[68] Also Croatia works with a fixed age. In Croatia, the early retirement age is 60.[69] One could argue thus that in Croatia the early retirement window is 5 years below normal or reference retirement age. But when it comes to the voluntary DC schemes in Croatia the earliest age is 55 and thus even 5 years lower that the statutory early retirement.
- The access to early retirement is a combination of age and length of career. Such is the case in Belgium with age 60 with a career of 44 years, 61 years with a career of 43 years and 63 with a career of 42 years. The link with occupational pensions is inflexible: early statutory retirement means taking up occupational retirement. However, there are strong tax consequences meaning that early retirement leads to a higher taxation of the occupational pension.
- The access to early retirement is a combination of conditions whereby the date of early retirement is a moving target. In Austria for example the early retirement age differs between 60 and 62 years depending on the sex, date of birth, insurance term and the type of early retirement benefit. Germany has a similar approach with 63 years for the long-service old age pensions and 62 for the severe disability old age pensions. Here again the early take up of the statutory pension means the take up of the occupational pension. Thus the strictest legal limit to early retirement is set by Germany, where the company/occupational pension scheme is paid out at the end of the contractual term. This is usually at the end of a person's working life. Early retirement is fully coordinated with the statutory retirement age, as an employee can only claim the occupational pension when it is linked to claiming the full statutory pension and fulfilling a waiting period.

[68] Example: In the construction industry, there are collective agreements on early retirement schemes with specific early retirement ages (ranging from 60 to 62), paying a temporary pension as well the OP retirement savings contributions till the present legal reference retirement age of 65.

[69] At least for men in 2024 and during transitional period until 2030 lower for women.

In most of the countries in our study, early retirement is conditional upon long(er) insurance periods or careers. This is the case in Austria (e.g. 480 insurance months, i.e. 40 years, for the so-called "corridor pension"), Belgium (44 years in case of early retirement at the age of 60), Croatia (35 years) and Germany (35 years for long-service old age pensions and severe disability old age pensions). In Finland and Switzerland, however, early retirement is possible regardless the career length or insurance periods of a person. The reasons for these age conditions and possible link with a career or insurance period are mainly linked to the status of the labour market. Depending on the state of the general economic condition of a country, governments will tend to relax or tighten the rules. All in all, this is also obviously linked with the general narrative of sustainability. When it comes to occupational pensions the rationale is less linked to the rationale of sustainability but also linked to life-style, health and work life balance.

4.3 Does Early Retirement Induce a Malus?

To prevent early exit from the labour market or facilitate late exit, mali or boni can be used. The idea is simple: if you work longer, you get more pension, and if you retire earlier, you get less pension. Early retirement will shorten the period of insurance—at least in full retirement and only to a certain degree in partial retirement—and therefore reduce the benefits to be accrued. At the same time, the retirement period is extended. Consequently, the benefits should cover a longer period.[70] However, this simple idea is more complex than it seems. Especially when it comes to the malus. In our study, Belgium is the only country that does not foresee any maluses for early retirement in statutory pensions. As stated earlier, the UK and the Netherlands don't have early retirement schemes in statutory pensions. Malus measures are foreseen in:

- Austria (for example for the "corridor pension":–0.425% for each month that a person retires before the standard retirement age; up to 5.1% reduction per year; in total up to 15,3% reduction of the pension);
- Croatia (–0.2% per month, maximum pension reduction up to 12%)[71];
- Germany (–0,3% per month, maximum pension reduction up to 14,4%)
- Finland[72] (–0,4% for each pension month taken before the minimum pension age) and
- Switzerland (the reduction rate is determined actuarially, from 0,6 for one month up to 13,6% for 24 months).

---

[70] Van Solinge, H. and Henkens, K. (2009). "Living longer, working longer? The impact of subjective life expectancy on retirement intentions and behaviour". *European Journal of Public Health*, 47–51.

[71] As the maximum early retirement window is 5 years (i.e. 60 months).

[72] For the earnings-related statutory pension scheme.

Having a malus for early retirement is perfectly reasonable for the countries in our study. Governments looking at stable economic turnovers with pressures on sustainability will find it reasonable to explain the link between the malus and the earlier exit of the labour market.

The possibility of early retirement is often connected to "malus measures" in the sense that statutory pension benefits are being reduced analogous to the periods (months or years) a person is taking up the pension earlier than the "normal" or "reference" pension age. The main idea is that the earlier the pension is taken up, the bigger the malus should be.

The question whether early retirement also entails a malus, first of all requires an analysis of what exactly the word 'malus' means. In other words, some nuance is in order. A malus can refer to several dimensions. These dimensions are determined by two things. First, by what is understood by a normal pension calculation and, second, by how the reduction is calculated.

A malus implies getting less pension than 'normally' considered. That 'normal' nature means that there is some kind of calculation of how much one would get if one does not retire early. The reduction then involves a deduction from this normal amount.

Depending on the narrative or "ratio legis" of the reduction different legal interpretations of a malus can be given. For example, if the malus is placed in a narrative of actuarial correction, the deduction is going to be linked to the cost to the government of the reduction. If people leave the labour market early, there will be a number of effects including, among others—and not exhaustively—that, first, there is less income and contributions in personal income tax and social security, second, average economic growth falls and, third, the pension bill remains at least as high because life expectancy remains at least the same. Concretely, this narrative translates into a reduced pension amount as a function of reduced contributions and/or life expectancy usually expressed as a percentage of the so-called normal pension amount. And that percentage is variable as a function of reduction and advancement. An actuarial reduction is often based on factors such as mortality. In the case of a life annuity, an actuarial reduction means that the accrued benefits have to be spread over a longer period of time and therefore the amount paid out on a monthly/annual basis will be lower. If there is no life annuity, the actuarial reduction may also result in the benefits being depleted over time.

Actuarial reductions cannot only be found in statutory pensions but also in occupational pensions. This is the case for example in Switzerland, Germany and the UK. Swiss occupational pensions proceed with actuarial reductions on early retirement annuities. However, there is a difference in the reduction between the annuities in the mandatory BVG/LPP scheme and in the supplementary schemes. The minimal BVG/LPP annuity is calculated initially along actuarial factors set by law, with a component of generational solidarity, whereas supplementary schemes set less generous actuarial factors which are applied if the supplementary benefit englobes the mandatory benefits. The actuarial reductions will thus vary for the pensioners of purely mandatory plans or those benefitting from a voluntary supplementary plan. The United Kingdom's defined benefit schemes set their own rules on the typical actuarial reduction. The Civil Service Pension Scheme offers the early retirement option with an actuarial reduction of the pension, which can however be bought out by making a lump sum payment.

At the other end of the spectrum, a malus might not always be framed in the narrative of an actuarial correction but as a retribution and might also be seen as a mere political and even ideological decision which is loosely based on actuarial calculations. This involves reducing the pension without a direct link to life expectancy or prepayment. It is really about retributing by giving less.

Between the actuarial correction and the retribution there is a wide range in which the reduction is applied according to how the narrative is fleshed out. Thus, it is clear that even a supposedly purely actuarial correction by measuring reduced social contributions or taxes, for example, also involves a certain retribution. Only the narrative is different. Essentially, it is about a certain ideology being packaged.

In PAYG schemes the volume of a malus is thus mainly a political measure. After all, in PAYG systems it is overall far more difficult to define a coherent malus in actuarially neutral way. The malus in a PAYG scheme tries to define some link between longevity, paid contributions, loss of non-paid contributions due to the early retirement and the final pension amount. But such calculations are often complicated by the mere fact that statutory pensions are not merely based on social security contributions or individually paid taxes. An actuarially correct malus is thus easier to delineate in a system of individually funded schemes where there might be a clearer link between the contributions paid and the final pension paid out. Moreover, defining the malus is even more easy if the funded pension is paid out in a lump sum rather than then when it is paid out as an annuity.

In some cases, the malus is combined with a "ceiling" of the permanent reduction of the pension (or a maximum pension decrement). Such is the case in e.g. Croatia and Germany. This idea of limiting the malus is also a political decision.

But there is more to it. One should not approach the malus—actuarially or otherwise calculated—as a standalone element. Similarly, much depends on how the pension is or is not taxed on early retirement. Is the early pension taxed differently or not? As a function of different taxation—despite a different narrative—one can still look at the same effect in particular: is there more or less early exit from the labour market due to taxation?

4.4 Working While on Early Retirement?

Conceptually, retirement suggests that a person exits the labour market when taking up a pension. Equally is this true on a conceptual level when retiring "early" as in "before the "normal or reference pension age"". Hence it might seem contradictory at first sight to work while on early retirement. In reality, statutory old-age pension schemes often allow a person on early retirement to continue working while receiving some form of pension benefit. Several narratives can play a role in this set-up. The most imminent example is of course partial retirement. Or even that some people just want to work less and still maintain adequate financial resources while with the same employer. Other people want to take a different path in their career and start working in a different job or work environment. The dynamics of the national labour market, the cultural background and pension systems'sustainability play a defining role in the possibilities to work while in early retirement.

However, the countries in this study show differences in terms of to what extent working is allowed. Several models can be recognized and are valid for both statutory and occupational pensions. Some fiscal differences can occur though. Occupational pensions are often treated differently from a fiscal point of view than statutory pensions and this can have an effect on the possibility to combine work and early retirement. This is for example the case in Belgium, Germany, and Finland. In Switzerland, and in the UK, early retirement can be allowed without restrictions or limits. However, a dissuasive effect may be found in tax law. In Croatia, on the other hand, occupational pension can be combined with work and other earnings with no limitations.

The limitations may be based on the number of working hours, the amount of wage revenue, the status of the pensioner (employee, civil servant, self-employed), etc. First, some countries do not really allow working in practice. This is the case for example in Austria where the maximum wage threshold for persons on statutory early retirement is comparably low. Besides, there has to be no compulsory insurance in pension insurance in Austria while receiving an early pension. This goes along with gainful employment above the marginal threshold.

The second group consists of countries in which working is limited on certain grounds. For instance, in Belgium the limitations are ceilings to the amount a person can earn during early retirement. If one surpasses these ceilings, then pension amount is reduced with the same amount as the excess above the ceiling.[73]

A variant of this second group is a model in which it is allowed to combine a full pension with part-time work (see also below). This is the case in Croatia. All old-age, early retirement pension receivers and survivor's pension receivers are allowed to work (as employees) part-time up to 20 h per week, with a parallel right to full pension benefit in payment. Longer working hours lead normally to pension payment suspension (with the exception for partial disability pensioners and old-age police and military pensioners). Concerning the form of permitted work, only work within an employment relationship and earnings through so-called other income is permitted. (e.g. occasional income based on a contract for service or author's contract, or receipts based on the activities in supervisory company boards). Engaging in independent work—i.e. self-employment (such as tradesmen or registered professional activities)—is not allowed, and will result in suspension of pension payments.[74]

[73] In Belgium there are different ceilings when working as an employee or as a self-employed. The ceilings to work as a self-employed are more attractive from a fiscal point of view due to incentives build into the system.

[74] However, in May 2025 Government proposed the new Pension Insurance Act, which from January 2026 significantly expands the possibility to combine work with retirement.

In the third model there are no limitations for working at early retirement. This is the case in Finland, Germany and Switzerland. However, although there are no pension system-based limitations for working while on early retirement in these countries, working and wage revenue have, of course, fiscal repercussions.

In the countries where working fully or part-time is allowed while on early retirement, the person on early pension pays social security or pension contributions as usual. In Finland, Germany and Croatia this also means that the person's pension benefit increases. In Finland, for instance, where the early retirement is only possible as partial retirement, the contributions that are based on wage revenue and paid during the early retirement increase the future part of the pension, i.e., the part that has not yet been claimed. The same applies for Germany. In Croatia, due to the benefit formula the effect on the benefit level within mandatory PAYGO DB scheme (first pillar) is quasi absent. However, there is a clear effect on the benefit level within mandatory funded DC scheme pension (second pillar) due to the contributions paid. However, Belgium and Switzerland have different rules. There, the pension contributions paid while on early retirement, albeit in case of full and not partial early retirement in Switzerland, do not increase the pension benefit.

Paying social (or pension) contributions while on early retirement without benefiting from extra pension benefits makes working during early retirement obviously less attractive from a personal perspective, compared to when there is benefit accrual. But then again, there might be other reasons than financial gain to retire early and keep on working. This is for example the case when somebody decides on a career switch and turns a hobby into a job as retiree.

As mentioned earlier, irrespective of the type of combination between work and early retirement, taxation can play a very important role. Two countries—not surprisingly with large occupational pensions—influence the combination of work and retirement on a clear tax basis: the Netherlands, the UK and Switzerland. In the Netherlands early retirement is possible with regard to occupational pensions. The law does not require to reduce income generating activities to the same extent, while being on early retirement. However, from a fiscal point of view it might be less interesting as, e.g., the normal tax rates apply to the income earned (which still includes the AOW tax contribution).[75] In the United Kingdom, the tax regime introduced by the Finance Act 2004 does not prohibit the combination of receiving a pension whilst also making contributions from gainful income to a pension scheme. However, this is most likely to be done by people who have reached their normal pension reference age, otherwise they will have a reduction in pension and be treated like an early leaver. However, income tax will apply and there is a limit on tax-exempt retirement savings contributions. Individual pension may have additional limits. In the public sector, the Civil Service Scheme uses the term 'partial retirement' to allow a person to be both an active member and a pensioner member of the scheme, but they must change their job—and reduce their pay by at least 20%. In Switzerland, the AVS pension can be drawn as partial of full early retirement from age 63. But there is

[75] See for the tax rates that will apply once receiving the Dutch statutory pension (AOW): Dutch country report, Section 3.4.

no link with the payment of an occupational pension benefit, nor limits to continued gainful work.

5 Partial Retirement

The increase in mandatory retirement ages in the countries examined in this study has frequently been accompanied by a reassessment of partial retirement systems. A particular new focus on the gradual, step-by-step, reduction of gainful activity till full retirement is at the heart of many pension policy debates. This evolution raises new questions linked to partial retirement as well as the combination of formal retirement with continued gainful activities.

5.1 *Narratives for Partial Retirement in Statutory and Occupational Pension*

Historically, the partial pension compensated for the reduction in salary caused by switching to part-time work. The International Labour Organisation (ILO) defines "partial retirement" as the "*combining of part time employment with receipt of a reduced pension*".[76] However, more contemporary trends illustrate an encouragement to partial retirement whilst allowing the beneficiary to continue gainful activity.[77]

Part-time pension is a system tailored to employees and civil servants. In principle, it is not for the self-employed. After all, the underlying idea is that there will be a restriction on mandatory working hours. Self-employed people do not have a limitation on hours to be worked in any of the countries surveyed. This makes the part-time pension a construction in line with the world of employees and civil servants. This does not mean that self-employed people are *ipso facto* always excluded from access to a part-time pension. However, it does mean that regulations are usually included in social protection law rather than labour law for determining the minimal number of hours to be worked. After all, for self-employed people, it makes no sense to talk about part-time work.

The narratives for partial retirement are manyfold.

The main purpose of the part-time pension was to give older workers the opportunity to combine part-time working and being retired, given changes in health but also

[76] International Labour Organization (ILO) (2020), "ILO Thesaurus", Geneva, https://metadata.ilo.org/thesaurus/1848370168.html (accessed June 19, 2025).

[77] European Social Policy Analysis Network (ESPAN) (2025), "Flexible retirement pathways. An analysis in 28 European countries", Publications Office of the European Union, 92p.

personal preferences such as lifestyle and work life balance.[78] Indeed, the sudden transition from full-time work to full retirement was, and can sometimes be, perceived as a shock. Part-time retirement thus allows people to have a kind of softer landing, as it were, towards retirement. Another narrative is of course that partial retirement can help maintaining savings and offer a higher income during retirement if all conditions are met.

From the employers' or entrepreneurs' standpoint, there is another narrative. For them partial retirement has the advantage of maintaining in-house skills whilst reducing the individual workload. This is especially valid in ageing societies and even more so in times when there are labour market shortages. A clear example of this reasoning can be found in Germany where the so-called "Flexi-Pensions Act," was introduced in 2017 with the intention to contribute to keeping older people in employment as long as possible. The reasoning was that older employees are indispensable because they make a valuable contribution to combating the shortage of skilled workers with their potential to have additional experience.[79]

A more recent concept, is the narrative that partial retirement might be in the general interest of the economy, thereby also contributing to the financial stability of retirement schemes.[80] In this manner partial retirement is devised as an incentive for continued labour market participation of older workers but with less hours than in full time employment.

5.2 *Possible or Not?*

Belgium is the only country included in the study that does not have a system of partial retirement. Austria knows a system of partial retirement (in the sense of receiving a part of a pension, while earning income above a certain threshold), currently only for disability pensions, which are not included in this book. However, a new statutory partial pension is on the political agenda, supposedly effective as of 2026. Since 2014 Croatia adopted a model of partial retirement in the form of the right to full pension benefits in payment combined with part-time work. Partial retirement in the sense that there is reduced working activity combined with partial pension pay-out exists only in two cases: for partial disability pensioners and for pensioners from the police or military force who have retired with a preferential age treatment if they continue working full-time. In Finland, Germany and Switzerland partial retirement is possible for all employee groups and self-employed alike.

[78] See also: Neumark, D., Burn, I. and Button, P. (2019). "Is It Harder for Older Workers to Find Jobs? New and Improved Evidence from a Field Experiment". *Journal of Political Economy* 127 (2), doi.org/10.1086/701029.

[79] Reasoning of the Act on the flexibilisation of the transition from working life to retirement and to strengthen prevention and rehabilitation in working life ("Flexible Pensions Act") from 8 december 2016, with effect from 1 January 2017; see also: Country report Germany.

[80] Message du Conseil fédéral relatif à la stabilisation de l'AVS (AVS21), 28th August 2019, Feuille Fédérale 2019, 5979.

In the Netherlands and in the UK the possibility of a partial pension exists only within the occupational pension schemes, but not in the statutory pension scheme (see below). Both countries integrate the possibility of partial retirement with some form of early or deferred retirement. In the Netherlands for example, occupational pension schemes may allow participants to retire either before or after the retirement age set out in the pension scheme.[81] In the UK, the possibility for (partial) occupational pensions starts at the age of 55 with a possible deferment until the age of 75. In Switzerland partial retirement is allowed from age 63 in the statutory AVS and from age 58 in occupational pensions.

5.3 *Annuities and/or Lump-Sum Partial Retirement Benefits*

In Finland, Germany and Switzerland, the partial pension is always an annuity in the statutory pension systems. In Switzerland, occupational pension institutions can provide for a partial lump-sum benefit instead of a partial annuity, with the limit that lump-sum partial benefits are paid out in a maximum of three steps and not more.

5.4 *Different Models of Partial Retirement*

At least two models of partial retirement within statutory pension schemes can be discerned. The first model can be called the "fixed percentages model". For instance, in Finland, the amount of the partial early old-age pension is either 25% or 50% of the accrued pension depending on the choice of the pensioner.[82] The second model can be called the 'flexible percentage model'. In Switzerland, for example, the minimum partial amount is 20% and the maximum amount is 80% of the AVS pension and the beneficiary may choose a partial pension of anything between these percentages.[83] Also Germany has this second model. Old-age pensions can be flexibly paid as partial pensions.[84] The proportion of the partial pension must be at least 10% or 99.99% at most of the full pension.

[81] Please note that certain restrictions must be taken into account (see country report).

[82] In Finland, the income-tested minimum pension schemes i.e. national pension and guarantee pension, do not recognize partial retirement.

[83] The means-tested supplementary retirement benefits can be granted fully in case of partial AVS retirement.

[84] § 42 Book VI German Social Code.

5.5 Partial Pension with Early or Deferred Retirement

Combining partial pension with early or deferred retirement is possible in Finland, Germany, and Switzerland. In Finland early retirement is only possible as partial retirement. In Finland the partial pension is either 25% or 50% of the full pension. In Germany, eligibility for early retirement is foreseen for recipients of *long-service old age pensions* (at age 63) and *severe disability old age pensions* (at age 62). However, this is only possible with negative (permanent) adjustments to pension benefits, amounting to 0,3% a month.[85] In Switzerland a beneficiary may choose between full pension and partial pension when retiring before the reference age of 65. In this case, the partial early pension can be anything between 20% and 80%. In Switzerland, a partial pension is possible before or after the "normal" or reference retirement age, allowing the deferral of the remaining part of the pension. The Austrian policy discussions on a new partial pension include old-age as well as early retirement pensions.

5.6 Gradual Increase of the Level of the Partial Pension

Both in Finland and in Switzerland the partial retirement decision is irrevocable meaning that a person cannot lift the partial pension apart from when taking full retirement. But in both countries the beneficiary can gradually increase, within specific legally prescribed steps, the level of the partial retirement pension. In Finland, regarding earnings-related pension schemes it is possible to increase the partial pension once, i.e., from 25% to 50%. Partial pension continues as long as the pensioner decides to claim full pension. If the pensioner defers the full pension beyond the life expectancy-bound minimum retirement age, each month increases the "not-yet-claimed" part of the full pension by 0.4%. After the age of 70, income from work does not accrue the full pension anymore.

In Switzerland, the possible increase from 20% to 80% and then full retirement can also occur in three steps from ages 63 up till 70 (in AVS). Occupational pensions have to offer the identical possibilities but are allowed to provide in their regulations for more fine-tuning and therefore more partial steps till full retirement, as well as an earlier starting date from age 58. However, if the partial pension benefits are paid out in the form of lump-sums and not annuities, the three steps limit is mandatory.

---

[85] The German "flexi pension" gives insured persons the opportunity to pay additional contributions into the statutory pension scheme earlier as well as flexibility to compensate for pension reductions. This enables early retirement to be planned and secured more effectively. If a person chooses to defer his/her pension, the positive permanent adjustment to pension benefits are 0,5% per month.

5.7 *Combining Partial Pension with Working*

In Finland, Germany and Switzerland, the partial retirement does not affect the beneficiary's right to work. In other words, the beneficiary may continue working full-time if they so choose. But they can of course also work part-time.

However, full-time work obviously affects the person's taxation. In Switzerland, the AVS does not require a reduction in working time when a partial pension is paid. However, in occupational pensions, tax rules do not allow a person to continue accruing benefits, with employer and employee contributions, on the salary insured in the same institution without considering the partial pension in payment, unless the insured salary is increased with the employer's consent. Full-time work for another employer and an insurance in another institution is legally possible, as labour and social security law do not register working times.

Previously, in Finland one of conditions for partial retirement was that the beneficiary would have to reduce their working hours so that their earnings from the part-time work were 35–70% of the established earnings from full-time work. From 2017 onwards, this has no longer been the case, and the beneficiary can work full-time.

In Germany, partial pensions had been quite unpopular in the past due to the strict income ceilings. These applied to retired persons below statutory retirement age who made use of the options for partial retirement.[86]

These legislative reforms in Finland and in Germany attest to the paradigmatic change described above. Today, one of the main objectives of partial retirement is to function as an incentive for continued labour market participation of older workers, in the general interest of the economy, thereby also contributing to the financial stability of retirement schemes.

The Austrian policy discussions involve a reduction in working hours but staying in employment to some extent while receiving a partial pension.

6 Retirement Regimes for Persons in Arduous and Hazardous Jobs

Retirement regimes for persons in arduous and hazardous jobs refer to special retirement schemes designed for workers whose jobs are exceptionally (physically and/or psychologically) demanding or dangerous.[87] These regimes typically offer earlier retirement ages, enhanced pension benefits, or both, recognizing the toll such work

[86] The income ceiling increased during the Corona pandemic and was completely abolished with effect from 1. January 2023.

[87] Zwick, T., Bruns, M., Geyer, G. and Lorenz, S. (2022). "Early retirement of employees in demanding jobs: Evidence from a German pension reform". *Journal of the economics of ageing* 22, 100,387. http://doi.org/10.1016/j.jeoa.2022.100387.

can take on health and longevity.[88] Although the narratives are quite straightforward, the legal frameworks prove to be complicated.

6.1 Narratives for Arduous and Hazardous Jobs

The main historical justification for the special retirement treatment of persons performing arduous (strenuous) and hazardous (dangerous) jobs is that they both have possible negative effect on health and life expectancy.[89] People performing these jobs "merit" a distinctive pension approach.[90] In this line of reasoning, it can also be argued that the economic narrative behind it was to compensate for insufficient health and safety measures,[91] which can be seen as a valid argument for mortality and health risk-bearing occupations, i.e. inherently dangerous jobs that may shorten life expectancy (e.g. heavy construction work), or strenuous occupations that usually cannot be performed at an older age (e.g. ballerinas, opera singers). A second common justification is that people in these jobs need a compensation for their labour that is not fully covered by their (higher) wages, their (lower) working hours, their (higher) number of holiday days or other elements of human resources and labour law/labour market policy during the active career.[92]

However, in addition to harsh occupations, preferential treatment rules sometimes have a broader scope due to other reasons, such as:

- cultural reasons (e.g. in the case of musicians (e.g. Croatia in this study but also a lot of other former eastern European countries)),
- political reasons wanting to give a boost to employment in specific sectors (e.g. school teachers) by recognizing the arduous or hazardous character of the job and thus creating a more attractive remuneration package,

[88] Vermeer, N., Mastrogiacomo, M. and Van Soest, A. (2016). "Demanding occupations and the retirement age". *Labour Economics* 43, 159–170.

[89] Pestieau, P. and Racionero, M. (2016). "Harsh occupations, health status and social security". *Journal of Economics* 117, 239–257.

[90] Zaidi, A. and Whitehouse, E. (2009), "Should Pension Systems Recognise "Hazardous and Arduous Work"?", *OECD Social, Employment and Migration Working Papers*, No. 91, OECD Publishing, Paris, pp. 4, 6–8.

[91] Existence of privileged pension treatment for persons in arduous and hazardous jobs can be also perceived as an excuse for not doing enough to make jobs less arduous (Vukorepa, I. (2017), "Retirement policy changes for workers in arduous and hazardous jobs: comparative overview and lessons for Croatia", *Zbornik Pravnog fakulteta u Zagrebu*, 67 (1), 5–28 (https://hrcak.srce.hr/176827), p. 10.).

[92] Rosen, S. (1986), "The theory of equalizing differences". In Ashenfelter, O.C. and Layard, R. (eds), *Handbook of Labor Economics*, Elsevier, Vol. 1, pp. 641–692.

- deservingness reasons for workers e.g., in specifically sensitive (public) sectors (such as police, customs or army)[93] and/or with increased safety risks (e.g. Germany and Austria),
- solidarity and additional hardship reasons as to compensate for health deficiencies not necessarily related to work injuries (e.g. in Croatia for blind workers, workers with multiple sclerosis, etc.).[94]

All in all, the recognition of hazardous or arduous work in retirement schemes can have many reasons. Not all of them are linked to the historical reason of health and life expectancy. These different narratives give rise to three issues.

First of all, this mixture of narratives often leads to the—at least legally—sensitive issue of defining the qualification criteria of hazardous or arduous work. Our comparative analysis shows that there is no clear-cut definition to be found in any of the countries.[95] The arduousness and the hazardousness can be linked to:

- Physically demanding work and straining circumstances in which the work is being performed (e.g. factors like hot, cold or noisy working conditions, chemical exposure etc.)
- Burdensome work organisation and organisational factors such as modality in which the work is being performed (e.g. shift work or night work),
- Increased safety risks in a variety of unsafe situations (e.g. soldiers, firefighters or policemen). Such work requires workers to risk their lives to protect the public in armed confrontations, pursuits, riots, raids, accidents, fires, rescue operations and so on.
- Mental or emotional strain due to long working hours, working with traumatised people due to abuse, addiction, mental illness and the like. Long-term psychological effects such as PTSD or burnout can be caused by this.

These different qualifications lead to questions about weighing these different elements and then combining them with the preferential treatment. Legally these qualifications are often discussions on equality and discrimination.

Secondly, the link between hazardous or arduous occupations and the premature erosion of working ability, bad health and lower life expectancy is not always straightforward, as it may depend on the nature of the job, its actual content, working conditions and the duration of exposure to such jobs.[96] In order to have an equitable

[93] Van Oorschot, W. (2000). "Who should get what, and why? On deservingness criteria and the conditionality of solidarity among the public". *Policy & Politics*, 28, 33–48.

[94] Similarly: Vukorepa I. (2017). "Retirement Policy Changes for Workers in Arduous and Hazardous Jobs: Comparative Overview and Lessons for Croatia". *Zbornik Pravnog fakulteta u Zagrebu*, 67 (1), 5–28 (https://hrcak.srce.hr/176827), p. 9.

[95] Vukorepa I. (2017). "Retirement Policy Changes for Workers in Arduous and Hazardous Jobs: Comparative Overview and Lessons for Croatia". *Zbornik Pravnog fakulteta u Zagrebu*, 67 (1), 5–28 (https://hrcak.srce.hr/176827), pp. 8–9.

[96] Vukorepa I. (2017). "Retirement Policy Changes for Workers in Arduous and Hazardous Jobs: Comparative Overview and Lessons for Croatia". *Zbornik Pravnog fakulteta u Zagrebu*, 67 (1), 5–28 (https://hrcak.srce.hr/176827), p. 10.

instrument of measuring all parameters, the law requires an intricate matrix of conditions and provisions defining the exact criteria. It goes without saying that this also gives rise to discussions on equal treatment and discrimination.

Thirdly, even if such a fine-grained matrix is developed, it might be quickly out-dated. The scope of arduousness and hazardousness changes over time due to technological advancements and development of health and safety measures. From a legal perspective, this also can lead to questions on equal treatment and discrimination. After all, some jobs are catalogued as arduous or hazardous at a certain moment, while others are not. Furthermore, society changes and other jobs occur with perhaps tougher working conditions without formal recognition of the arduousness and hazardousness of the job.

6.2 *Preferential Approaches*

Within the statutory pension systems in this study, we can differentiate between three groups of countries:

- with no special treatment such as the UK, Belgium,[97] the Netherlands,[98] and Switzerland,
- with more favourable pension rules for persons in arduous and hazardous jobs (Austria, Croatia, Finland) and
- with limited rules just for one profession (Germany just for miners).

Closely related to this is also their normative approach: there are countries that have adopted respective legislation within state mandatory schemes (e.g. Austria, Croatia, Finland) while other countries leave it to social partners in collective agreements (e.g. Switzerland) and private occupational schemes (e.g. UK).

While some countries list harsh and arduous jobs and occupations either in their national legislation (e.g. Croatia) or collective agreements (e.g. Switzerland), other

---

[97] Some civil servants have some kind preferential treatment whereby they can retire earlier. The professions of these civil servants are often (historically) linked to arduous and hazardous jobs, but they are not legally qualified as being hazardous or arduous jobs. Its more seen as a generally known rationale that for example policemen can retire earlier because of the unsafe job. However, it is not that these known rationales for these civil servants aren't questioned.

[98] The Netherlands do not have a specific system in place for arduous and hazardous jobs but there are two mechanisms worth mentioning: the "RVU" (Regeling Vervroegde Uittreding) and "verlofsparen". Both are mechanisms designed to give employees more flexibility regarding their work and retirement. "RVU" is an arrangement allowing the employee employees to stop working before they reach the official retirement age and "verlofsparen" (leave savings) allows employees to save up leave days over a long period. This latter system helps employees to accumulate a significant amount of paid leave, which they can use for various purposes, including early retirement or sabbaticals. (see country report of The Netherlands)

countries mostly apply quantitative and qualitative criteria to measure arduous conditions related to various factors such as heaviness, energy expenditure, temperature, and pressure exposure (e.g. Austria and Finland).

From an administrative perspective, to establish whether the requirements are met is rather demanding. For example, it is not easy to validate the calorie consumption in the case of heavy labour. This is probably the reason, why nevertheless some kinds of lists with certain professions do exist, where the fulfilment of preconditions is at least assumed in the first place (e.g. Finland[99] and Austria[100]).

The preferential treatment takes two forms. First there is the right an earlier retirement than at the normal or reference retirement age. In Austria,[101] Croatia,[102] Finland[103] this is for example the case. Secondly there can be a more advantageous pension accrual rates (e.g. in Croatia in the form of insurance period counted with extended duration that affects also pension benefit) or smaller deductions (Austria, 1.8% a year to a maximum of 9%). In Switzerland collective agreements can also provide, as in the Swiss construction industry, for a temporary bridging retirement pension until the AVS reference retirement age.

By and large, it can be debated if the more generous pension approach towards hazardous or arduous occupations is legally justifiable for some jobs. No wonder that some countries have adopted different policy approaches to this legally tricky and disputable area of pension rights for hazardous and arduous jobs.[104] After all, health and mortality risk problems related to arduous and hazardous jobs can be dealt with through various social security and labour market policy pathways. An example is the promotion of workability and employability of persons in hazardous or arduous occupations by job counselling or by engaging those persons in other similar jobs (the ballet dancer becoming a dance teacher or the police(wo)man working

---

[99] In Finland there are no official lists.

[100] For Austria, the lists can be found at the website of the Pensionsversicherung and accessed via link. www.pv.at/web/pension/pensionsarten/schwerarbeitspension (accessed 18 June 2025).

[101] With age 60 as lowest.

[102] In Croatia the retirement age decrease depends on the years worked in hazardous jobs and arduous occupations, as well as on the degree of insurance period extension for each of these occupations. Hence, the pension age for persons in arduous and hazardous jobs is in Croatia reduced as follows: (1) by one year for every six years of work in jobs or professions in which the insurance period of 12 months is counted as 14 months, (2) by one year for every five years of work in jobs or occupations in which the insurance period of 12 months is counted as 15 months, (3) by one year for every four years of work in jobs or professions in which the insurance period of 12 months is counted as 16 months, and (4) by one year for every three years of work in jobs or professions in which the insurance period of 12 months is counted as 18 months.

[103] In Finland, the earnings-related schemes include an early retirement regime for persons who have worked in arduous jobs. Currently, a person has a right to the 'years-of-service pension' (työuraeläke) at the age of 63 if: (1) they have done mentally or physically strenuous and consuming work for at least 38 years, (2) their ability to work is permanently reduced but they are not eligible for work disability pension, (3) they are born in 1955 or later.

[104] This has also been pointed out by the OECD (OECD, *Pensions at a Glance 2023: OECD and G20 Indicators*, OECD Publishing, Paris, Chap. 2, p. 97).

as security desk officer).[105] But also the instalment of disability benefits, sickness benefits, special benefits related to accidents at work or occupational diseases.[106]

7 Retirement Regimes Based on Means or Income Testing

Apart from statutory and occupational pensions, it is rather common in modern welfare states to have certain forms of poverty alleviation amongst the elderly. This is often combined with certain forms of means or income testing.[107] The focus of the study is on retirement age in combination with work. In this section the narratives of means or income tested benefits are looked at in combination with the narratives for the "normal" or reference retirement age. Obviously, the combination of work and a pension that is aimed at poverty alleviation taps into a totally different spectrum. Precisely because there is either an income test or a wealth test, income generated by work is going to have a direct impact on the amount of the benefit.

7.1 Overall Narratives for Retirement Regimes Based on Means or Income Testing

The general goal of means or income tested benefits is clear: to provide financial support to those who do not have sufficient income or assets to support themselves in retirement. This helps to reduce poverty among the elderly, ensuring they have a basic standard of living. These types of retirement schemes are often part of the so-called social assistance and hence also means or income tested. They can be found in all of the countries involved in the study in this book.

There are several intertwined different narratives behind means or income tested benefits for the elderly to be found in the countries in this study.

---

[105] Vukorepa I. (2017). "Retirement Policy Changes for Workers in Arduous and Hazardous Jobs: Comparative Overview and Lessons for Croatia". *Zbornik Pravnog fakulteta u Zagrebu*, 67 (1), 5–28 (https://hrcak.srce.hr/176827), p. 14; Natali, D., Spasova, S. and Vanhercke, B. (2016), "Retirement regimes for workers in arduous or hazardous jobs. A study of national policies", European Social Protection Network (ESPN), Brussels, European Commission, pp. 17–20. For more detailed national reports see country thematic reports on retirement regimes for workers in arduous or hazardous jobs (2016) (Website of the European Commission: Analytical support and exchange of information in social protection and inclusion - Country Reports, http://ec.europa.eu/social/main.jsp?catId=1135&intPageId=3589).

[106] Vukorepa I. (2017). "Retirement Policy Changes for Workers in Arduous and Hazardous Jobs: Comparative Overview and Lessons for Croatia". *Zbornik Pravnog fakulteta u Zagrebu*, 67 (1), 5–28 (https://hrcak.srce.hr/176827), p. 13.

[107] Börsch-Supan, A., Härtl,K. and Leite, D. (2018). "Earnings test, non-actuarial adjustments and flexible retirement". *Economics Letters* 173, 78–83.

- The first and most common one is that the limited public resources are allocated efficiently. By focusing on individuals who need it the most, means or income tested pensions ensure that efficient allocation of resources. In other words: targeting helps to maximize the impact of welfare programs on the most vulnerable groups of populations. This narrative is based on a budgetary rather than a legal reasoning.
- Another narrative is that of addressing income inequality and having an equitable society. Means or income tested benefits are thus seen as redistributing wealth from the more affluent members of society to those in need. This can help to address income inequality and provide a safety net for those who have had lower lifetime earnings. This is clearly legal because it deals with the question on coverage. Who should, is or can be covered and are there equality issues?
- Another approach is that of a means or income tested approach discouraging overdependence on state support. In this kind of a narrative, it is reasonable to provide benefits only to those who truly need them. This is then believed to motivate people to remain in the workforce longer or to save more during their working years. There is often also a legal narrative linked to this approach in the sense that abuse of the support is penally or fiscally sanctioned. Often, a set of rules on inspection and scrutiny of people is at hand.

All these narratives can be countered though. After all, public resources are at all times limited and thus a lot depends on the so-called poverty ceilings used within these schemes. With a very low ceiling, the poverty alleviation will be higher and vice versa. Furthermore, from a welfare point of view it is well established that most programs for the poor end up in being inadequate programs if the budget allocations are too low.[108] And above all, the overdependence on state support should not be presented as a choice for people. People in poverty often lead their lives without having the possibility to save more or to remain longer in the workforce. That is exactly the reason why they are in poverty.

7.2 *Means or Income Tested Retirement Regimes*

Poverty alleviation amongst the elderly can be done in several ways. In the UK there is no separate means tested pension, the current state pension is paid at a flat rate basis,[109] although there is an option for those who fall below a set threshold to apply for an increase to their pension up to a set amount, but that increase is termed a pension credit rather than a separate means tested pension. Austria and Finland have some kind of income testing, while Germany has for example some form of means testing. Switzerland, the Netherlands and Belgium have a mixed system: both income

[108] M. Friedman (1966), "The Case for the Negative Income Tax: A View from the Right". In *Proceedings of the National Symposium on Guaranteed Income*, pp. 49–55.

[109] People who retired under the previous regime may be entitled to an earnings related state pension as well as a basic state pension, see Country Report for further details.

and means tested. In Croatia poverty alleviation is targeted within the mandatory PAYGO DB scheme (first pillar) through so called minimum pension that is neither means tested nor income-tested. Outside the pension system there is special social assistance measure for persons over 65 with no right to pension benefit (national allowance for elderly) that is income tested. Means testing goes a lot further than the income testing because other assets such as housing or bank accounts can be taken into account under certain conditions and with clearly defined ceilings. While the income testing relates more to the incoming revenue at a certain moment in time.

7.3 *The Link Between the Entitlement to Means or Income-Tested Benefits and the Retirement Age of the General Scheme*

From a legal and structural point of view, it is interesting to see how countries have linked the means or income tested benefit to the general retirement scheme regarding the age at which the benefit can be received.

The countries included in this study have adopted different policies for the situation in which the pension or total income of a pensioner remains so low that it does not meet the social minimum of the respective country. In Finland, pensioners whose earnings-related pension income remains low, are entitled to a statutory minimum pension (national pension and/or guarantee pension).[110] In Belgium and in the Netherlands, there are statutory means-tested social assistance type of benefits for pensioners. In both countries a person can end up receiving a combination of some kind of minimum pension and a means or income-tested benefit for the elderly until a certain ceiling. In Croatia, a pensioner may be entitled to an income-tested social assistance benefit for the elderly if they don't have right to any pension.

Apart from the UK, all countries in this study have a direct or indirect link with the so-called normal retirement age or with the receipt of a certain pension amount. In Austria, Switzerland, the Netherlands and Belgium the benefit received can be seen as a kind of supplement to the pension received. Hence there is a direct link with the requirement of receiving a pension. The link being that you cannot receive the benefit if you are not entitled to some kind of pension form. Only in the UK such a link is absent. In all other countries the schemes are connected either through the age requirement or the need to be a pensioner. If the latter is the case, usually, minimal previous contributory period to the statutory pension scheme are required. The latter is the case for Switzerland (at least 11 months AVS insurance).

The linking of the retirement age or pension receipt with receiving an income or means tested retirement benefit already indicates the strong link with the pension system in general. That leads to the conclusion that all in all, the narratives for means or income-tested benefits are the same as with the "normal" or reference pensionable

[110] In Finland, pensioners whose total pension income remains low may also be entitled to the general means-tested income support.

age. All in all, we discern five main legal narratives in the countries examined besides the obvious poverty alleviation: stable economic turnover, sustainability, leisure after work, equal treatment and upholding the social contract. In general, one could state that in principle persons who have reached the "normal" or reference retirement age of the statutory old age pension scheme can apply for a means or income-tested benefit because of one or more of these five reasons.

8 Taxation

Statutory pension and occupational pension schemes must not be seen apart from their tax regimes. There is no uniform EU approach on how to tax pensions, as taxation remains the sovereignty of the member states. Therefore, different tax regimes can be distinguished between and even within counties.

8.1 Taxation at Normal Retirement Age

With regard to tax, a different approach is taken compared to social law. In all countries, statutory pensions are taxed. From a legal perspective, a tax can be considered to be a financial charge or levy imposed by the government on the taxpayer without receiving a direct individual benefit from that government. Taxes are meant to support the government's functioning and to provide funding for public and (agreed) national needs.[111] In other words, one of the functions of taxation is the financial support of the government so individuals can use the national public services. Therefore, it might seem reasonable not to exempt statutory pensions from taxation in general but to treat them—at least from a tax perspective—similarly to wages, which is the case in, for example, Austria, Belgium, the Netherlands, the UK, Croatia, Finland, and Switzerland. After all, pensioners also use national public services.

Occupational pensions are often treated more favourably as special rules apply for the contributions paid and/or the benefits. The premiums/taxes in the accumulation phase of the occupational pension are in many countries not (fully) subjected to social security contributions or tax (Austria, Belgium, Croatia, Finland, Germany, the Netherlands, Switzerland, United Kingdom). As soon as occupational pensions are paid out, some countries, such as Belgium and Switzerland, apply specific rules compared to the general tax scheme. Other countries differentiate between lump-sum benefits and periodic payments (e.g. the United Kingdom and Switzerland). In Austria and Germany, occupational pensions are subject to income tax (as statutory pensions).

[111] Lymer, A., "Tax and social policy landscape". In Lymer, A., May, M., Sinfield, A., *Taxation and social policy*, Bristol University Press, Bristol, 2023, 23–24; also interesting with regard to social-goods allocation: Musgrave, R.A. and P.B. Musgrave, P.B (1989). *Public Finance in Theory and Practice* (fifth ed.). New York: McGraw-Hill, 59–60.

However, in Austria the employees own contributions are partially tax-privileged when paid out.

A more favourable tax regime for occupational pensions can encourage people to save for their retirement in addition to the statutory pension. This is based on the nudging principle familiar from behavioural economics: one is not obliged to save for their retirement, but the government installs some incentives to encourage the behaviour they consider to be 'good'.[112] At first sight, it seems logical to state that such an encouragement only makes sense if participation in the pension scheme is voluntary or one can opt-out. After all, why encourage participation in an occupational pension scheme if participation is already mandatory? Nevertheless, this view might be too simple. Let's give an example with occupational pensions for employees as the central theme. Making participation mandatory for employees, doesn't automatically imply that the employer is obliged to offer an occupational pension scheme. In Belgium, e.g. the decision of whether or not to offer an occupational pension scheme is given to the social partners (collective level) and/or employer (individual level). If the government doesn't oblige employers to offer their employees an occupational pension scheme, tax benefits such as tax deductions may convince employers/ social partners to offer such a pension scheme.[113] After all, employers are interested in reducing wage costs and offering competitive compensation packages. But even if employers are obliged to offer a pension scheme, and employees are obliged to participate, tax measures can still be relevant to 'justify' the mandatory system, in other words: to make the obligation to participate 'more acceptable for those to whom it applies'.

However, the effect of tax measures does not always necessarily align with the underlying policy intentions and/or can be affected by other (non-)tax measures, such as tax ceilings, indexation regimes, matching contributions, competing saving mechanisms, etc. Such measures can strengthen or weaken the effect of the tax measures taken. Whether saving in an occupational pension scheme is encouraged, depends on multiple factors. Tax measures can be a (in)direct incentive intended (or even unintended) by policymakers. Also, treating occupational pensions more favourably doesn't automatically imply that people's overall savings will increase. The impact of tax measures can also be a shift in savings rather than an increase.[114]

---

[112] For more on the nudging principle, see: Thaler, R.H. and Sunstein, C.R. (2008), *Nudge: Improving decisions about health, wealth and happiness*, Yale University Press, New Haven, 293 p.

[113] E.S. van Aggelen (2022), *Het personeel toepassingsgebied van aanvullende pensioenregelingen voor werknemers. Een rechtsvergelijkend en empirisch onderzoek naar de werking van aansluitingsregels*, Brugge, Die Keure, 164–165.

[114] E.S. van Aggelen (2022), *Het personeel toepassingsgebied van aanvullende pensioenregelingen voor werknemers. Een rechtsvergelijkend en empirisch onderzoek naar de werking van aansluitingsregels*, Brugge, Die Keure, 165–166; see also: Chetty, R., Friedman, J. N., Leth-Petersen, S., Nielsen, T. H., and Olsen, T. (2014). "Active vs. Passive Decisions and Crowd-Out in Retirement Savings Accounts: Evidence from Denmark". *Quarterly Journal of Economics,* 129(3), 1141–1220; see also: OECD (2018), "Financial Incentives and Retirement Savings", OECD Publishing, Paris, 296p.

8.2 *Taxation to Encourage Early Retirement or Discourage Deferred/Partial Retirement*

Taxation of statutory pensions might seem to offer opportunities to discourage early retirement -or encouraging deferred or partial retirement. After all, a tax increase may be a burden when opting for early retirement and/or encourage people to stay (partially) active on the labour market. The absence of tax measures encouraging or discouraging individuals from making certain retirement decisions brings with it a fundamental question. Is there an underlying rationale for this absence? There might not always be a clear answer to this question. After all, the reasons for not taking certain actions are not always clearly defined. Nevertheless, it is an open question that one can think about and reflect on. In some countries, such as the Netherlands and the UK, early retirement is not allowed in the statutory pension scheme, and partial retirement is only permitted in occupational pension schemes. Consequently, the question is less relevant or even irrelevant. The same can be said about Croatia, as there are no special taxation rules for early retirement. All countries involved in this study that allow early retirement do not use taxation as a measure. Switzerland, Germany, Austria, and Finland have installed a malus on annuity benefits to discourage early retirement. Belgium is the only country allowing early retirement without a malus. Nevertheless, the malus has been raised as a possible new measure to discourage early retirement in statutory pensions.[115] Furthermore, most of these countries—except for Belgium and Austria—allow partial retirement and even the combination of partial retirement with deferred retirement. Setting the framework and requirements for early retirement seems to remain a topic that governments prefer to tackle through social law instead of tax law. In other words, governments seem reluctant to interfere with social policy decisions regarding early retirement through tax measures. The countries studied opt for social law measures, such as bonus/malus combined with partial and/or deferred retirement.

With regard to occupational pensions, some countries, such as Croatia, Switzerland, Austria and Germany, do not distinguish between the tax treatment of pensions paid out at normal retirement age, early retirement age or deferred retirement. In Switzerland, it is also possible to pay tax-exempt personal contributions to an early retirement account.[116] However, in contrast to statutory pensions, some countries use taxation to discourage early retirement. We found such tax disincentives in the following countries:

- Belgium: higher tax rate (increase of 6,5%)
- UK: tax penalties if certain thresholds are breached
- Finland: age limits for drawing out the pension benefits in a tax-friendly way.

---

[115] Federal coalition agreement 2025–2029 www.belgium.be/nl/publicaties/regeerakkoord_van_de_federale_regering_bart_de_wever (accessed 30 May 2025).

[116] Art. 79b § 1 Loi sur la prévoyance professionnelle vieillesse, survivants et invalidité (LPP), art. 1b Ordonnance sur la prévoyance professionnelle vieillesse, survivants et invalidité (OPP2).

8.3 *Interconnectivity Between Statutory and Occupational Pensions from a Tax Perspective*

Statutory and occupational pension schemes allow individuals to save for retirement through different pension forms. From a tax perspective, these pension types can be treated completely separate from each other, meaning that there is no connection/link between the tax framework of both pension types. In other words: different pension types receive different tax treatment. In Finland, for example, from a tax perspective, the different pension forms are not, at least not directly, interconnected.

Interestingly, in some countries, elements of interconnectivity between the statutory pension and the occupational pension can be found. In Belgium, e.g., there is a shift towards the incorporation of statutory and occupational pensions in the same legal framework. In this country, various elements of the statutory pension schemes and the occupational pension schemes are fiscally interconnected. The first element is the fiscal contribution limit to occupational pensions. The contributions paid to occupational pensions cannot exceed a certain ceiling. This ceiling is calculated as follows: the contributions to an occupational pension cannot lead to an amount whereby the occupational pension, together with the statutory pension, exceeds 80% of the last earned wage. This means that the contributions to occupational pensions are always linked to the level of statutory pensions. The reason behind it is clear: the fiscally advantageous nature of the contributions paid into occupational pensions. The second element includes two different levies: the solidarity levy and the levy special for the healthcare sector. The solidarity levy amounts to a maximum of two percent of the pension income, including statutory and occupational pensions. The special levy for the healthcare sector is equal to 3.55% of the total pension income, also consisting of statutory and occupational pension schemes.[117] The third element is the bonuses for those who work longer. There will be no bonus if the total pension amount, including statutory and occupational pensions, goes above a certain ceiling.[118]

In the Netherlands, there is a shift towards the incorporation of occupational and individual pension schemes in the same legal framework. With the Dutch pension reform the tax treatment of individual pension accrual will be largely aligned with the tax treatment of occupational pension accrual. The connection between statutory and occupational pension schemes, is not based on a strive towards a similar legal framework. A part of income is expected to be covered by the state pension (i.e. the franchise). There are no occupational or individual pension rights accumulated in relation to this franchise.

[117] Stevens, Y. (2025), "Deel IX. Pensioenen'. In Put, J., Verdeyen, V., Stevens, Y, *Praktijkboek sociale zekerheid. Voor de onderneming en de sociale adviseur*, Wolters Kluwer, Mechelen, 676–679, pp. 736–738; Stevens, Y. (2025), "Deel VI. Pensioenen'. In Put, J., Verdeyen, V., Stevens, Y, *Praktijkboek sociale zekerheid. Voor de onderneming en de sociale adviseur*, Wolters Kluwer, Mechelen, p. 850 and pp. 875–877.

[118] Stevens, Y. (2025), "Deel IX. Pensioenen'. In Put, J., Verdeyen, V., Stevens, Y, *Praktijkboek sociale zekerheid. Voor de onderneming en de sociale adviseur*, Wolters Kluwer, Mechelen, 627–739.

In Switzerland the connection between the statutory pension and the occupational pension is not legal in nature. There is, however, a strong political link. Tax-exempt retirement savings contributions on gainful income are allowed up to up to 25% of the annual taxable income ceiling of CHF 907′200. The law also provides for a very high level of tax-exempted additional voluntary contributions (AVC) allowing a benefits buy-back up to the amount of the regulatory benefits. The possible AVC can be calculated on the basis of the current insured income with up to 25% savings contributions that would have been paid since age 18. *De facto,* this represents a defined benefit last income approach. The calculated AVC is entirely deductible from the ongoing yearly taxable income. AVC's are also allowed to finance, under certain limits, a supplementary early retirement option. Benefits resulting from an AVC buy-back may not be paid out in the form of a lump sum by the pension schemes before three years have elapsed, this limit was introduced to address the favourable taxation of such lump-sums. High contributory income ceilings and AVC's in occupational pensions are very potent tax optimisation measures or, critically, tax subsidies favouring higher incomes, which however politically compensate for the very high level of income solidarity in AVS due to the absence of any ceiling on the contributory gainful income.

In Austria, all pensions, no matter if statutory or occupational, are subject to the same income or wage tax regulations when paid out and therefore treated equally to a large extent. Statutory and occupational pensions are even taxed together by law (joint taxation). The wage tax is to be deducted from the highest benefit by the institution who pays out the highest benefit (mostly statutory pension insurance institutions) for all statutory and occupational benefits. Employees own contributions are also treated (favourably) in the same way, with being tax exempt up to 100%.

References

Legislation

Algemene Ouderdomswet (National Old Age Pensions Act)

Act on the flexibilisation of the transition from working life to retirement and to strengthen prevention and rehabilitation in working life ("Flexible Pensions Act") from 8 december 2016

Directive 2008/94/EC of the European Parliament and of the Council of 22 October 2008 on the protection of employees in the event of the insolvency of their employer

German Social Code

Loi sur la prévoyance professionnelle vieillesse, survivants et invalidité (LPP)

Ordonnance sur la prévoyance professionnelle vieillesse, survivants et invalidité (OPP2)

Case Law

European Court of Justice, 25 January 2007, Robins e.a., C-278/05
European Court of Justice, 25 April 2013, Hogan e.a., C-398/11
European Court of Justice, 24 November 2016, Webb-Sämann, C-454/15
European Court of Justice, 6 September 2018, Hampshire, C-17/17
European Court of Justice, 19 December 2019, Günther Bauer, C-168/18

Literature

Anderson A, Markussen S, Roed K (2021) Pension reform and the efficiency equity tradeoff: impacts of removing the early retirement subsidy. Labour Econ 72:102050
Autor DH (2015) Why are there still so many jobs? The history and future of workplace automation. J Econ Perspect 29(3):3–30
Barr N, Diamond P (2008) Reforming pensions: principles and policy choices. Oxford University Press, Oxford, p 352p
Böckerman P, Skedinger P, Uusitalo R (2018) Seniority rules, worker mobility and wages: evidence from multi-country linked employer-employee data. Labour Econ 51:48–62. https://doi.org/10.1016/j.labeco.2017.11.006
Börsch-Supan A, Härtl K, Leite D (2018) Earnings test, non-actuarial adjustments and flexible retirement. Econ Lett 173:78–83
Clark RL, Mitchell OS (2005) The changing retirement paradigm. In: Clark RL, Mitchell OS (eds) Reinventing the retirement paradigm. Oxford University Press, 18p
Chetty R, Friedman JN, Leth-Petersen S, Nielsen TH, Olsen T (2014) Active vs. passive decisions and crowd-out in retirement savings accounts: evidence from Denmark. Q J Econ 129(3):1141–1220
D'Agostino F (2024) Contemporary approaches to the social contract. *The Stanford Encyclopedia of Philosophy* (online article). https://plato.stanford.edu/archives/spr2024/entries/contractarianism-contemporary/
Deroose M, Melyn W, Stinglhamber P, Van Parys S (2023) "Is public spending on pensions in Belgium sustainable? A comparison with other euro area countries". *NBB*. Econ Rev:30p
Dolls M, Krolage C (2023) Earned, not given? The effect of lowering the full retirement age on retirement decisions. J Public Econ 223:104909. https://doi.org/10.1016/j.jpubeco.2023.104909
Ebbinghaus, B. (2006), Reforming early retirement in Europe, Japan and the USA, Oxford University Press, Oxford, 352 pg. ISBN: 978–0–19–928611-9
Engels B, Geyer J, Haan P (2017) Pension incentives and early retirement. Labour Econ 47:216–231
French E, Jones JB (2017) Health, health insurance and retirement: a survey. Annual Review of Economics 9:383–409. https://doi.org/10.1146/annurev-economics-063016-103616
Friedman M (1966) The case for the negative income tax: a view from the right. Proceedings of the National Symposium on Guaranteed Income:49–55
Gierusz A, Kowalczyk-Rólczyńska P, Pobłocka A, Rutecka-Góra J (2022) Changes in approach to risk sharing in supplementary pension schemes. In: Kolaczkowski J, Maher M, Stevens Y, Werbrouck JM (eds) The evolution of supplementary pensions. Edward Elgar, pp 410–438
Hakola T, Uusitalo R (2005) Not so voluntary retirement decisions? Evidence from a pension reform. J Public Econ 89:2121–2136
Hess M (2017) Rising preferred retirement age in Europe: are Europe's future pensioners adapting to pension system reforms? J Aging Soc Policy 29(3):245–261. https://doi.org/10.1080/08959420.2016.1255082
Hofäcker D (2015) In line or at odds with active ageing policies? Exploring patterns of retirement preferences in Europe. Ageing & Society 15:1529–1556

Kosonen H, Keskinen K, Nikander P, Lumme-Sandt K (2000) Employment exits near retirement age: an agency-analysis. Nord J Work Life Stud 11(1):63–83

Lymer A (2023) Tax and social policy landscape. In: Lymer A, May M, Sinfield A (eds) Taxation and social policy. Bristol, Bristol University Press, pp 23–45

Mastrobuoni G (2009) Labor supply effects of the recent social security benefit cuts: empirical estimates using cohort discontinuities. J Public Econ 93(11–12):1224–1233

Musgrave, R.A. and P.B. Musgrave, P. B (1989). Public finance in theory and practice (5th ed.). New York: McGraw-Hill, 627p

Neumark D, Burn I, Button P (2019) Is it harder for older workers to find jobs? New and improved evidence from a field experiment. J Polit Econ 127(2). https://doi.org/10.1086/701029

Noordam, F. (1998), "Sociale verzekeringen 1890-1950" in J. van Gerwen en M. van Leeuwen (ed.), *Studies over zekerheidsarrangementen*, Nederlands Economisch Historisch Archief, Amsterdam/Den Haag, 570–604 (in Dutch)

O'Higgins N (2017) Rising to the youth employment challenge: new evidence on key policy issues. International Labour Organization, Geneva. https://www.ilo.org/publications/major-publications/rising-youth-employment-challenge-new-evidence-key-policy-issues

Pestieau P, Racionero M (2016) Harsh occupations, health status and social security. J Econ 117:239–257

Rabaté S (2019) Can I stay or should I go? Mandatory retirement and the labor-force participation of older workers. J Public Econ 180:104078. https://doi.org/10.1016/j.jpubeco.2019.104078

Reeskens T, Van Oorschot W (2013) Equity, equality, or need? A study of popular preferences for welfare redistribution principles across 24 European countries. J Eur Publ Policy 20:1174–1195

Rodrik, D. (1997), "Has Globalization Gone Too Far?". *Washington, DC: Peterson Institute for International Economics* (also known as the Institute for International Economics), 128 pages, ISBN 0–88132-2415

Rosen S (1986) The theory of equalizing differences. In: Ashenfelter OC, Layard R (eds) *Handbook of labor economics*, Elsevier, vol 1, pp 641–692

Wu C, Odden MC, Fisher GG, Stawski RS (2016) Association of retirement age with mortality: a population-based longitudinal study among older adults in the USA. J Epidemiol Community Health 70(9):917–923. https://doi.org/10.1136/jech-2015-207097

Staubli S, Zweimuller J (2013) Does raising the early retirement age increase employment among older worker? J Public Econ 108:17–32. https://doi.org/10.1016/j.jpubeco.2013.09.003

Stevens, Y. (2002), *Equality and solidarity in occupational pensions for employees: from remuneration to social protection* (in Dutch), PhD, Faculty of Law, Leuven, 588 p. + 56 p. appendix

Stevens Y (2019) The role of the government in creating or enhancing the access to funded or unfunded pensions in the modern welfare state. In: Da Costa Cabral N, Cuncha Rodrigues N (eds) The future of pension plans in the EU internal market. Springer International Publishing, Cham, pp 55–74

Stevens, Y (2022a), "On the origin of pensions". In Kolaczkowski, J, Maher, M. J., Werbrouck, J. and Stevens, Y. (eds)., In *the evolution of supplementary pensions: 25 years of pension reform*, London, Edward Elgar Publishing, 10–36

Stevens Y (2022b) EU pension law, vol 2022. Edward Elgar Publishing, London, p 308

Stevens Y (2025a) Deel IX. Pensioenen. In: In Put J, Verdeyen V, Stevens Y (eds) Praktijkboek sociale zekerheid. Voor de onderneming en de sociale adviseur. Wolters Kluwer, Mechelen, pp 627–739

Stevens Y (2025b) Deel VI. Pensioenen. In: In Put J, Verdeyen V, Stevens Y (eds) Praktijkboek sociale zekerheid. Voor de onderneming en de sociale adviseur. Wolters Kluwer, Mechelen, pp 827–883

Thaler RH, Sunstein CR (2008) Nudge: improving decisions about health, wealth and happiness. Yale University Press, New Haven, p 293 van Aggelen ES (2022) Het personeel toepassingsgebied van aanvullende pensioenregelingen voor werknemers. Een rechtsvergelijkend en empirisch onderzoek naar de werking van aansluitingsregels, Brugge, Die Keure, p 341p

van der Valk, L (1998), "Overheid en de ontwikkeling van het verzekeringswezen 1500-1815". In van Gerwen, J., van Leeuwen, M. (ed.), *Studies over zekerheidsarrangementen*, Nederlands Economisch Historisch Archief, Amsterdam/Den Haag, 23–48

Van Langendonck J, Jorens Y, Louckx F (2023) *Handboek socialezekerheidsrecht* (11de editie). Intersentia, Brussel, p 685p

Van Oorschot W (2000) Who should get what, and why? On deservingness criteria and the conditionality of solidarity among the public. Policy Polit 28:33–48

Van Solinge H, Henkens K (2009) Living longer, working longer? The impact of subjective life expectancy on retirement intentions and behaviour. Eur J Pub Health:47–51

Vermeer N (2016) Age anchors and the expected retirement age: an experimental study. De Economist 164:255–279. https://doi.org/10.1007/s10645-016-9276-1

Vermeer N, Mastrogiacomo M, Van Soest A (2016) Demanding occupations and the retirement age. Labour Econ 43:159–170

Vukorepa I (2017) Retirement policy changes for Workers in Arduous and Hazardous Jobs: comparative overview and lessons for Croatia. Zbornik Pravnog fakulteta u Zagrebu 67(1):5–28. https://hrcak.srce.hr/176827

Weaver RK (2016) Privileging policy change? Sustaining automatic stabilizing mechanisms in public pensions. Soc Policy Adm 50(2):148–164

Werbrouck, J.M., Het multidimensionale pensioenbegrip, Boom Juridisch Antwerpen, 2022, 514p (in Dutch)

Werding, M. (2011), "Incentive effects of public pension schemes". In Meszaros, J. (ed.), Life-cycles and pension systems, Progress, Budapest, 2011, 71–80

Whitehouse, E., D'Addio, A., Chomik, R. and Reilly, A. (2009), "Two decades of pension reform: what has been achieved and what remains to be done?". *The Geneva Papers on Risk and Insurance–Issues and Practice*, 34, 515–535

Woss J (2011) The impact of labour markets on economic dependency ratios. In: Meszaros J (ed) Lif*e-cycles and pension systems*. Progress, Budapest, pp 63–70

Zwick T, Bruns M, Geyer G, Lorenz S (2022) Early retirement of employees in demanding jobs: evidence from a German pension reform. Journal of the economics of ageing 22:100387. https://doi.org/10.1016/j.jeoa.2022.100387

Reports

Borsch-Supan A (1998) Incentive effects of social security on labor force participation: evidence in Germany and across Europe. NBER Working Paper 6780. https://doi.org/10.3386/w6780

Butler, M., Huguenin, O., Teppa, F. (2004), "What Triggers Early Retirement? Results from Swiss Pension Funds", Center for research on pensions and welfare policies, Working paper 35/04, April 13, 2004

Dorn D, Sousa-Poza A (2005) Early retirement: free choice or forced decision? CESifo Working Paper Series No 1542

European Social Policy Analysis Network (ESPAN) (2025) Flexible retirement pathways. In: An analysis in 28 European countries. Publications Office of the European Union, 92 p

European Commission (2024a) Directorate-General for Employment, Social Affairs and Inclusion, "long term projections of pension adequacy in a selection of countries: report produced in the context of the 2024 pension adequacy report". Publications Office of the European Union, p 40p

European Commission (2024b) Directorate-General for Employment, Social Affairs and Inclusion, "the 2024 pension adequacy report–current and future income adequacy in old age in the EU", vol I. Publications, Office of the European Union, 195p

International Labour Organization (ILO) (2020), "ILO Thesaurus", Geneva, https://metadata.ilo.org/thesaurus/1848370168.html

International Labour Organization (ILO) (2014) World of work report 2014: developing with jobs, Geneva. https://www.ilo.org/publications/world-work-2014-developing-jobs

Natali D, Spasova S, Vanhercke B (2016) Retirement regimes for workers in arduous or hazardous jobs. A study of national policies. In: European social protection network (ESPN). European Commission, Brussels, p 52p

European Commission (2015) The 2015 ageing report. Economic and budgetary projections for the 28 EU member states 2013-2060. Eur Econ 3:397p

European Commission (2021) The 2021 ageing report. Economic and budgetary projections for the EU member states (2019-2070). Institutional Paper 148:375p

OECD (2006) Ageing and employment policies: live longer, work longer. OECD Publications, Paris, p 146p

OECD (2018) Financial incentives and retirement savings. OECD Publishing, Paris, p 296p

OECD (2019) Pensions at a glance 2019: OECD and G20 indicators. OECD Publishing, Paris, p 224p

OECD (2021) Pensions at a glance 2021: OECD and G20 indicators. OECD Publishing, Paris, p 222p

OECD (2023) Pensions at a glance 2023: OECD and G20 indicators. OECD Publishing, Paris, p 233p

Ponds E, en Webers, E. (2024) Solidarity buffer and solidarity preferences. Netspar Design Paper 238:87p

Zaidi, A. and Whitehouse, E. (2009), "Should pension systems recognise "hazardous and arduous work"?", OECD social, employment and migration working papers, No. 91, OECD Publishing, Paris, 56p

Other

Algemene Rekenkamer, Ouderdomsregeling ontleed, 2019, pp 27–28. https://www.rekenkamer.nl/publicaties/rapporten/2019/11/13/ouderdomsregelingen-ontleed

Federal coalition agreement 2025–2029 www.belgium.be/nl/publicaties/regeerakkoord_van_de_federale_regering_bart_de_wever

Künzler G, Knöpfel C (2002) *Les pauvres vivent moins longtemps. Couche sociale, mortalité et politique de l'âge de la retraite en Suisse,* Lucerne. Caritas Suisse 100p

Message du Conseil fédéral relatif à la stabilisation de l'AVS (AVS21), 28th August 2019, Feuille Fédérale 2019, 5979

Movie: "Historique des retraites en France" (in French) at. https://enseignants.lumni.fr/fiche-media/0000001741/historique-des-retraites-en-france.html

Website of the Pensionsversicherung. www.pv.at/web/pension/pensionsarten/schwerarbeitspension

Website of the European Commission: Analytical support and exchange of information in social protection and inclusion—Country Reports, http://ec.europa.eu/social/main.jsp?catId=1135&intPageId=3589

Pension Law and Labour Market: Key Features of the Narratives

Emma Suzanne van Aggelen

In the chapter 'To retire or to work? That's the question: choice or necessity!?' different perspectives and narratives were examined regarding the legal relationship between pensions and the labour market. But what are typical characteristics of narratives?[1] Three characteristics are notable. First, far from being standalone, the narratives are embedded in the political, cultural and historical context of a country and, therefore, have particular legal effects within it. Second, some narratives obviously transcend multiple themes. Third, narratives interact with each other and, therefore, affect each other (in)directly.

1 Key Features of the Narratives

1.1 Narratives Are Embedded Within a Country's Specific Context

Although narratives can be similar for multiple countries, the legal framework in each of the countries is not. It's, therefore, interesting to see how often rather similar narratives can lead to differences in the concrete regulations when it comes to interactions between pensions and work within each of the countries. Each of the analyzed

[1] In order to investigate the typical charachteristics of the narratives, this chapter is mainly based on the chapter 'To retire or to work? That's the question: choice or necessity!?'. References with regard to particular narratives can be found in that chapter, without always making internal references. This is inspired by optimal readability.

E. S. van Aggelen (✉)
Faculty of Law, UHasselt University, Hasselt, Belgium
e-mail: emmasuzanne.vanaggelen@uhasselt.be

Faculty of Law and Criminology, KU Leuven, Leuven, Belgium

E. S. van Aggelen (ed.), *Retirement and Employment*, Ius Gentium: Comparative Perspectives on Law and Justice 145, https://doi.org/10.1007/978-3-032-33561-6_11

countries has, e.g., different rules on early retirement, partial retirement and deferred retirement. Even though at first sight some countries might be similar when answering the question 'is early, partial and/or deferred retirement allowed', the way the narratives are reflected in concrete legal rules is not. In turn, different legal requirements can lead to variations in for example the degree of freedom.[2]

1.2 Narratives Are Theme-Transcending

Narratives can—and often will—transcend specific themes.

Throughout Europe, pension experts are familiar with challenges regarding economic and financial sustainability. Economic and financial sustainability is clearly a transcending narrative pinpointing several themes simultaneously. For example, it does not only impact the 'normal' retirement age, but may also affect early and/or partial retirement.

Another example of such a theme-transcending narrative is the narrative of leisure after work. This narrative is relevant with regard to, e.g., the normal retirement age, early retirement, deferred retirement and means or income-tested benefits. Also, narratives such as equality, social contract, personal preferences or health are clearly theme-transcending narratives. Health as a narrative, e.g., does not only play an important role when it comes to retirement regimes for hazardous and arduous jobs, but also when talking about early and/or partial retirement.

Transcending themes, however, do not necessarily mean that each of the narratives is of equal importance for or within each of the themes discussed. For example, the narrative of discouraging overdependence on state support is definitely relevant when talking about retirement regimes based on means or income testing, but will be less of influence when talking about the partial retirement. Furthermore, the national contexts define the narratives even if transcending.

Taxation is clearly omni-present but with different effects and policy needs. Taxation of pension contributions and/or pension benefits has an impact on the level of retirement incomes as well as on the (re-)distribution of those incomes. Furthermore, it affects the future development of pension adequacy.[3] Therefore, one could state that pension taxation is connected to most, if not all, of the themes discussed. The same could be said about non-taxation. The choice, whether deliberate or inadvertent, not to tax pension contributions or benefits in a specific situation (such as, e.g., early retirement), affects the future development of pension adequacy as well as level and (re-)distribution of retirement incomes.

---

[2] Chapter 'To retire or to work? That's the question: choice or necessity!?', Sect. 3, 4 and 5.

[3] European Commission (2024), Directorate-General for Employment, Social Affairs and Inclusion, "The 2024 pension adequacy report—Current and future income adequacy in old age in the EU", Volume I, Publications Office of the European Union, 133.

1.3 Interaction Between Narratives

Narratives interact with one another. If, e.g., in a PAYG system the labour market shrinks (low birth rates, aging, emigration and early labour market exit), fewer contributors support more pensioners. Consequently, both sustainability and adequacy can be at risk, particularly if pensioners also tend to live longer. Adequacy is the counterpart of sustainability in many perspectives. Reducing pension benefits might be a good idea for sustainable pensions but then pensions might no longer be adequate and provide decent income. At the same time, this means that although adequacy and sustainability can be seen as counterparts from many perspectives, they remain interconnected. The pursuit of more adequate pensions cannot be separated from the need to ensure (fiscal) sustainability. Neither can it be separated from labour market developments. In many countries pension rules differ between employees and the self-employed. Given the rising number of non-standard forms of employment, the topic of adequate pensions for those in non-standard forms of work has been growing in importance in recent years and is unlikely to lose its importance anytime soon. While the labour market is evolving rapidly, changing pension policy is a process that requires more time, which may in turn bear on sustainability and adequacy.[4]

2 Final Reflection on Changing Narratives

Changing (pension) legislation can reflect changing narratives. At the same time, the existing legal framework can provide boundaries that must be taken into account when implementing new measures that reflect these changing narratives.[5] Shifting narratives can also lead to changes in responsibilities within the pension framework, reflecting a particular socio-economic policy perspective. Pension law can thus serve as an instrument of socio-economic policy, and the way this instrument is applied often reflects a political perspective shaped by demographic and labour market developments. Challenges regarding sustainability and/or adequacy of the pension system can trigger changes in pension law. There are, e.g., several ways of trying to enhance economic sustainability of pension schemes. Creating a more open approach towards work and retirement is one of them. Nowadays in many countries, 'retirement' or 'pension' no longer necessarily implies 'leaving the labour market'. The appropriate measure, however, to deal with a specific problem is always open for political debate. One should not forget that every pension system is embedded in a national cultural history and has known its own country specific evolution. Due to path-dependencies it can be difficult to substantially change the system. Shifting narratives and political

[4] European Commission (2024), Directorate-General for Employment, Social Affairs and Inclusion, "The 2024 pension adequacy report—Current and future income adequacy in old age in the EU", Volume I, Publications Office of the European Union, 3 and 170–177.

[5] Such as, e.g., legislation on equal treatment.

perspectives, therefore, do not often result in rewriting the entire pension system.[6] Measures taken are often, in a certain way, adapted to the existing pension framework.

References

European Commission (2024) Directorate-general for employment, social affairs and inclusion. The 2024 pension adequacy report—Current and future income adequacy in old age in the EU, vol I. Publications Office of the European Union, p 195.

Stevens Y, van Aggelen ES (2021) Pension reform in Belgium. In: Van Popta B, Steenbeek O (eds) Transition to a new pension contract in the Netherlands: lessons from abroad, pp. 91–96, Netspar Occasional Paper 03/2021, https://www.netspar.nl/en/knowledge-hub/transition-to-a-new-pension-contract-in-the-netherlands-lessons-from-abroad/. Accessed 29 May 2025

[6] Parametric reforms are often easier to explain, at least from a political point of view (Stevens, Y. and van Aggelen, E.S. (2021). 'Pension reform in Belgium'. In: Van Popta, B. and Steenbeek, O. (Eds.) *Transition to a new pension contract in the Netherlands: Lessons from abroad* (pp. 91–96), Netspar Occasional Paper 03/2021, https://www.netspar.nl/en/knowledge-hub/transition-to-a-new-pension-contract-in-the-netherlands-lessons-from-abroad/ (accessed 29 May 2025).

Conclusions and Insights from a National Perspective

The purpose of the conclusions and insights is for each author to reflect on the other countries included in this book through the lens of their own national perspective. The central question is: what lessons do you take home from the individual country reports and the common part on work and retirement? The reflections presented in the chapters are, of course, purely personal.

Given the focus of the question, however, some knowledge of the author's national context may be required to fully grasp these individual reflections. The country reports again provide a solid basis for the readers' understanding.

Austria

Verena Zwinger

1 Insights

The most salient distinctions between the Austrian and most of the other compared pension systems is the degree of allowed gainful activity while receiving an early retirement pension as well as the absence of a partial (old-age) pension. However, in the meantime there have been ongoing policy discussions for a new statutory "partial pension".

The Austrian general rule currently is that you may be active on the labour market unlimitedly while receiving a full/standard old-age pension at the "normal" retirement age. When it comes to early retirement, however, working or any kind of gainful activity is possible, if it is not subject to compulsory pension insurance and to the extent of certain—relatively low—income level ("marginal earnings", EUR 551,10/ month in 2025, indexed every year[1]).[2] Otherwise, the early retirement pension is suspended.

From this point of view, other countries in this study have been more flexible in comparison and allow for instance (for non-self-employed) to work up to twenty hours per week (such as Croatia) or do not limit the combination of gainful activity and early retirement at all, such as e.g. Finland, Germany and Switzerland. Belgium installed income ceilings, above which the pension benefit is reduced. This is the same for Austria's disability pensions. One of the rationales of the other systems is, that arguably, very restrictive rules could lead to a growing black/grey economy and,

---

[1] Different, more generous, rules apply in the case of invalidity pensions, which are not part of this publication.

[2] OGH, 12.05.2009, 10ObS26/09 k = DRdA 2010,72 = SSV-NF 23/36 = RdW 2009,737 = DRdA 2011,136/14 (Resch).

V. Zwinger (✉)
Austrian Pension Insurance, Business Division for Legal Affairs and Research, Vienna, Austria
e-mail: verena.zwinger@pv.at

E. S. van Aggelen (ed.), *Retirement and Employment*, Ius Gentium: Comparative Perspectives on Law and Justice 145, https://doi.org/10.1007/978-3-032-33561-6_12

hence, shrinking contributions/tax revenue instead of achieving its foremost goal of allowing for more personal flexibility within the pension system.

While it was truly intriguing to learn what the other compared countries provided for, the question remains why in Austria, the rules seem to have been stricter for a longer time than in other countries. One consideration comes to mind immediately: the pension system designs differ a lot in its specificities in the compared countries. Those countries in which a (mostly) tax-financed residence based pension exists (e.g. the Netherlands), complemented by an occupational pension, tend to be more generous when it comes to personal choice.[3] In comparison, in Austria, up to this point around 90% of pensioners rely solely on their statutory pension when exiting the labour market, which is based on contributions.[4] Hence, the balance between sustainability and flexibility needs to be maintained especially careful. Correspondingly, occupational pensions are not as pronounced in Austria compared to other countries up to this point.[5] The number of occupational pensioners, however, is growing, as around one million people (of approximately 4,4 million insured persons in statutory pension insurance) are currently participating in an occupational pension plan and will therefore be entitled to future occupational pension benefits.[6]

Moreover, while it is true that the other Countries in this study have more generous rules combining early retirement and income from gainful activity, it is also apparent that Austria has been "somewhere in the middle" from an overall EU perspective, with seven member states not providing for a combination of early statutory pensions and labour market flexibility.[7]

The political discussion and media reports with regards to the new "partial pension" include the possibility to take-up a partial pension while staying in employment for old-age pensions, regardless if these are early retirement pensions or standard retirement pensions. The idea is, for example, to take 50 percent of the pension and continue to work also for 50 percent. If the legal act will be adopted, the interesting questions at first target the specific requirements and design of the new benefit

---

[3] For instance in the Netherlands, early retirement exclusively exists in the occupational pension schemes, but the occupational schemes allow for a maximum of flexibility when it comes to the combination with gainful employment.

[4] Another angle to be considered are the expectations of future pensioners, since Austrian statutory pensions tend to be among the highest among EU countries. In that respect, to promote pension literacy was among the top runners in terms of social policy. The respective legal amendments targeted not only the information of cohorts close to retirement about their pension rights, but also to prevent younger cohorts from making short-sighted decisions which might affect their future pensions.

[5] In 2022, around 10% of pensioners received an additional occupational pension. Statistics Austria (2025), Pensionen. www.statistik.at/statistiken/bevoelkerung-und-soziales/sozialleistungen/pensionen/pensionen. Accessed 10 April 2025.

[6] Financial Market Authority Austria (2024), Quarterly report on pension funds (www.fma.gv.at/pensionskassen/offenlegung/quartalsberichte. Accessed 11 July 2025.

[7] Spasova S, Deruelle T, Airoldi F (2025) Flexible retirement pathways—An analysis of policies in 28 European Countries p 20. Available via European Commission https://employment-social-affairs.ec.europa.eu/document/download/667f3ed0-2999-40c7-a295-4bebe33b8c1b_en?filename=KE-01-24-028-EN-N.pdf. Accessed 10 April 2025.

as well as the uptake of the new partial pension. Ultimately, it will mainly depend on whether there will be noticeable effects on the pension system and the labour market.

The third perception taken away from the group writing journey, is the Finnish system's approach to retirement age and life expectancy. In place since 2017, the system tells each cohort its standard retirement age ("minimum" retirement age as it is called in the Finnish setting) at age 62. One can only imagine how the reactions to similar regulations of a standard retirement age that moves alongside life expectancy would be in Austria, even so, if the principle of trust is upheld with sufficiently long transition periods.

Currently in Austria, there is no (semi-)automatic mechanism to adjust the standard retirement age to reflect life expectancy. Since 2017, there is a "commission on the long-term financing of pension systems"[8] ("*Alterssicherungskommission*") in place.

The members of the commission are representatives of employees/employers as well as administration and research. The primary mandate is to issue expert opinions every year and report on cost development and long-term financial viability of the Austrian pension system every three years. In doing so, deviations of the reference-life expectancy (set currently until 2050) have to be evaluated. If a deviation of more than 3% on average is determined, proposals and recommendations to ensure the long-term viability of the Austrian pension system ought to be made, including contribution rates, standard retirement age, pension adjustment, etc. Recently in May 2025, a sustainability mechanism has been proposed which stipulates that if the pensions to be paid exceed legally defined thresholds by more than 0.5% during a reference period, manifold measures may be adopted. Among them, the increase of the required insurance prerequisites for the "corridor pension" or other measures that may, for example, affect the contribution rate or the retirement age.

Although also the Finnish system is not comparable to the Austrian system as such, since the system parameters differ by a lot, it was intriguing to learn about other ways to approach questions of sustainability and intergenerational fairness, which every European country currently has to deal with.

References

Official documents and decisions

Alterssicherungskommissions-Gesetz, BGBl I 2017/29

OGH, 12.05.2009, 10ObS26/09k = DRdA 2010,72 = SSV-NF 23/36 = RdW 2009,737 = DRdA 2011,136/14 (Resch)

[8] *Alterssicherungskommissions-Gesetz*, BGBl I 2017/29.

Literature

Österreichische Finanzmarktaufsicht (FMA) 2024/1, quarterly report on pension funds (www.fma.gv.at/pensionskassen/offenlegung/quartalsberichte)

Spasova S, Deruelle T, Airoldi F (2025) Flexible retirement pathways—An analysis of policies in 28 European Countries p 20. Available via European Commission https://employment-social-affairs.ec.europa.eu/document/download/667f3ed0-2999-40c7-a295-4bebe33b8c1b_en?filename=KE-01-24-028-EN-N.pdf

Statistics Austria (2025) Pensionen www.statistik.at/statistiken/bevoelkerung-und-soziales/sozialleistungen/pensionen/pensionen

Belgium

Yves Stevens

1 Insights

Belgium—like so many countries—has struggled with the relationship between retirement and work. The issues may seem similar but, of course, there is always the national context that is culturally historically important. This chapter is written from a personal and national law perspective. From this perspective, there are three sections:

1. What Belgium does (relatively) well compared to other countries?
2. What Belgium should study further as an interesting train of thought?
3. What is really difficult in a Belgian context?

1.1 What Belgium Does (Relatively) Well Compared to Other Countries

The first positive element of which other countries could learn is the link between the retirement age for statutory pensions and occupational pensions. Occupational pensions and statutory pensions always have the same legal start. There is but one common retirement age. This change was introduced in Belgium in 2015.[1] Compared to the other countries it is clear that this change creates simplicity and transparency. Having one common date to retire instead of several mechanisms also leads to a clear

[1] Wet van 18 december 2015 tot waarborging van de duurzaamheid en het sociale karakter van de aanvullende pensioenen en tot versterking van het aanvullend karakter ten opzichte van de rustpensioenen, *B.S.* 24 december 2015.

Y. Stevens (✉)
Catholic University of Leuven, Faculty of Law and Criminology, Department of Social Security & Labour Law, Institute for Social Law, Leuven, Belgium
e-mail: yves.stevens@kuleuven.be

E. S. van Aggelen (ed.), *Retirement and Employment*, Ius Gentium: Comparative Perspectives on Law and Justice 145, https://doi.org/10.1007/978-3-032-33561-6_13

fiscal construction whereby early retirement leads to a lower pension due to higher taxes on occupational pensions. The increased connectivity between the pension forms is a situation far more easy to understand. Beforehand one could retire at a different age for the occupational pension than for the statutory pension. This led to strange situations whereby people tried to retire purely in function of the fiscal consequences of their choice.

The second positive element is the absence of partial retirement in the Belgian set-up. Looking at the other countries, these systems are highly complicated in practice. In theory, the idea of a partial retirement is obviously very simple. And the reasoning behind it, is also easy: allowing people to remain in the labour force for a longer while instead of being pushed out. However, when we look at the countries involved in this study we see highly complicated systems with possible negative side-effects. The main reason thereto is of course that partial retirement is seen as an instrument for labour market policy. But pension law is not (always) a good instrument for shaping the labour market. It is as if you want to use a hammer as a screwdriver. The countries with partial retirement are having difficulties with for example self-employed or bogus-self employed. These people often can continue working without any loss of income. This goes against the basic idea of allowing people to "land more softly at the end of their career". So instead of installing partial retirement, it would be better to install workplace regulations allowing people to work less.[2] Fiscal incentives can help as well. Pensions are not ideal instruments for regulating labour market policies.

1.2 What Belgium Should Study Further as an Interesting Train of Thought

Belgium only recently re-installed a bonus.[3] If people remain in the labour force after their early retirement age, then they can earn a bonus. This bonus is paid out in the form of a lump sum. If one stay three years longer in the workforce this can even lead to an amount of more than 23,000 € paid out in the form of a lump sum.[4] However, in statutory pensions there is no real malus. The only malus is fiscal and in occupational pensions only. The occupational pension paid out as a lump sum is taxed 6,5% higher at early retirement than at the normal retirement age. However, there is no "true" malus in the sense that the statutory pension declines with early retirement. Belgium

[2] Nonetheless, two relatively recent Belgian governments tried to install some form of partial retirement. The last time was in 2020 when it was even mentioned in the so-called Governement agreement (Federaal Regeerakkoord, 2020), page 21.

[3] Wet 25 april 2024 houdende de hervorming van de pensioenen, *B.S.* 16 mei 2024.

[4] For the exact amounts, see the website of the pension office: www.sfpd.fgov.be

used to have such a system for employees until 1990[5] and until 2014[6] for self-employed. Other countries in this report have some kind of malus. This is intriguing from two perspectives. The first one is the link between the contributions paid and the pensions received. This link is obscured in Belgium by the interference of both minimum pensions and the number of equalized periods. Both these mechanisms lead to an absence in the insurance principle whereby there is some kind of link between contributions paid and pensions received. Re-installing a pension malus in Belgium opens automatically the question on the height of the minimum pension and on the free rides of equalized periods. Secondly the malus opens the debate on the link between statutory pensions and occupational pensions. They are currently not linked in amount like in Finland, but of course if there is a malus in the statutory pension by retiring early then the question arises whether the current fiscal malus of 6,5% in occupational pensions can be maintained as such.

From the Belgian perspective the Dutch basic pension (AOW) is truly interesting. This Dutch citizenship pension has a major advantage: there is no difference between employees, self-employed and civil servants. Belgium has been struggling with harmonization processes for at least the last four decades.[7] The Dutch statutory pension system is truly neutral towards the labour form. There is no difference between an employee, a civil servant, a housewife, a prisoner or any other status. It is a true citizenship pension. This is a clear asset in transparency. The main obstacle is of course the financing method. The Dutch system is financed on the basis of taxes, while the Belgian system is still mainly based on social insurance. So in order to install a system similar to the Dutch one, the entire Belgian social security system and fiscal system would need to be revised. This is politically impossible. The stakes are too high for all kinds of groups. We would first need a revolution before such an overall evolution could take place.

The minimalism in the Dutch system is definitely not present in the Finish system. However, the Finish system is truly inspiring on the interconnectivity of the pension forms. There is no true occupational pension in Finland but pensions are partially funded. All in all this leads to a very strong logical set up of the Finish system. That is to say: at least compared to the Belgian system. The Finish system is like a jigsaw puzzle but it is - comparatively—very coherent. Linking the different pension forms is a good idea. Belgium could learn from the Finland by installing mechanisms whereby statutory, occupational and individual pensions are truly linked in social law and fiscal law. The current links are mainly limited to some ceilings for.pension bonusses, some taxes which are the same for occupational and statutory pensions but individual pensions remain truly out of scope in Belgium.

---

[5] Wet 20 juli 1990 tot instelling van een flexibele pensioenleeftijd voor werknemers en tot aanpassing van de werknemerspensioenen aan de evolutie van het algemeen welzijn, *B.S.* 15 augustus 1990.

[6] KB 15 december 2013 tot uitvoering van artikel 3/1 van de wet van 23 december 2005 betreffende het generatiepact, *B.S.* 23 december 2013.

[7] The first law on harmonizing pensions already dates back from 1984 (Wet 15 mei 1984 houdende maatregelen tot harmonisering in de pensioenregelingen, *B.S.* 22 mei 1984).

Compared to the UK and Switzerland Belgium is still struggling with the lump of labour fallacy. Early retirement still means that the possibilities to work are refrained. The UK and Switzerland have far larger degrees of freedom. Anyone who wants to work can do so in all liberty and freedom without any specific regulations or fiscal limits. Only recently (2015) did Belgium let go of these financial limits after retirement age. Anyone older than the retirement age (65 in 2024 and 66 in 2025 and 67 in 2030) can work without limits in combination with the receival of a pension. Hence Belgium recognized for the first time in pension policy the lump of labour fallacy. However, when comparing the current situation with Switzerland with its flexible retirement age, then Belgium still has some leagues to go.

Austria, Finland and Switzerland have a bonus system linked to deferral. This is similar to Belgium: the later you retire the higher your pension bonus is. Belgium even has a lump sum bonus. Switzerland even combines this with partial retirement. In Belgium bonus systems are often tackled from the perspective of the so-called Matthew effect. In this reasoning the bonusses will be given mainly to the people that were already delaying their retirement. Hence the real effect is rather limited. According to this idea the extra pension money goes to those who didn't want to retire anyhow. So the question arises whether this is a smart way to organize deferral given the budgetary impact of the system. Apparently this kind of reasoning is far less present in Austria, Finland and Switzerland.

1.3 What Is Really Difficult in a Belgian Context

From a Belgian perspective there are two rather "outlandish" elements in the Austrian pension system. There is on the one hand the still valid gender inequality in the pensionable age (age 65 for men and age 60,5 for women). In Belgium this legislation was already changed in 1997 (with a very long transitional period up to 2009). Still the Austrian situation seems rather discriminatory from a Belgian perspective. Another element that is most peculiar is the impossibility to combine work with early retirement. So it is not possible to retire early and work. In Belgium such a situation might lead quick quickly to forms of grey economy. People would take up their early retirement but work undeclared and thus escaping fiscal and social levies.

Similarly as in Austria, Croatia still upholds the belief in the lump of labour fallacy. In Croatia for example a person on early retirement can work up to 20 hours per week without their pension benefit being suspended. One could argue that in Belgium a similar limitation exists. It may not be in hours but it is in financial ceilings.[8] Someone who retires early can only gain up to a certain amount. Despite the similarity, the difference between Belgium and Croatia is manifest. There is the obvious difficulty of correct registration of the number of hours. How are the 20 hours registered? Who does it correctly? And how do self-employed people register their

[8] For the exact current amounts, see the website of the pension office: www.sfpd.fgov.be

number of hours? The Belgian financial ceiling seems easier to check then the Croatian hourly registration. But then again, the entire Croatian pension system has a rather complex set-up from a Belgian perspective. The difference between Croatia and countries such as the UK and the Netherlands on set-up and format of the statutory pension system is immense. Whereby the UK and the Netherlands have a very limited number of exceptions on the overall system, the Croatian system looks like a juxtaposition of exceptions. That is at least from the Belgian perspective. For example, the impossibility to combine work and pension after the retirement age in Croatia for self-employed, seems strange from a Belgian angle.

Within the Finish system there is a longevity coefficient whereby the retirement age is dependent on the longevity of a given age cohort. From a Belgian perspective such a system would easily again lead to discussion on possible Matthew effects. Belgium has a rather low Gini index and the reasoning behind a possible Matthew effect lies in the idea that within a certain age cohort huge differences can occur. That is to say that a university professor and a mason might be of the same age cohort but they do not have the same longevity prospect and hence the masons are paying for the professors. From an economic point of view the Finish longevity coefficient might seem interesting to discuss but in Belgium it will lead rather quickly to the legal discussion on unequal treatment or even discrimination.

Switzerland introduced a flexible retirement age between ages 63 and 70. In the nineties of last century, Belgium had a similar system.[9] It didn't work. Everybody took their retirement at the earliest age possible. However, the system works in Switzerland. But in my opinion, this is due to the strong Swiss malus. The Swiss system is very much based on the insurance principle meaning that a lot depends on the social insurance contributions paid. The number of years worked is not the main determinant or driver of the system. In Belgium—with its system of equalized periods and complex minimum pension schemes—this idea is far from present. As stated before, the political will to install a malus is far from present in Belgium. Similarly to Switzerland, Austria has a rather strong belief in linking contributions to benefits. In Austria this strong belief in "deservedness" works with very high average replacement rates at 80% of the average earnings. When Austria is compared to Belgium and definitely when compared to Croatia it appears very strictly regulated with very little flexibility.

References

Wet 15 mei 1984 houdende maatregelen tot harmonisering in de pensioenregelingen, *B.S.* 22 mei 1984

Wet 20 juli 1990 tot instelling van een flexibele pensioenleeftijd voor werknemers en tot aanpassing van de werknemerspensioenen aan de evolutie van het algemeen welzijn, *B.S.* 15 augustus 1990

[9] Wet 20 juli 1990 tot instelling van een flexibele pensioenleeftijd voor werknemers en tot aanpassing van de werknemerspensioenen aan de evolutie van het algemeen welzijn, B.S. 15 augustus 1990.

Wet van 18 december 2015 tot waarborging van de duurzaamheid en het sociale karakter van de aanvullende pensioenen en tot versterking van het aanvullend karakter ten opzichte van de rustpensioenen, *B.S.* 24 december 2015
Wet 25 april 2024 houdende de hervorming van de pensioenen, *B.S.* 16 mei 2024
KB 15 december 2013 tot uitvoering van artikel 3/1 van de wet van 23 december 2005 betreffende het generatiepact, *B.S.* 23 december 2013
Governement agreement 2020 (Federaal Regeerakkoord, 2020)
Website of the pension office., www.sfpd.fgov.be

Croatia

Ivana Vukorepa

1 Insights

Regarding broad organisational structure, I believe the three-pillar system existing in Croatia (consisting of mandatory PAYG DB part, mandatory funded DC part and voluntary funded DC part) is appropriate. It is result of structural reform undertaken from 1998 to 2002. The problem is that since that time there have been several rounds of parametric reforms and more than 25 legislative changes of the main laws in addition to changes of bylaws which all jeopardizes trust in the system, reasonable expectations, and sustainability.

Within the first PAYG DB pillar simplification and more transparency is needed. Namely, there are too many groups within the pension system with special arrangements. This results in too much redistribution and incoherence in the pension system.

Regarding retirement age, firstly within mandatory schemes it can be argued that the normal retirement age of 65 (in force for women only in 2030)[1] needs to be raised. This can be justified by long-term demographic trends of low fertility rates and increased longevity combined with generous retirement conditions that resulted in labour shortages and low employment rate of older workers being considerably below the EU average.[2] Some countries have prudentially raised normal retirement age as to ensure pension systems sustainability (e.g. Belgium, Germany and UK, or Finland by linking it to life expectancy changes).[3] Secondly, there is a problem

[1] Art. 33 and 180 of the Pension Insurance Act.

[2] Similarly: European Commission (2024, p. 45).

[3] Based on information provided in country reports.

I. Vukorepa (✉)
Department for Labour and Social Security Law, Faculty of Law, University of Zagreb, Zagreb, Croatia
e-mail: ivana.vukorepa@pravo.unizg.hr

E. S. van Aggelen (ed.), *Retirement and Employment*, Ius Gentium: Comparative Perspectives on Law and Justice 145, https://doi.org/10.1007/978-3-032-33561-6_14

of age-related incoherence between mandatory and voluntary schemes. Namely the mandatory normal retirement age is 65 (early retirement age is 60),[4] while voluntary retirement age rules (occupational and individual pension retirement) are not linked to statutory pension in Croatia. They are set too low, only at 55 for temporary pension and 60 for life-time annuities.[5] This lack of interconnectivity has a negative consequence that persons usually taking temporary pension spend all their voluntary savings before normal retirement age.

Concerning early retirement, there are several lessons that can be learned. Firstly, the size of early retirement window in Croatia amounts to 5 years. It is worth reflecting about it being lowered (e.g. in Finland it is only 3 years), while some countries do not allow early retirement within their statutory systems (e.g. UK and Netherlands). Secondly, malus could be set higher as to be closer to actuarial neutrality (currently it is only 0.2% per month of early retirement).[6] For example, in Germany malus amounts to 0.3%, in Finland to 0.4% and in Switzerland to even 0.6% per month of early retirement. Belgium has abolished malus a long time ago.[7] I do not think that abolition of malus would be a good example for Croatia, (especially considering the possibility to combine part time work and full pension benefit in payment even in the case of early retirement).

Deferred retirement is possible without limit in Croatia; however, the bonus is limited to maximum 5 years of deferral (the bonus amounts to 0.45% per each month of later retirement, maximum for 5 years amounting to 27%).[8] Unlike Croatia, Finland Germany and Belgium are good examples since there is no limit for the bonus for pension deferral. In Finland it amounts to 0.4% per month of late retirement, while in Germany it is even higher: 0.5% per month. Belgium has bonus in fixed lump sum amounts, also with no age limitations.[9] I am of the opinion that 5-year bonus limitation in Croatia should be eliminated in order to stimulate pension deferral even more.

Partial retirement with partial pension in payment exists in many countries. However, since 2014 Croatia adopted an irrationally generous model: partial retirement in the form of right to full pension benefit (old-age pension, early retirement pension and survivorship pension) combined with the right to do part-time work for up to 20 h per week. There are lessons to be learned regarding partial retirement's theoretical purpose which is phased retirement, hence reduction of working hours compensated by income replacement in the form of partial pension benefit.[10] However, I doubt that such changes directed towards reduction of current pensioner's rights would be politically feasible in Croatia since the rule now allows part-time work combined with the right to full pension benefit. A further problem linked to

[4] For women there is transitional period until 2030.

[5] Art. 115 of the Act on Pension Insurance Companies.

[6] Art. 85, para 2 of the Pension Insurance Act.

[7] Based on information provided in country reports.

[8] Art. 85, para 3 of the Pension Insurance Act.

[9] Based on the information provided in the country reports.

[10] Vukorepa (2023, pp. 425–433).

limitations in the form of part-time work is that pensioners and employers might be stimulated to underreport working hours (declare formally work as part-time, although full-time) thus concealing part of the work and earnings in the shadow of the grey economy.

Regarding arduous and hazardous jobs, Croatia undertook reform in 2018 however keeping for such workers double advantages (lower retirement age depending on the duration of work in such jobs and increased insurance period).[11] The Croatian generosity of pension law measures for such workers is questionable, especially since some comparative countries do not have them any more (e.g. Belgium, Netherlands, and Germany only for miners), while some have left it within occupational schemes subject to negotiations among social partners (Switzerland and UK). I think that Croatia should firstly consider limiting the scope of jobs and occupations considered as arduous and hazardous, and secondly, reduce the generosity of double advantages in the form of lower retirement ages and increased insurance period.

References

Legislation

Act on Pension Insurance Companies (Zakon o mirovinskim osiguravajućim društvima, NN 22/14, 29/18, 115/18, 156/23)

Act on the Insurance Periods Counted with Extended Duration (Zakon o stažu osiguranja s povećanim trajanjem, NN 115/18, 34/21)

Pension Insurance Act (Zakon o mirovinskom osiguranju, NN 157/13, 151/14, 33/15, 93/15, 120/16, 18/18, 62/18, 115/18, 102/19, 84/21, 119/22)

Literature

European Commission (2024) The 2024 Pension Adequacy Report—current and future income adequacy in old age in the EU, vol II. Publications Office of the European Union. https://data.europa.eu/doi/10.2767/550848

Vukorepa I (2015) Lost between sustainability and adequacy: critical analysis of the Croatian pension system's parametric reform. Revija za socijalnu politiku 22(3):279–308

Vukorepa I (2023) Hrvatski model djelomičnog umirovljenja: kritički osvrt (The Croatian model of partial retirement: a critical review). Zbornik Pravnog fakulteta u Zagrebu 73(2–3):423–456

Vukorepa I (2017) Retirement policy changes for workers in arduous and hazardous jobs: comparative overview and lessons for Croatia. Zbornik Pravnog fakulteta u Zagrebu 67(1):5–28

Part I in this book with country reports

---

[11] Act on the Insurance Periods Counted with Extended Duration (Zakon o stažu osiguranja s povećanim trajanjem, NN 115/18, 34/21); Vukorepa (2017).

Finland

Toomas Kotkas

1 Reflections on the Life Expectancy Model

The question about learning from other countries' pension systems is not an easy one. Although more or less comprehensive reforms are occasionally carried out, most existing pension systems are nevertheless a result of a long historical development defined by numerous incremental changes, prevailing economic realities, and political compromises. What works in one country does not necessarily work in another. So, instead of trying to answer the question of what Finland might learn from other countries, I will have a closer look at the one feature that seems to stand out in the Finnish old-age pension schemes in comparison to other countries included in this study, i.e., that the minimum retirement age depends on the changes in the life expectancy.[1]

The life expectancy-based minimum retirement age model came into force in 2017. It was preceded by a careful evaluation of the strengths and weaknesses of the then existing system. Several national and international reports were commissioned.[2] The reform was agreed in the tripartite negotiations between the government, employer confederations, and trade union confederations. For this reason, the reform did not really give rise to political opposition amongst wage earners, the self-employed or the general public. It can be argued that a pension system based on a life expectancy-bound minimum retirement age is less likely to cause political controversy in the long run, compared to a system in which the minimum retirement age is fixed. In the latter, every new rise in the minimum retirement age is open for political debate whereas in the former, changes in the retirement age occur 'automatically'.

[1] In the Netherlands, too, the reference retirement age is linked to life expectancy.

[2] See, e.g., Barr (2013), Ambachtsheer (2013) and Lassila et al. (2013).

T. Kotkas (✉)
Faculty of Law, University of Helsinki, Helsinki, Finland
e-mail: toomas.kotkas@helsinki.fi

E. S. van Aggelen (ed.), *Retirement and Employment*, Ius Gentium: Comparative Perspectives on Law and Justice 145, https://doi.org/10.1007/978-3-032-33561-6_15

In order for a life expectancy-bound retirement age pension system to achieve its goals, i.e., extending working careers and increasing public tax revenue, entry into early retirement must be made stricter or less attractive. This is what the malus of 0.4% in the partial early old-age pension scheme is designed for. On the other hand, a life expectancy-bound retirement age pension system also needs a 'safety valve' mechanism because the rise in minimum retirement age does not treat all professions and trades equally. In the Finnish system the 'years-of-service pension' (*työuraeläke*) functions as such a mechanism.

From the point of view of an individual, a system in which the minimum retirement age is a 'moving target' may cause confusion. Each age cohort's minimum retirement age is only confirmed in the year when they turn 62. However, a website maintained by the Finnish Centre for Pensions includes a 'retirement age calculator' (*eläkeikälaskuri*) with the help of which everyone may check their estimated minimum retirement age.[3]

The bill on the 2017 pension reform was referred the Constitutional Law Committee of the Parliament for pre-legislative constitutional review. The Committee found that the grounds for the reform were acceptable and well-founded. The Committee saw no constitutional problems in the life expectancy-based pension model either because the reform would be implemented during a transitional period within which the minimum retirement age would first rise gradually. Furthermore, individuals would know their minimum retirement age well in advance, and the minimum age could rise by two months per year at the most.[4]

In regard to the Finnish life-expectancy-bound minimum retirement age model, it is too early to evaluate its overall impact. However, as was already mentioned in the chapter on the Finnish system, there is evidence that the reform has prolonged working careers.[5] On the other hand, it will be interesting to see whether the number of persons applying to get on the 'years-of-service pension' will rise in the future.

References

Official Documents

PeVL 5/2015 vp [Constitutional Law Committee's statement on the 2017 pension reform bill]

---

[3] See, https://www.tyoelake.fi/.

[4] PeVL 5/2025 vp p. 3.

[5] Nivalainen and Ilmakunnas (2023).

Literature

Ambachtsheer K (2013) The pension system in Finland: institutional structure and governance. Finnish Centre for Pensions. Evaluation of the Finnish Pension System/Part 2. 2013. https://urn.fi/URN:ISBN:978-951-691-177-2

Barr N (2013) The pension system in Finland: adequacy, sustainability and system design. Finnish Centre for Pensions. Evaluation of the Finnish Pension System/Part 1. 2013. https://urn.fi/URN:ISBN:978-951-691-175-8

Lassila J, Määttänen N, Valkonen T (2013) Eläkeiän sitominen elinaikaan – miten käy työurien ja tulonjaon? [Tying retirement age to life expectancy: what happens to working careers and income distribution?]. Finnish Centre for Pensions, Reports 05/2023. https://urn.fi/URN:ISBN:978-951-628-590-3

Nivalainen S, Ilmakunnas I (2023) Pension reform 2017: impact of rising old-age pension age on employment and other labour market states, summary. Finnish Centre for Pensions, Studies 02/2023. https://urn.fi/URN:ISBN:978-951-691-362-2

Germany

Stamatia Devetzi

1 Reflections on the "Flexi-Pension"

It is quite difficult to compare (pension) systems from the point of view "what can one country learn from the others". A pension system is after all the result of (long) historical developments and various political trade-offs. The (still) Bismarckian character of the German pension system could certainly be criticized for many reasons, the most important being the exclusion of larger groups such as the self-employed. In this section, however, only one aspect of the German pension system, the one that "directly affects" work and retirement, will be discussed: The "flexi-pension".

The flexi-pension law incentivises people to work longer. Insured persons can continue to build up their pension entitlements and improve their financial situation through the opportunity to continue working and receive additional supplements of 0,5% per month or 6% per year.

The flexi-pension also allows early retirees to continue working alongside their pension before reaching the standard retirement age of 67. This could offer both financial benefits and promote social integration. There is also the possibility to work not only part-time, but also full-time again if necessary.

On the other hand, there has also been critique in the sense that the flexi-pension is a complex system with various regulations and requirements. There are therefore difficulties in understanding all the options and effects. Sufficient information is needed to make the right decision.

It is also argued that the flexi-pension leads to injustices, particularly for people with low incomes. This mainly relates to the regulations on additional earnings and pension deductions. In addition, pensioners who already receive a higher pension could benefit more from the flexible instruments than people with lower pension

S. Devetzi (✉)
Department of Social and Cultural Sciences, Fulda University of Applied Sciences, Fulda, Germany
e-mail: stamatia.Devetzi@sk.hs-fulda.de

E. S. van Aggelen (ed.), *Retirement and Employment*, Ius Gentium: Comparative Perspectives on Law and Justice 145, https://doi.org/10.1007/978-3-032-33561-6_16

entitlements, who may not have the same conditions to work longer in order to increase their pension entitlements. In this context, the political party 'DIE LINKE' criticised the fact that the flexi-pension does not reach some occupational groups at all.[1] In addition, there are typical occupational differences that need to be taken into account. For example, employees in physically demanding professions, such as in the metal industry or building cleaning, retire on average early, whereas for example office workers have a longer working life. The flexi-pension law pursues "the spirit of working until you drop", it said in a statement. "It is not about combating poverty in old age".[2]

In 2022, a study evaluating the flexi-pension was conducted on behalf of the German Federal Ministry of Labour and Social Affairs.[3] The project results showed that, despite positive developments in terms of demand and actual take-up, the flexi-pension was still barely known five years after the introduction in 2017. In this context, a third of respondents aged 60 to 70 stated that they had not yet heard of the flexi-pension. The most unfamiliar option was the option to combine income and a partial pension.[4] Given the low level of awareness and the lack of information, the flexi-pension could hardly have contributed to an increase in employment in old age since its introduction.

Maybe the flexi-pension is financially not attractive enough, especially when taken before the regular pensionable age. Applicants can receive a supplement of 0.5 per cent but retirement before regular pensionable age reduces the pension for 0.3% per month, so the factual gain is very modest.

It is true that 13 percent of retirees above pensionable age are working.[5] However, they mostly choose working in a so called "mini-job" and prefer cash payments instead getting additional pension points.

A lesson that can be learned from this is that information is very important. As mentioned in the country report on Germany, all insured persons receive every year their personal pension information with the current status of their accrued pension entitlements. However, this is not enough in order to understand more "complex" models such as the flexi-pension.

A starting point for better information can be seen in the online area. The German Pension Insurance's online service is a first and important point of contact for many insured persons. Even if insured persons rely almost exclusively on individual financial advice for detailed planning of their own pension transition, the online service is often used at an early stage to get an overview of possible options and the associated financial implications. There is therefore potential here to make insured persons

[1] *Legal Tribune Online*, Bundestag beschließt Flexi-Rente, https://www.lto.de/recht/nachrichten/n/bundestag-beschluss-flexi-rente/.

[2] *Legal Tribune Online*, ibid.

[3] BMAS/Destatis, Evaluierung der Flexirente, https://www.bmas.de/SharedDocs/Downloads/DE/Rente/abschlussbericht-flexirente.pdf?__blob=publicationFile&v=3.

[4] Ibid, p. 16.

[5] Federal Statisticial Office of Germany, https://www.destatis.de/DE/Presse/Pressemitteilungen/Zahl-der-Woche/2025/PD25_05_p002.html (Last update 13 March 2025).

aware of structuring alternatives to the "classic" pension transition at an early stage through a good information structure. The information currently available on the subject of flexi-pension is sometimes difficult for insured persons to understand and should be tailored even more closely to individual needs. Improvements in these areas can be achieved, for example, through customisable information, descriptive model comparisons or a standardised pension calculator.[6]

References

BMAS/Destatis, Evaluierung der Flexirente, https://www.bmas.de/SharedDocs/Downloads/DE/Rente/abschlussbericht-flexirente.pdf?__blob=publicationFile&v=3

Legal Tribune Online, Bundestag beschließt Flexi—Rente, https://www.lto.de/recht/nachrichten/n/bundestag-beschluss-flexi-rente/

Federal Statisticial Office of Germany., https://www.destatis.de/DE/Presse/Pressemitteilungen/Zahl-der-Woche/2025/PD25_05_p002.html (Last update 13 March 2025)

[6] BMAS/Destatis, ibid., p. 41.

Switzerland

Jacques-André Schneider

1 Pensions and Direct Democracy: Another Political Game?

Switzerland is characterized by two specific political institutions of direct democracy. Firstly, the constitutional initiative allows 100'000 citizens to sign, during an 18 month period, a proposed constitutional change which may, or not, lead to an immediate legislative change,[1] in case of approval by a double majority of voters nationally and canton by canton. Any constitutional change decided by parliament is also automatically subject to this double majority popular vote.[2] Secondly, a federal law approved by parliament can be revoked by a national majority of voting citizens, if a referendum is signed by 50'000 citizens within a 100 day period.[3]

Therefore, any changes to national mandatory pension schemes often give rise to a general vote, which necessarily strongly impacts the political parliamentary debates. Even then, pension law reforms have historically often been rejected. This specificity partially explains the inherent structural complexity of Swiss pensions. Through successive popular votes, Swiss constitutional law enshrined the so-called three pillar system for retirement provision and gave rise, more particularly, to the effectively dominant but confusingly generous voluntary tier of funded occupational pensions. Therefore, conceiving and adapting Swiss mandatory pension schemes is a risky endeavour, especially in our brave new pensions ageing world of rising expectations and falling financials. Therein lies a major difference with other countries, particularly Finland with its simple, transparent and generous pension system.

[1] Art. 138-139b Constitution fédérale de la Confédération suisse, RS 101, 1999.

[2] Ibid, Art. 140.

[3] Ibid, Art. 141.

J.-A. Schneider (✉)
University of Lausanne, Lausanne, Switzerland
e-mail: jas@jaschneider.ch

E. S. van Aggelen (ed.), *Retirement and Employment*, Ius Gentium: Comparative Perspectives on Law and Justice 145, https://doi.org/10.1007/978-3-032-33561-6_17

I'm reminded here of Guy Perrin's prescient sociological remark that social protection systems generally tend towards coordination, generalization, harmonization and administrative centralization as a response to the secular need for equal and transparent protection at a reasonable cost. But this supposes, in Switzerland, a broad political majority. The recent approval of the constitutional 13 month AVS pension payment initiative, despite its major and presently unfinanced supplementary cost, shows that political symbolic simplicity combined with specific social demands can have a major impact on the evolution of a pension system, in line with the traditional sociological trends applicable to social security.

2 Partial and Gradual Retirement: An Effective Path?

The remark is also valid for the retirement age increase proposal as a response to ageing. Switzerland recently approved the introduction of partial and gradual retirement from ages 63 to 70 in the September 2022 popular vote on the AVS21 reform law, which was opposed by referendum. Confronted by rising uncovered costs, the mandatory AVS had to be reformed. However, a general rise of the retirement age from 65 to 67 with a transition period, as set by other European countries, would however have represented an impossible political mission as popular rejection was a very high probability. The chosen alternative was thus the proposal of a gradual and step-by-step voluntary path to full retirement till age 70 at the latest, in the hope of encouraging continued work after the reference retirement age of 65. This reform was also extended to the mandatory and high voluntary levels of occupational pensions. If one excepts the German flexible retirement set-up, which hasn't gained much traction yet, the validity of this approach still needs to be practically tested and does not, at least for now, seem to attract similar reforms elsewhere.

The Netherlands

Emma Suzanne van Aggelen

1 The Underlying Question for the Dutch Pension System

The answer to the question whether combining work and pension is possible in the Netherlands depends entirely on whether one is referring to the statutory pension or the supplementary pension. In this regard, the comparison of the analyzed countries highlights an existing fundamental question for the Dutch system. Is it flexible or inflexible? That's the question.

1.1 The Statutory Pension Characterized by Homogeneity with a Minimum of Exceptions

The Dutch statutory pension (AOW) follows mainly a Beveridgian approach.[1] The statutory pension can be considered as a 'basic state pension', providing a flat-rate amount to all residents who have reached the normal retirement age.[2] Based on the Beveridgian approach, the Dutch pension system aligns most closely with the UK and Switzerland.

Similar to the UK, the statutory pension system in the Netherlands operates with minimal exceptions. In contrast to countries such as Switzerland, Belgium, and

[1] van Aggelen, E.S. (2022), *Het personeel toepassingsgebied van aanvullende pensioenregelingen voor werknemers. Een rechtsvergelijkend en empirisch onderzoek naar de werking van aansluitingsregels*, Brugge, Die Keure, pp. 20–21.

[2] Country report 'The Netherlands', section 1.

E. S. van Aggelen (✉)
Faculty of Law, UHasselt University, Hasselt, Belgium
e-mail: emmasuzanne.vanaggelen@uhasselt.be

Faculty of Law and Criminology, KU Leuven, Leuven, Belgium

E. S. van Aggelen (ed.), *Retirement and Employment*, Ius Gentium: Comparative Perspectives on Law and Justice 145, https://doi.org/10.1007/978-3-032-33561-6_18

Austria, there are no provisions for early or partial retirement within the statutory scheme. Furthermore, the Netherlands has not implemented a preferential framework for individuals in arduous or hazardous occupations, as seen in several other countries such as Germany, Croatia and Finland.[3] This absence of exceptions has resulted in a statutory system characterized by a high degree of homogeneity for all citizens.

This homogeneity has the advantage of transparency. Compared to other countries, the AOW may not win the prize for the most complex statutory pension system. However, it also comes with a drawback. The degree of choice an individual has within the statutory pension system is limited. For example, early retirement is not possible, and also deferral of retirement is not interesting.

1.2 Occupational Pensions Under Reform with a Greater Emphasis on Individual Choice and Labour Market Evolutions

The Dutch pension system, with relatively low statutory pension amounts financed through taxes,[4] puts emphasis on additional savings. No wonder that occupational pensions play an important role in the Netherlands. With regard to its occupational pension system, the Netherlands is currently experiencing an interesting era due to the ongoing reform. Looking at the recent pension reform, which largely (but not exclusively) impacts occupational pensions, some narratives prevail. First of all, there is the narrative of sustainability of the pension system aiming to make the system more responsive to economic changes. Also, the system will be more personalized/individualized aiming—among other things—to strengthen the relationship between the contributions paid and the individual pension amount received as well as to introduce more choice for the individual. A third narrative is the alignment of the pension system with today's labour market, in which people change employers and types of employment more frequently than in the past.[5]

What is interesting in the perspective of the latter narrative is the idea of strengthening the interconnectivity between the occupational and individual pensions in order to achieve more labour market neutrality within the pension system. Tax has been explicitly chosen as a tool to diminish the impact of individual labour market choices

---

[3] See Chapter 'To retire or to work? That's the question: choice or necessity!?', section 6.

[4] The amounts of the statutory pension can be found at the website of the 'Sociale Verzekeringsbank (SVB)': https://www.svb.nl/nl/aow/bedragen-aow/aow-bedragen (accessed 5 May 2025).

[5] Memorie van toelichting bij de Wet toekomst Pensioenen, Tweede Kamer der Staten Generaal 2021–2022, 36,067, nr. 3, p. 16–18 [House of Representatives of the Netherlands, Parliamentary documents 2021–2022, 36,067, nr. 3]; see also: Sociaal-Economische Raad, *Naar een nieuw pensioenstelsel*, (2019), https://www.ser.nl/nl/Publicaties/naar-nieuw-pensioenstelsel (accessed 9 May 2025).

on additional pension savings.[6] Also interesting is that, given the fact that people need to work longer, the government agreed to allow more flexibility with regard to early retirement in occupational pension schemes. This is reflected in the fact that the maximum age for early retirement has been prolonged from 5 years to 10 years before retirement age (or the age stipulated in the pension scheme) and that it has been made possible to combine early retirement and work without the requirement of adding a statement of intent not to engage in paid work from the moment their pension starts.[7] Even though the Netherlands doesn't provide a fixed age as in the UK and Switzerland, the pension provider has an important role to play in setting the concrete conditions for early retirement, similar to these countries.[8]

1.3 Flexibility or Inflexibility?

Based on the above observations two important fields of tension can be distinguished in the Dutch pension system:

- The flexibility of the occupational pension system[9] and the predominantly paternalistic nature of the Dutch pension system. Elements of solidarity and collectivity may face pressure due to growing flexibilization and individualization affecting the pension identity of the country.[10]
- The inflexibility of the statutory pension system and the desire for individual choice.[11] The question has been raised whether the statutory pension system requires more flexibility as is already the case in many other countries.[12] However, one cannot deny the background of the statutory pension system (Beveridgian).

[6] Memorie van toelichting bij de Wet toekomst Pensioenen, Tweede Kamer der Staten Generaal 2021–2022, 36,067, nr. 3, p. 138–147 [House of Representatives of the Netherlands, Parliamentary documents 2021–2022, 36,067, nr. 3].

[7] Memorie van toelichting bij de Wet toekomst Pensioenen, Tweede Kamer der Staten Generaal 2021–2022, 36,067, nr. 3, 16–18 [House of Representatives of the Netherlands, Parliamentary documents 2021–2022, 36,067, nr. 3], p 247 en 432.

[8] See Chapter 'To retire or to work? That's the question: choice or necessity!?', section 4.

[9] For a detailed analysis of the flexibility with regard to membership of occupational pension schemes for employees: van Aggelen, E.S. (2022), *Het personeel toepassingsgebied van aanvullende pensioenregelingen voor werknemers. Een rechtsvergelijkend en empirisch onderzoek naar de werking van aansluitingsregels*, Brugge, Die Keure, 341 p.

[10] Stevens, Y. (2023), "Hoe de WTP de identiteit van Nederland verandert", Netspar Occasional Paper 03.

[11] Vandenbroucke, F. (2022), "Collectiviteit, solidariteit en zekerheid in het pensioenakkoord". In Maatman, R.H., Heemskerk, M., Knoef, M.G., Nijman, Th. E. (red.), *Pensioen 2025*, Nijmegen, Wolters Kluwer, p. 78.

[12] Vandenbroucke, F. (2022), "Collectiviteit, solidariteit en zekerheid in het pensioenakkoord" In Maatman, R.H., Heemskerk, M., Knoef, M.G., Nijman, Th. E. (red.), *Pensioen 2025*, Nijmegen, Wolters Kluwer, 42–79.

Both fields of tension have one element in common: even if people may prefer individual choice, it requires a properly informed participant to make a well-considered choice. Information is, in other words, essential. At the same time this leads to another field of tension: the one between providing the information as clearly and usefully as possible and providing information in the most legally accurate way.[13]

References

Memorie van toelichting bij de Wet toekomst Pensioenen, Tweede Kamer der Staten Generaal 2021–2022, 36067, nr. 3

Sociaal-Economische Raad (2019) Naar een nieuw pensioenstelsel. https://www.ser.nl/nl/Publicaties/naar-nieuw-pensioenstelsel. Accessed 9 May 2025

Stevens Y (2023) "Hoe de WTP de identiteit van Nederland verandert", Netspar Occasional Paper 03, December 2023

van Aggelen ES (2022) Het personeel toepassingsgebied van aanvullende pensioenregelingen voor werknemers. Een rechtsvergelijkend en empirisch onderzoek naar de werking van aansluitingsregels. Brugge, Die Keure, p 341

van Aggelen ES, en Stevens Y (2021) Diverse rechtsperspectieven over passende informatie. In: van Aggelen ES (ed) Informatie en recht. Diverse rechtsperspectieven, Hoogstraten-Brussel, Lefebvre Sarrut Belgium NV, p 333

Vandenbroucke F (2022) Collectiviteit, solidariteit en zekerheid in het pensioenakkoord. In: Maatman RH, Heemskerk M, Knoef MG, Nijman TE (red.), Pensioen 2025. Nijmegen, Wolters Kluwer, pp 33–90

[13] van Aggelen, E.S. en Stevens, Y. (2021), "Diverse rechtsperspectieven over passende informatie". In van Aggelen, E.S. (ed.), *Informatie en recht. Diverse rechtsperspectieven*, Hoogstraten-Brussel, Lefebvre Sarrut Belgium NV, 332–333.

The United Kingdom

James Kolaczkowski

1 Insights

When looking at the question of retirement and pensions, the experiences of other countries in this study highlight the role of 'individualism' and 'freedom' in the UK pensions narrative. In the UK, the expectation to save through an occupational or private pension in order to provide adequate savings for retirement shows the obligation upon the individual to take action, rather than the state mandating specific provision for them. The separation of public and private responsibility raises important questions, such as where should the line be drawn between the role of the state and the role of employers and what should fairly be expected from an individual. In the UK there is a relatively large amount of freedom of choice for employees when making decisions on retirement and pensions. With a relatively low state pension designed to encourage individuals to provide for themselves,[1] it is necessary to have flexibility within the legal framework.

The extent to which these two concepts can be seen in the UK are reflected upon in relation to two areas of choosing when to retire, and the approach taken by the government to raising the retirement age. In comparison with the other countries in this study, there appears to be a greater expectation upon the individual coupled with more freedom of choice within the system. Whether this is generally desirable is a larger question for public policy, but from a legal perspective, the system appears to facilitate and arguably encourage these two elements within the pension system. Legal complexity and policy choices have in some instances raised difficulties, arguably, such issues merit a legal response through legislation or regulatory

[1] Beveridge, Social Insurance and Allied Services, November 1942, Cmnd 6404.

J. Kolaczkowski (✉)
James Kolaczkowski, Law School, University of Exeter, Exeter, UK
e-mail: J.Kolaczkowski@exeter.ac.uk

E. S. van Aggelen (ed.), *Retirement and Employment*, Ius Gentium: Comparative Perspectives on Law and Justice 145, https://doi.org/10.1007/978-3-032-33561-6_19

action, which would move the balance of responsibility more towards the state than the individual.

2 Choosing When to Retire

The lack of state involvement means that occupational pensions make up a significant part of the pensions landscape in the UK, much more so than in other countries such as Finland or Croatia where occupational defined benefit pensions are not permitted. Retirement choice in the UK is therefore supported to some extent by overriding law such as the removal of a default national retirement age and no restriction on receiving benefits and a salary, although there are practical consequences from a taxation perspective. However, a notable feature of the UK system when compared to other countries is its flexibility within a broader framework, rather than the state directing, or facilitating, certain retirement patterns. For example, partial retirement is used in some occupational pension schemes in the UK because it is not prohibited by the taxation rules. The use of partial retirement is therefore possible but not necessarily well understood by individual employees where different employers will have varying approaches. A defined contribution pension scheme will now allow cash to be drawn down or payment in lump sums at different times after the relaxation of the rules in 2015. In a defined benefit arrangement the scheme rules would need to permit partial retirement. Whilst employers may want to promote flexible retirement, it is unlikely to be seen as an obvious option as it may be in a country that has explicitly introduced it into its statutory schemes. Here the individual responsibility requires them to understand the options and consequences and to take action. In their response to a government consultation on the law relating to partial retirement, a trade union reported there was little take up of partial retirement.[2] Whilst there is freedom within the system, it is perhaps not 'real' freedom of choice if the individual does not have the necessary information and understanding to make the decision.

Other countries have introduced partial retirement as a feature of their statutory system such as Finland and Switzerland. The practise is therefore specifically permitted, promoting transparency within the system. Employees may be more aware of the option to retire and with an arguably stronger role of the state in pensions, this may promote a culture of flexible retirement that is beneficial for employees. Writing at the time of the abolition of the default retirement age in the UK, with their analysis based upon statistical evidence, Barret and Sargant observed that the availability of a pension may have been a significant part of employee decision making

[2] Department for Work and Pensions Flexible Retirement and Pension Provision, 10 December 2009, https://webarchive.nationalarchives.gov.uk/ukgwa/20130128102031/http://www.dwp.gov.uk/docs/flexible-retirement-responses.pdf. Accessed 8 April 2025, p11.

when deciding to work past retirement age.[3] Public understanding of the options is important to develop an open culture of flexible working.

3 Rising Pension Age

The state pension age has been equalized for men and women, it is currently age 66. It is due to increase according with a set timetable that is periodically revised, the next increase is to age 67 with phasing in according to age to be completed in 2028. There have been significant complaints and legal challenges regarding the communication of the changes to women's state pension age, particularly how it has affected women born between 6 April 1950 to 5 April 1960 who claim not to have been given fair notice of the changes. The Parliamentary and Health Services Ombudsman has issued two reports on the issue and has called for compensation to be paid to those affected,[4] the issue was sent to Parliament for its consideration, but the government has rejected that there was 'injustice' and has refused to pay compensation.[5] The campaign group behind this cause (Women Against State Pension Inequality or *WASPI*) has instigated judicial review proceedings in the High Court challenging the government grounds for refusing to pay compensation. The communication methods of the increases in the state retirement age and the rationales behind of the pace of change have therefore been under scrutiny in the UK.

In terms of communication of the new ages, in the UK the government states that there is a 10 year period in which to inform the public of the changes, there is 5 years in the Netherlands. However, despite a longer period, there is ongoing dissatisfaction with the process concerning not just timing but quality of communication, that can be seen through the *WASPI* campaign. Other countries have not reported such issues with communication of the changing age. Poor communication makes it harder for individuals to make informed retirement choices, particularly those on low incomes who rely upon the state pension.

In the Netherlands and Finland both countries have decided to link the state retirement age with longevity statistics. This has already been introduced in Finland and is due to be introduced in the Netherlands. This specific connection provides a clear rationale and a transparent concept that should give some certainty and be

---

[3] Barrett, Sargeant (2015) 'Working in the UK Without a Default Retirement Age' Industrial Law Journal, Vol 44 No1, 75 at 79.

[4] For the final decision see Parliamentary and Health Services Ombudsman, Women's State Pension age: our findings on injustice and associated issues (21 March 2024), https://www.ombudsman.org.uk/publications/womens-state-pension-age-our-findings-department-work-and-pensions-communication-0. Accessed 29 April 2025.

[5] Department for Work and Pensions, Government Response to the Parliamentary and Health Service Ombudsman's investigation into Women's State Pension and associated issues, (December 2024) https://www.gov.uk/government/publications/government-response-to-parliamentary-and-health-service-ombudsmans-investigation-into-womens-state-pension-age-communications-and-associated-issues. Accessed 29 April 2025.

positive for those wishing to plan flexible retirement. In contrast, the pace at which the UK age rises currently takes various factors into account. The recommendations have been based upon life expectancy, demographic evidence and fiscal, economic and labour market factors.[6] However, linking to life expectancy is under consideration as part of the current review of the state retirement age. This may result in a more transparent system that improves understanding of how the state pension age rises.

References

Reports

Beveridge, social insurance and allied services, November 1942, Cmnd 6404
Department for work and pensions flexible retirement and pension provision (10 December 2009) https://webarchive.nationalarchives.gov.uk/ukgwa/20130128102031/http://www.dwp.gov.uk/docs/flexible-retirement-responses.pdf. Accessed 8 April 2025
Department for work and pensions, government response to the parliamentary and health service Ombudsman's investigation into women's state pension and associated issues (December 2024) https://www.gov.uk/government/publications/government-response-to-parliamentary-and-health-service-ombudsmans-investigation-into-womens-state-pension-age-communications-and-associated-issues. Accessed 29 April 2025
Parliamentary and health services ombudsman, women's state pension age: our findings on injustice and associated issues (21 March 2024) https://www.ombudsman.org.uk/publications/womens-state-pension-age-our-findings-department-work-and-pensions-communication-0. Accessed 29 April 2025

Literature

Barrett S (2015) Working in the UK without a default retirement age. Ind Law J 44(1):79

[6] Policy Paper, State Pension Age Review 2023 (March 2023), available at: https://www.gov.uk/government/publications/state-pension-age-review-2023-government-report/state-pension-age-review-2023. Accessed 12 July 2025.

The manufacturer's authorised representative in the EU is Springer Nature Customer Service Centre GmbH, Europaplatz 3, 69115 Heidelberg, Germany. If you have any concerns regarding our products, please contact ProductSafety@springernature.com

Printed and bound by CPI Group (UK) Ltd, Croydon, CR0 4YY
23/10/2026
02238439-0001